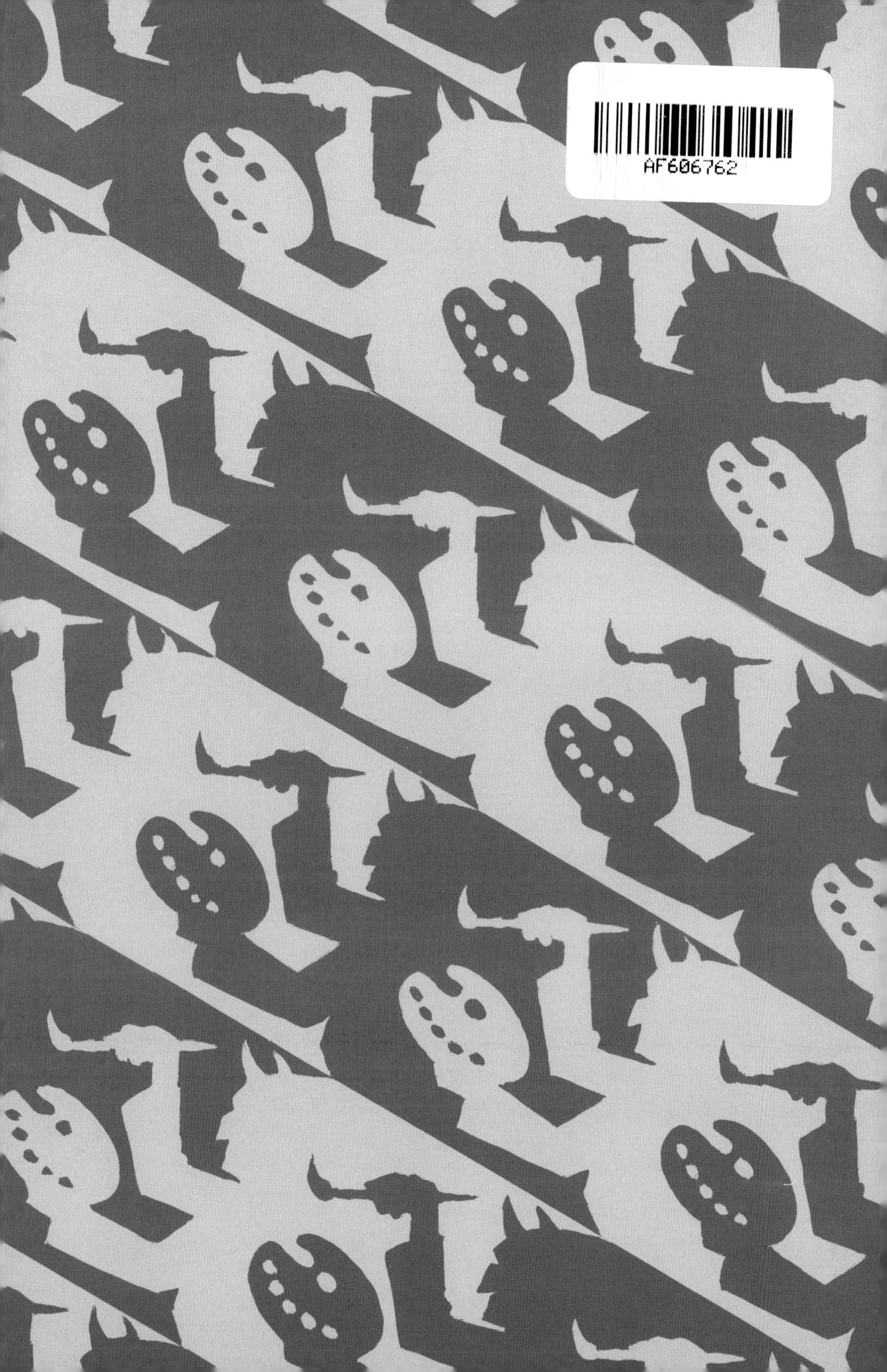

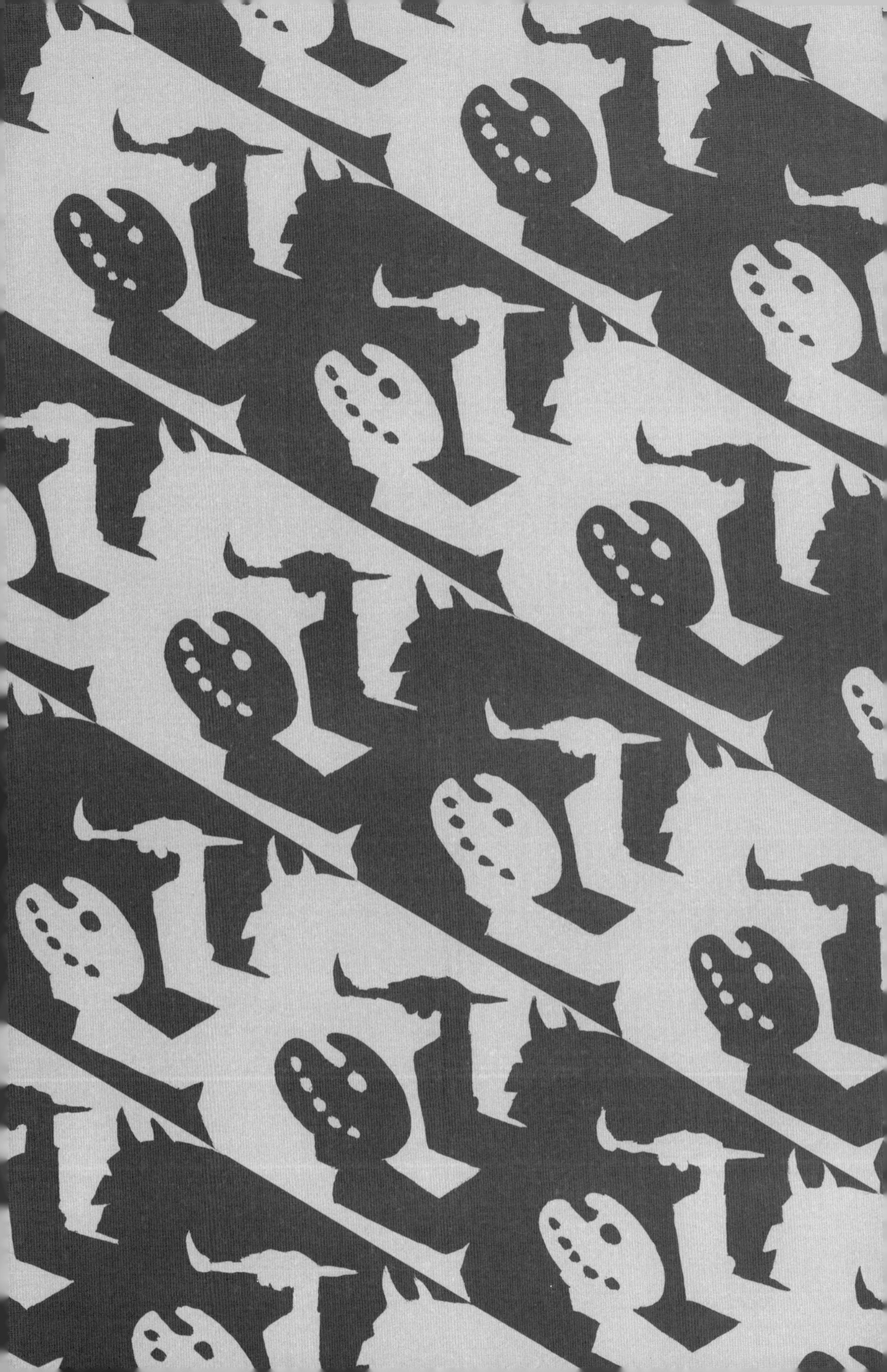

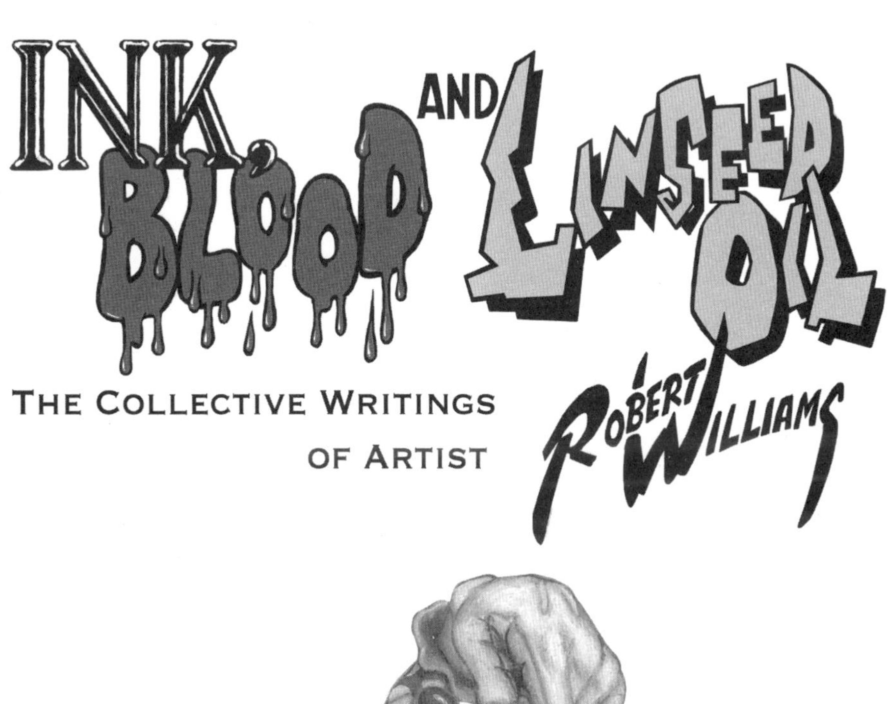
INK,
BLOOD
AND
LINSEED
OIL
THE COLLECTIVE WRITINGS
OF ARTIST
ROBERT WILLIAMS

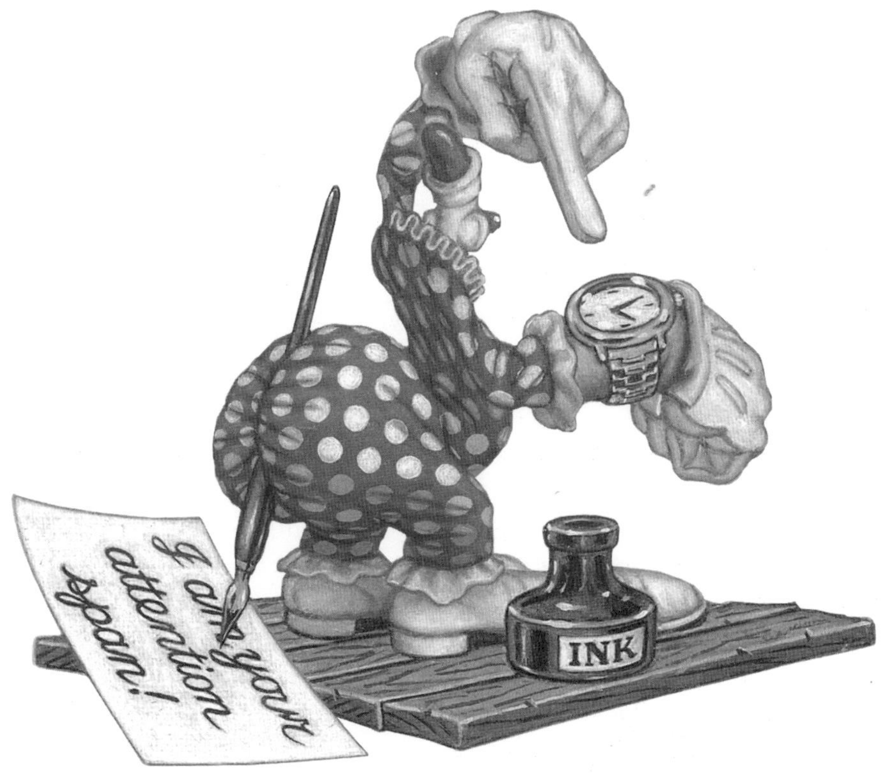
I am your attention span!
INK

Published by Last Gasp of San Francisco
777 Florida Street, San Francisco, California 94110.
www.lastgasp.com

ISBN 978-0-86719-887-4

Pre-press and design Art Works, Los Angeles

Printed in China by Prolong Press Ltd.

INK, BLOOD AND LINSEED OIL

INK. The medium for pen and brush drawings. But more symbolically the staple that gives the printing processes their reason for being and the image-making power to reach untold thousands of people both with text and reproduced prints. It is also the essential element used in physically making this book.

BLOOD. The word is not as overly dramatic as it may seem. The results and reaction to many of the works championed in this book have consciously or inadvertently caused bookstore arrests, unimaginable legal expenses and fights against federal indictments, a measure of social unrest and yes, physical confrontations. The supporters of underground and alternative artwork who defended some of the graphic works remember that decades ago controversial imagery was not so easily taken for granted. Blood would be a suitable descriptive.

LINSEED OIL. This vague and esoteric art supply is to many young artists essentially the premier medium for oil painting and is the traditional binder for the paint its self. Seeing usage for over four hundred years it has come to be a metaphor for authentic classical painting. The oil's odor, that might distract some, is a familiar and pleasant aroma to an experienced painter.

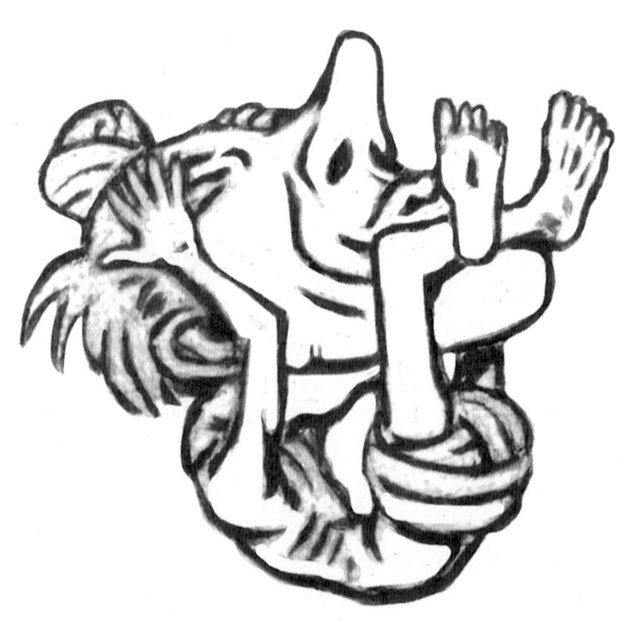

Table of Contents

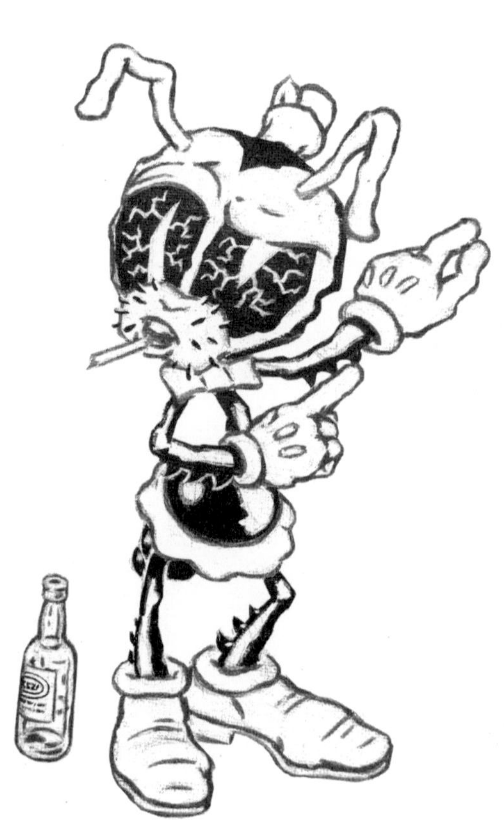

Introduction

Listening to an interview on Milk Street Radio, I marvelled at the humility and world view of renowned French Chef Eric Ripert. At the conclusion, host Christopher Kimball noted how Ripert perceives himself more artisan than artist, attributing that to the chef's sensibility of elevating craft above art: "One feeds mankind, the other feeds just one man." I immediately thought of Robert Williams, and yes, to use a popular phrase, "There's a lot to unpack here."

The title of this book, *Ink, Blood and Linseed Oil* shakes the senses, summoning the depth and immediacy of Williams' work. Remember the opening scene of the documentary *Mr. Bitchin'*? Robert's first words are not outrageous, nor self-aggrandizing, but speak about the difficulty of achieving the color purple. After so many years mixing and applying paint to canvas, he's still curious and relishes a challenge, enjoying the opportunity to observe and study all manner of arcane detail. Purple, which melds a mood between serene blue and passionate red, can ripple with rage but exude a commanding calm, like Robert, inking an indelible presence. He has a keen appreciation for materials like linseed oil and could easily explain how Jan van Eck adapted it in the 15th century to provide fluid depth in painting. And although a droplet of blood appears beneath Victim's nostril in Snafu (Acronym - Situation Normal, All Fucked Up), Williams delves more deeply than sanguinary scenarios. In his world, the protagonist and antagonist are almost interchangeable, managing and manipulating a world of threatening crimson skies, inflamed eyes, and hungry red lips. Hot-blooded or cold-blooded, his characters are on the alert, pulsating with fear, lust, hunger, cunning, and sometimes, cowering. Each of his pieces throbs with energy.

Maybe this is why my late husband Fausto slapped Robert's Make Your Obsession Palatable on the August 1988 cover of *Thrasher*, an image as passionately defiant as any of the traditional skateboard action photos that traditionally front the magazine. Fausto recognized a kindred spirit, someone who never took the easy route, who didn't just relish rattling cages but did the heavy lifting to prove a point, or at the very least, call out complacency. Frustrated by the East Coast "Elites" who pandered to self-absorbed, pseudo-intellectual emperors parading in expensive new clothes, and bolstered by his wife, the artist Suzanne Williams, Greg Escalante, C.R. Stecyk, and Lynn Coleman, Robert suggested that High Speed Productions partners Fausto Vitello and Eric Swenson add an art title to their publishing stable. San Francisco-based *Thrasher* had challenged the conventional Southern California surf and skate magazines literally an irreverent clarion by skaters and for skaters. Just as skateboarding didn't and doesn't have to be represented by a shaggy blonde stereotype, art shouldn't be decreed or delegated by a self-described intelligentsia. Comix, psychedelia, street art and figurative fantasy could finally have a platform. Robert saw the opportunity, and so did his cohorts. *Juxtapoz* launched in 1994, helmed by Williams and highlighted by his provocative editorials.

I'm happy to have a small part in introducing this treasure of *Juxtapoz* introductions that quicken the senses, dazzle with details, and captivate with their depth. His catalogs are like a thoroughly researched history of man, blemishes and all. And Williams is not afraid to let us all in on the secret.

Gwynned Vitello
Juxtapoz magazine

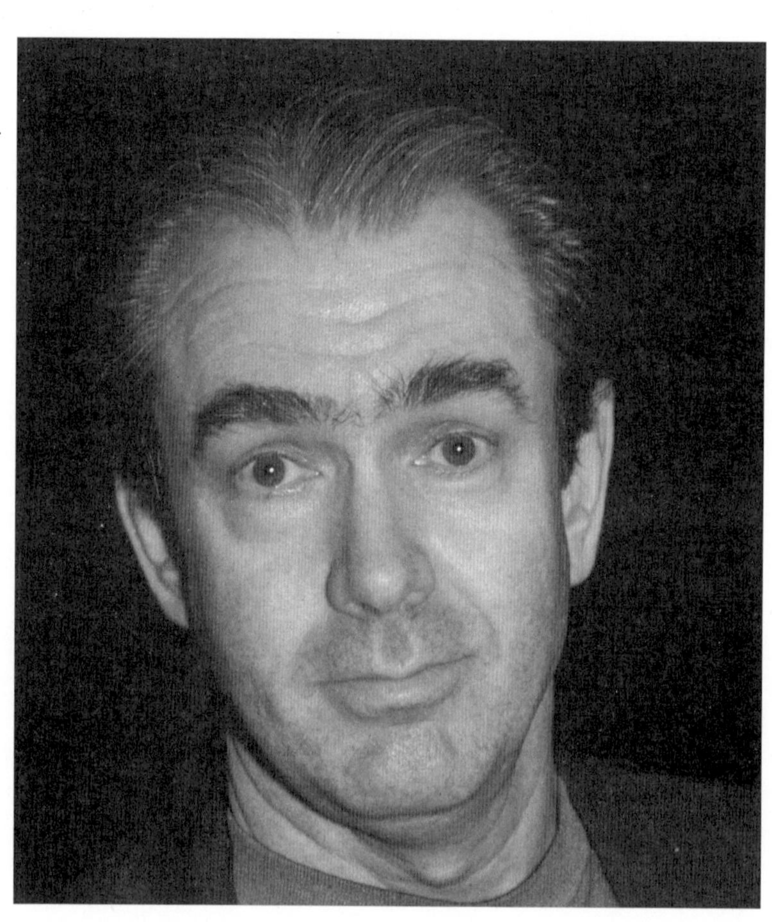

Preface

ART HISTORY WITH ONE FOOT ON A BANANA PEEL

Robert Williams

One was heard to ask, "Where have all the real artists gone?" A question proposed during a period of civilization when there are more fine arts artists and art students then any time in history. This leaves us with the question: What is the definition of "real artist." The word "real" is the problem here.

This dialogue takes us back to an obscure event in 1953; the release of a book titled "Seduction of the Innocent" by Doctor Fredric Wertham. This was a serious indictment that effected the graphic language allowed to be presented to the American public for years to come. In the case of comic books, the result was a Senate hearing and investigation under the pretext that salacious comic books could fall into the hands of children, creating juvenile delinquency followed in later life with perversion.

You're asking yourselves: "What have comic books got to do with high culture fine art?" Inadvertently quite a bit, but first fine art should be fully understood as it was in 1953. Let me further preface this text by explaining that it would be my belief that all art is inherently good and what is thought of as bad art is a violation of subjective reasoning. That being said, I can now explore darker aspects of what people call "taste." The international and American art scene during the late nineteen forties and early fifties was reveling in the progressive joys of nonobjective (totally abstract) art. A wonderful freedom that art liberators had been aiming for since the beginning of the twentieth century. This achievement democratized the arts to the point where thousands of hopeful artists could throw off the bonds of traditional disciplines: primarily drawing, craftsmanship and surface perfection.

Over time this graphic freedom created an unfortunately sizable class of skilled artists who needed to apply their talents in other directions. Consequently some went more in the direction of illustration, hence comic books. So over time the large family of fine arts lost at least a third of its skilled participants to what had been called the practical arts (commercial art). Since it was a slow process, nobody was up in arms about it. At any rate, commercial illustration already had a long and colorful history; its glory period being between the 1890s and 1945. So, disenfranchised artists always had this to fall back on although it was a rather restrictive business. Besides advertising, the movie, stage and television industry would help many. Some of the most talented and capable found a place in the eastern comics publishing world.

One must understand that comics in general were for children and moral standards had to be tightly observed. The forefather of comic books was the Sunday funnies section in newspapers. In fact, originally comic books were called "funny books." But as they evolved they slowly moved into what would be the genesis of today's graphic novels. Around the period of the Korean War (1950) publishers began to appeal to a small but growing intelligent older audience. With this increasingly dedicated readership imagination started to expand into more dramatic directions. One of these older influences was comic's more lurid cousin, pulp magazines, which were also the roots of science fiction. With this older market some comic publishers stepped away from puerile material like happy animals and innocent infantile buffoonery. Entertainment Comics was probably the most famous of the advanced comic book publishing groups.

However, the art world still resented comics. The literary arena saw no serious place for them either. And then, in 1954, the Kefauver Senate subcommittee put an end to comics as a viable form of expression. The most famous of these questionable comics that survived was, of course, *Mad Comics* because it went to a magazine format. So for fifteen years this seemed to be a dead issue. No one really cared.

I could almost understand the arts' reticence about comic books but it's their fear of cartoon and character exaggeration and distortion that puzzles me. Surrealism seemed to be okay at one time.

By the 1960s the arts had gone an entire generation free of any skill-based obligations, drawing in particular. Eventually, some repercussions were beginning to emerge. Lots of trained older artists remembered, and were greatly influenced by intelligent and intense comics that had been done away with in their past. And a number of these artists had no stomach for avant-garde fine arts. With the development of the Vietnam War in the mid-sixties psychedelic art appeared out of an already existing drug subculture. The fine arts world always claimed affiliation with a spirited Bohemian community, but ironically, the antiwar demonstrators couldn't dependably look to the prevailing arts for a narrative visual language–nobody could draw. However, the psychedelic poster artists as well as members of the drug culture still practiced a form of representational art that the academics had long forsaken. And with some of this small group there was a sense of revenge for the death of the old comics world, a part of the resentment that had been simmering for some time. By the end of the 1960s, a full-fledged American comic underground had evolved. In a sympathetic defense of the arts, a popular new form of realism did blossom during this period–pop art. Many felt this was a return to a realistic voice in fine arts. Maybe so, but pop art seemed to have a speech impediment. It spoke in a visual monotone. Its only statement was "I'm one of the objects around you." It could not formulate situations. But soon, conceptual art and conceptualists would preach the old 1839 quote of Paul Desarochs: "Painting is dead." Of course that meant drawing too.

After the psychedelic poster movement had waned, underground artists ushered in the most narrative and outspoken visual graphic trend of the twentieth century–underground comix. Although a few poster artists were in the early formation of underground comix, Robert Crumb is considered the founding artist. It also should be mentioned that almost all of the comix artists, at one time, had fine arts school backgrounds and all were in some way impacted by abstract expressionist curricula. Unfortunately, if you talk to a young person today and ask if they ever heard of underground comix they will just shrug or maybe mention Robert Crumb. This was despite the fact that these comix reached millions of young people nationally and internationally just a few decades ago, and especially surprising since a sizable number of people were arrested and went to jail. Newsstand and bookstore clerks were the primary victims.

There just hasn't been any such display of shear lurid gall in the liberal arts like *u.g.comix*. Yes, there has been pop art paintings, performance art, and photography shows that have exhibited frontal nudity, sex acts and outrageous behavior. But nothing that would violate basic logic more than depraved cartoon depictions. In fact, not even Dada or German expressionism dug so deeply into the civilized psyche. To many at the time, *u.g.comix* were just written-off as pornography. But these cartoonists weren't selling masturbatory fantasies. The premier *u.g.comix* was Robert Crumb's *Zap Comix*. The seven artists that made up *Zap's* talented roster had every intention of reaping vulgar revenge on the memory of the censorship agenda of the 1950s. The prevailing motto of *u.g.comix* artists was "You think the old E.C. Comics were bad, you haven't seen nothing yet!" The uninhibited transgressions against our sensitive mores and morals have never seen such an assault. In one story by S. Clay Wilson, a drunken pirate chops off the head of another sailor's penis and simply swallows it. In another well-written tale by Robert Crumb, an average American family spontaneously engages in incestuous sex with each other as if it were to be the beginning of a new family tradition. With these artists nothing was too sacred.

Remember, at this period of time the self-effected avant-garde art world is wrestling with esoteric questions like: "Is French ultramarine blue too strong to spatter next to warm earth colors or will slashes of grey bring out the ochre?"

I seriously thought alternative comix were here to stay and would eventually have an enormous influence on the art community. As it turns out my logic was simply too naive. I witnessed the psychedelic poster movement explode onto the American scene in the mid-sixties and dramatically influence graphics throughout the world with little or no response from the heralded art academics. These are some of the same art doyens who start to salivate when they hear the names of the old European poster greats: Toulouse-Lautrec, Gustave Klimt and Alphonse Mucha. But psychedelic poster interest among the same group of art officials was almost zero.

Nonetheless, it was my conclusion that if the Sixties posters were well received publicly and then the comix followed up with wild success this visual energy would spill over into painting and pleasantly contaminate the youth in art schools. With just a few exceptions, I couldn't have been more mistaken. Art students were totally absorbed in minimalism and conceptualism. Primarily assemblages, performance art, cinéma vérité and singularly large objects in big white spaces. For me, being a representational painter, the opportunities were bleak.

And then in 1980 there was hope. My salvation came in the form of a spectral hyena with rabies–punk rock. A nihilist Bohemian musical culture settled on the western world like a covey of pierced amateur berserkers. It was a youth movement that festered for the unrequited excitement of "now" with contempt for the future. And one of its main sacraments besides insane music was bad art. Coincidently, some of punk rock's more investigative practitioners were big fans of *Zap Comix*. Ironically, a large number of punk rockers had some form of art education. After attending a few of these inherently savage art shows I saw a remarkable possibility. Up until this point, because of the skillfully drawn nature of my work and its questionable narrative, I had no true peer group of painters. I could see, for the first time, a crack in this ridged wall of chronically sensitive abstract taste that fine art had always required. These young punkers would tolerate anything as long as it wasn't done too well or boring. They loved crazy realism, especially cartoons.

These modest galleries were basically rock clubs, after hours clubs or just rented store fronts. Originally they popped-up in New York City and Los Angeles, but soon appeared in other cities in some form. The most interesting aspect about them was the clientele–mostly adventurously dressed young men and women, somewhat aggressively behaved, generally intoxicated and receptive to any, and I mean 'any' kind of overt stimuli. As guests in the galleries their demeanor was punk rock appropriate. They would stumble against the art, vomit on the art, urinate on the work and in some cases steal the stuff. But, to have work in these unhallowed halls the work had to be spasmodically energetic. And I had just the graphic recipe–gratuitous eroticism blended with brute duress (sex & violence). There was no room here for pipe cleaner-spined pantywaists and art therapy. In no time at all this rough society gained me a sizable following and soon a talented group of other artists helped put together what could be considered a trend.

Now, to briefly change the subject. Some readers are probably asking themselves why all the distasteful use of overt licentiousness, why not happy fare? A good question. Simply put, art has to have the same cultural latitude with drama as does literature, poetry, music and motion pictures. The portrayal of the pathos of life doesn't always make a good wall decoration. Staying within the parameters of sophistication is great for weddings, church functions, cocktail parties and public presentations, but real life has texture and ribald adventure.

Back to my previous remarks. With my participation in this punk art experience more opportunities opened up. There were articles in music magazines, tattoo magazines, hot rod, surfing and skateboard periodicals and interviews on film and TV. I wasn't alone. My friends that were of the same mind were pulled along in the same tumultuous zeitgeist. By the early '90s, big group and solo shows were attracting a sizable following. Some of the punk and new wave galleries also had *Zap Comix* exhibitions. There was a feeling among a few that there was no need for the constipated kudos from the art world. As things grew the art work improved and the buyers were paying higher prices. The movement came to be colloquially known as 'low brow art', inspired by the name of my first book. Not a great moniker for a cultural phenomenon but left no doubt that this was coming up from the very bottom.

In the early '90s there was an attempt at a specialized art magazine that could serve our needs. Its title was *Art? Alternatives*. It was hit and miss without a clear direction. The New York publisher, Harvey Shapiro, had no real idea of an art conscious editorial thrust and it was considered just a zany money-maker.

After so much public attention and the many articles it became clear that a more serious and focused periodical was needed. Since I was the inspiration for *Art? Alternatives,* with Michelle Delio its first editor, I discussed buying the title. By this time some rather important people entered the low brow arena. During the late '80s a local Southern California art hero and art *bon vivant,* Craig Stecyk entered the picture as more or less artist, historical observer and documentarian. Later we were joined by one of Craig's surfer buddies and SoCal art cognoscenti, Greg Escalante. Both Stecyk and Escalante were actually credible and upstanding members of the West Coast fine arts community with reputable connections. And both felt this form of feral art was a phenomenon that needed important support. They understood my failed hopes for the magazine *Art? Alternatives* and my interest in bringing about a concise underground art magazine that would in some way act as a low brow manifesto. A rag much along the lines of the French surrealists magazines in the 1920s and '30s, but with the wild flavor of *Zap Comix.*

There was originally five of us that banded together to form a new magazine. The early conspirators were: Greg Escalante, Craig Stecyk, his wife at the time Lynn Coleman, my wife Suzanne and myself. We decided to contact the old underground publishers but they had long ago burned out on periodical ventures. Escalante suggested that I talk to Fausto Vitello, the adventurous publisher of the skateboard magazine *Thrasher* to see if he would be interested in purchasing the dead title to *Art? Alternatives* and hopefully breathe life into that dormant rag. Unfortunately the New York publisher had no interest in releasing the title. The next most logical option was to start with a clean slate and come up with our own art magazine. Suzanne and I flew up to the San Francisco office of *Thrasher* to negotiate the practicality and direction of an outlaw art magazine. I explained my ideas for the look of the magazine, the content, the layout and the editorial aims of the proposed magazine. Fausto was firm and businesslike but enthusiastically agreed with our intentions. With Fausto and High Speed Productions (*Thrasher* magazine), this brought in four more members in our happy little group. Besides Fausto himself, Eric Swenson and Ed Riggins joined, along with our first editor Kevin Thatcher. When Suzanne and myself returned to Los Angeles I set out to come up with a name. I wrote a list of 125 possible titles for our mag. Twenty were chosen to have researched by a lawyer to see what, if any were clean. We finally agreed on the name *Juxtapoz* and the magazine was born.

The first issue hit the stands in the winter of 1994. It was testing the sales as a quarterly with a print run of 23,000 copies. It must be explained here that if a magazine prints 10,000 and they are all distributed to newsstands a good 'sell-through' number would be about 40 to 45 percent of those originally printed. The rest would be returns or stock lost for a variety of reasons. The returns are probably recycled–that much waste is a common practice. But with *Juxtapoz* the 'sell-through' was outstanding from the start, having only 20 or 25 percent returns. Only a very few titles do that well. *Juxtapoz* was in the black right out of the shoot. The first ten or twelve issues weren't for the faint-hearted causing some newsstands to refuse to take them and art schools forbid students from bringing them into class. Within a year *Juxtapoz* had become something of an underground art institution.

But while *Juxtapoz* thrived the old American underground, as we knew it, slowly started to wither away. The cultural revolutions of the '60 were now nothing but a passé cliché. And unfortunately punk rock and new wave lifestyles seem to have youth complacency in its wake. Nonetheless, *Juxtapoz* sales were still climbing. With the changing times, magazine curator Greg Escalante said it perfectly, "*Juxtapoz* now has developed its own life." The old motto was "the art world needs an enema and *Juxtapoz* is the nozzle on the douche bag!" By 2010 *Juxtapoz* was in every art school classroom. To some students it became their bible. By the turn of the century *Juxtapoz* had outsold *Artforum* magazine. By 2012 it outsold *Art in America,* and soon after that *Juxtapoz* eclipsed the big one, *Art News.* Early on the magazine had aided some of the most talented artists in the country, with a few becoming quite famous and wealthy. But the most important achievement was what the magazine was created to do. It brought back a new, fresh representational art and the respect for the skills that allowed it to flourish. Furthermore, it did this without denigrating any of the other modernist art forms.

Now an artist can draw and paint or sculpt any unlimited vision they can sweep off the floor of their brain pan without having to face sanctioned repercussions. This freedom did not come easy but it can easily be lost under the feet of any new trend that adheres to a doctrine of dictatorial sophistication.

Juxtapoz is now at its most stable and respected position. Although it has been through many hands its editorial staff is at its best with the direction and guidance of Gywnned Vitello, who took on the publishing duties after the passing of her esteemed husband, Fausto Vitello in April of 2006. Fausto was the strong backbone for High Speed Productions, the father company to *Juxtapoz*. The editor in chief, Evan Pricco, a young man who has understood the turbulent legacy of *Juxtapoz,* is probably its longest lasting and dependable functionary. In the magazine's quarter century of life many kind people have come and gone, but none as helpful and dedicated as our magazine's champion, Greg Escalante who helped more young artists than can be counted.

To truly understand *Juxtapoz* art magazine and its intentions would best be explored by reprinting some of the magazine's old introductions. When I wrote them they were intended to instill a certain Bohemian charm into an art world that pampers and dotes over its acolytes but promises little. My forewards are rough-hewn and peppered with colorful expletives purposely avoiding any Pollyannaish pleasantries. Please understand that *Juxtapoz* magazine was an aspiration that was eventually realized–a rotten egg with a golden yolk. Thank you.

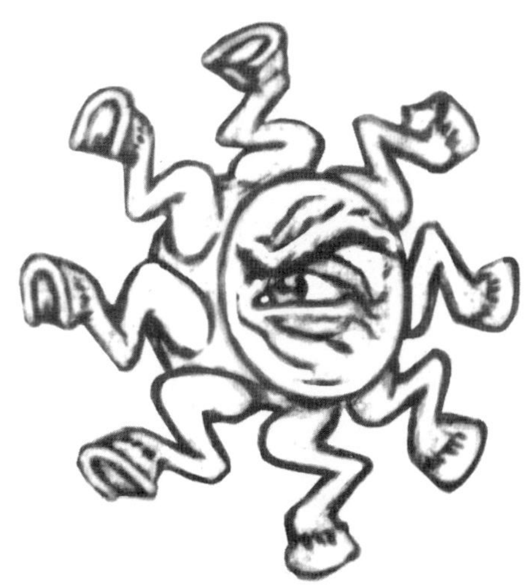

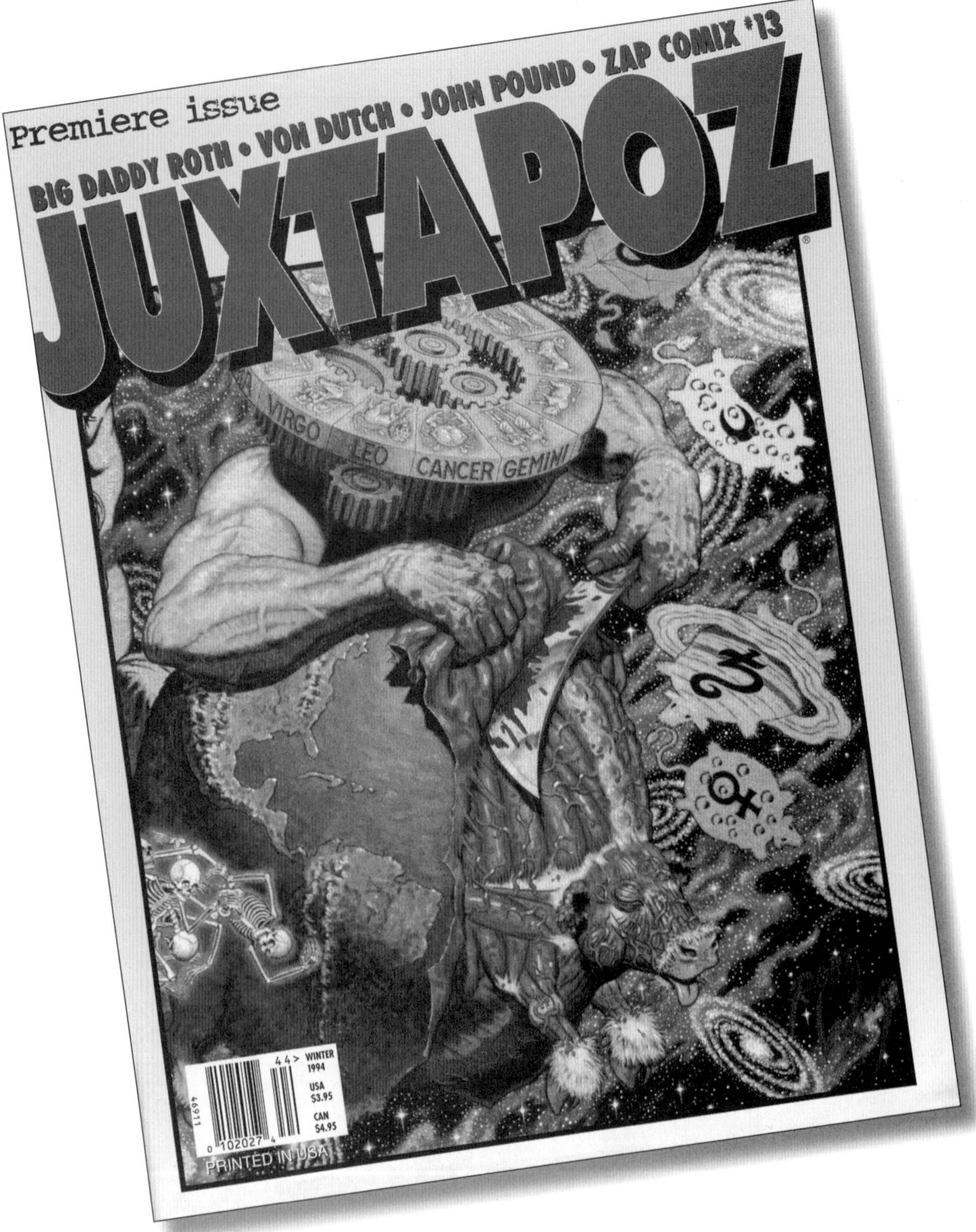

Cover art: Robert Williams *Nostradamus and the Astrological Planet Skinner*

Volume One Number One Winter 1994 (#1)

When you take a look at the history of modern art magazines, you see a direct link to the end of the First World War. From 1919 to 1924 Dadaists and poets put together a magazine called *Littérature*. In 1924, after the writing of the first surrealist manifesto, the surrealists came out with a magazine, *La Révolution Surrealiste*, which lasted until 1929. The next modern art magazine, *Le Surrealisme Au Servie De La Révolution*, came out in 1929 and stayed in circulation until 1933. Then, finally, the most famous of the art mags hit the newsstands; *Minotaure*, featuring cover art by Picasso, Dali, Magritte, Max Ernst, and Matisse. This magazine flourished until 1939.

All of these publications were French, as at that time France was the capitol of the art world. Since that time all art magazines strive to fall in behind the tradition established by these earlier French mags. I too envisioned a publication in this romantic and bohemian style, but unfortunately, the revolutions are over, the battles won, and everybody is now a rebel. We are free to do as we please, place a crucifix in a jar of piss or can our feces or whatever, and our work will enjoy the title of fine art. I have no criticism with this, I think the freedom good, and if it makes everyone an artist, so what?

But there are still other factors, what about the virtuosity of imagination, forethought and craftsmanship? What about all the capable people who can draw and paint and sculpt and shape? These artists have been relegated to the ranks of commercial drones, illustrators, draftsmen and functional lackeys.

In the last thirty years the most gifted artists have had to make do with occupations as illustrators, movie poster designers, comic book inkers, model makers, tattooists and other forms of commercial art. The fine art establishment has pretty well purged itself of resplendent and beautifully executed representational imagery. Art has become what Marcel Duchamp hoped for–whatever the artist points at is Art.

But the tide is changing. A lot of people want to see art that reflects a compulsion to stimulate thought with shape and color, be it abstract or representational, be it done crudely or be it done with chronic precision.

One factor of culture that has been excluded from the art world is the cartoon, yet cartoon imagery is the most powerful form of graphics in the twentieth century. With this magazine this wrong will be righted. We intend to create a publication that will stimulate investigation, activate imagination and (dare I use this term?) entertain the animal hunger in all of us.

In the graphic tradition of EC comic books, psychedelic rock posters, side show freak banners and *Zap Comix*, here is the first issue of *Juxtapoz*, the art magazine that plans to stay below everyone's dignity.

–Robert Williams

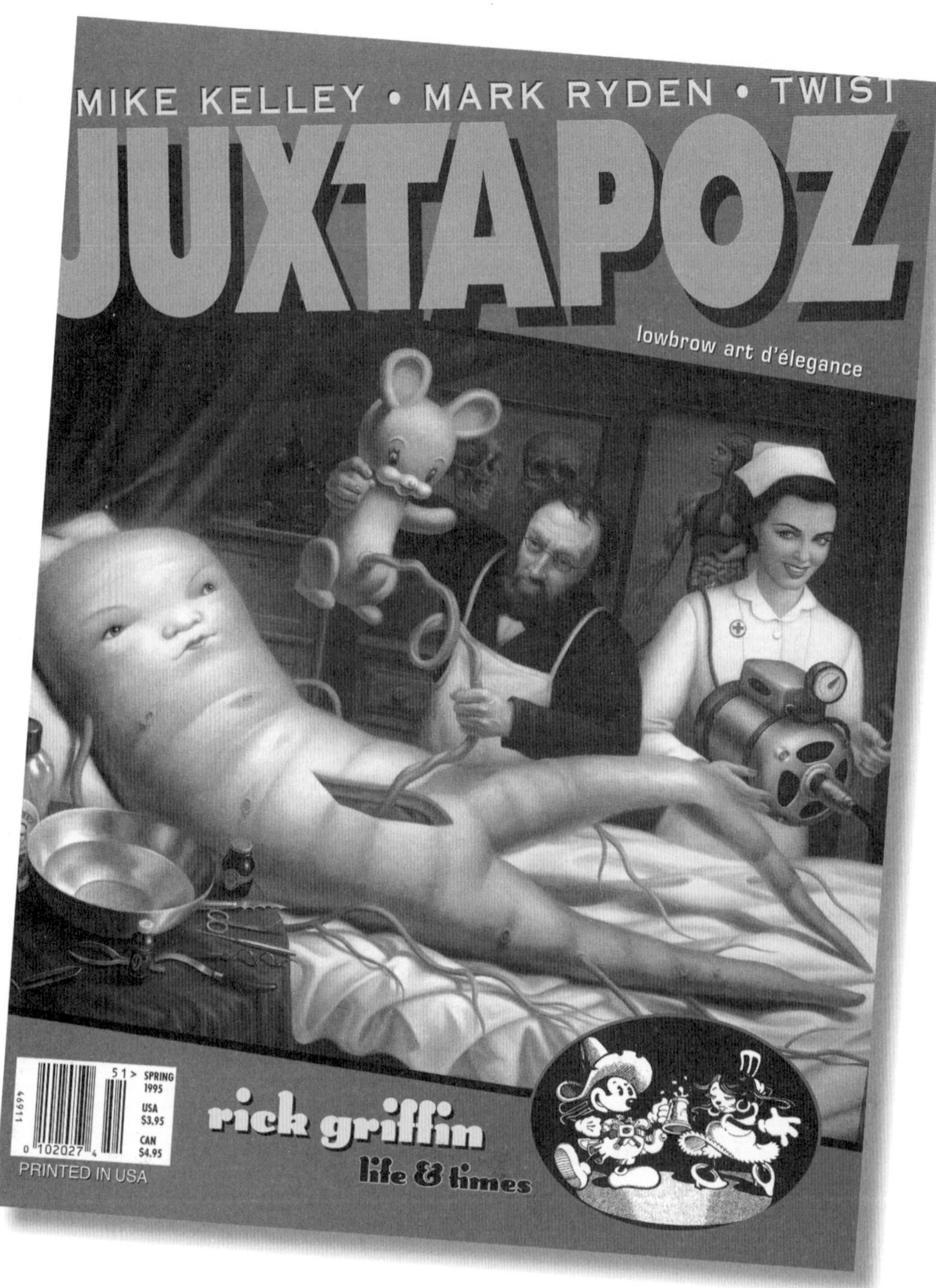

Cover art: Mark Ryden *The Birth*

Volume One Number Two   Spring 1995 (#2)

Just prior to the Second World War, the head critic for Chicago's leading newspaper visited the studio of the noted Polish sculptor, Stanislav Szukalski. This erudite little art reviewer was dressed in the high society attire of the time: bat wing collar, cutaway coat, corsage, pinstriped pants, grey spats and a thin greasy mustache. He walked from sculpture to sculpture, making his remarks on Szukalski's work. He would say, "Very strong nose," and tap the statue on the nose with his cane, "Bold pectoral muscles," tap, tap. Szukalski told him, "Don't tap the sculptures." The critic confronted a large bronze bust and said, "Magnificent. This zygomatic process is magnificent," as he tapped away at the bronze cheekbone. In an instant Szukalski grabbed this stuffy little bastard by the back of his neck and the seat of his pants and kicked him down three flights of stairs.

This is precisely what every artist has wanted to do to critics since the beginning of formal art criticism 400 years ago.

What defines a critic? Well, in theory, it's simple: a well-educated connoisseur who has a long term familiarity with the finer elements that make up our material culture. That's to say, a pearl is rare and resplendent so therefore it is good, and a turd is commonplace and drab so it is bad. That's understandable; I think we all agree with that. But in fact, critical judgments on art are nothing like that. Before the twentieth century, art was regulated by codes of craftsmanship, dexterity and mathematics. This constipated condition brought about a series of art revolutions that broke down the academic rules of so-called good art. In the 1900s, the art market grew more tolerant of modern abstraction, and foreign art from Asia and other lands. At the same time, the middle class grew to the point where the arts were no longer the province of the minority rich. By the 1960s, modern art had become the academic law of culture just like realism had 70 years earlier. This time, however, the governing rules for right and wrong weren't as easy to define. In fact, all that determined good and bad was the buying market and critics. Of course, it was in the best interest of the art establishment to give the general public the impression that all accepted art had been funneled down a road of proper cultural evolution. You've been told that it is the turd that is the prize and the pearl is the flotsam. What the art world doesn't know is that they are right–all art is relative.

Juxtopoz is the only art magazine that openly faces relative art values. Seventy percent of all art judgments are based on pure "zeitgeist," or what is the mode of the times. The other thirty percent of art values today are based on a genuine hunger for something interesting.

In this issue we feature two artists who represent two worlds that seem far apart, but under the skin are directly related. At one end we have the late Rick Griffin, who is the underground hippy artist personified. On the other end is Mike Kelley, the artist laureate who is the strongest force in the art world today. Both of these artists were molded by the same popular culture, music and movies. Rick was an absolute free spirit, unbelievably imaginative, yet completely irresponsible–the true Bohemian. On the other hand, Mike is an artist whose wild creative compulsions are brought into a conceptual realm of logic in the finest Dadaist tradition. Both Kelley and Griffin think in cartoons. Both artists have generated gigantic followings.

It's our responsibility to present an open forum. It's your job to keep an open mind and ignore the critics who claim to separate the pearls from the turds.

–Robert Williams

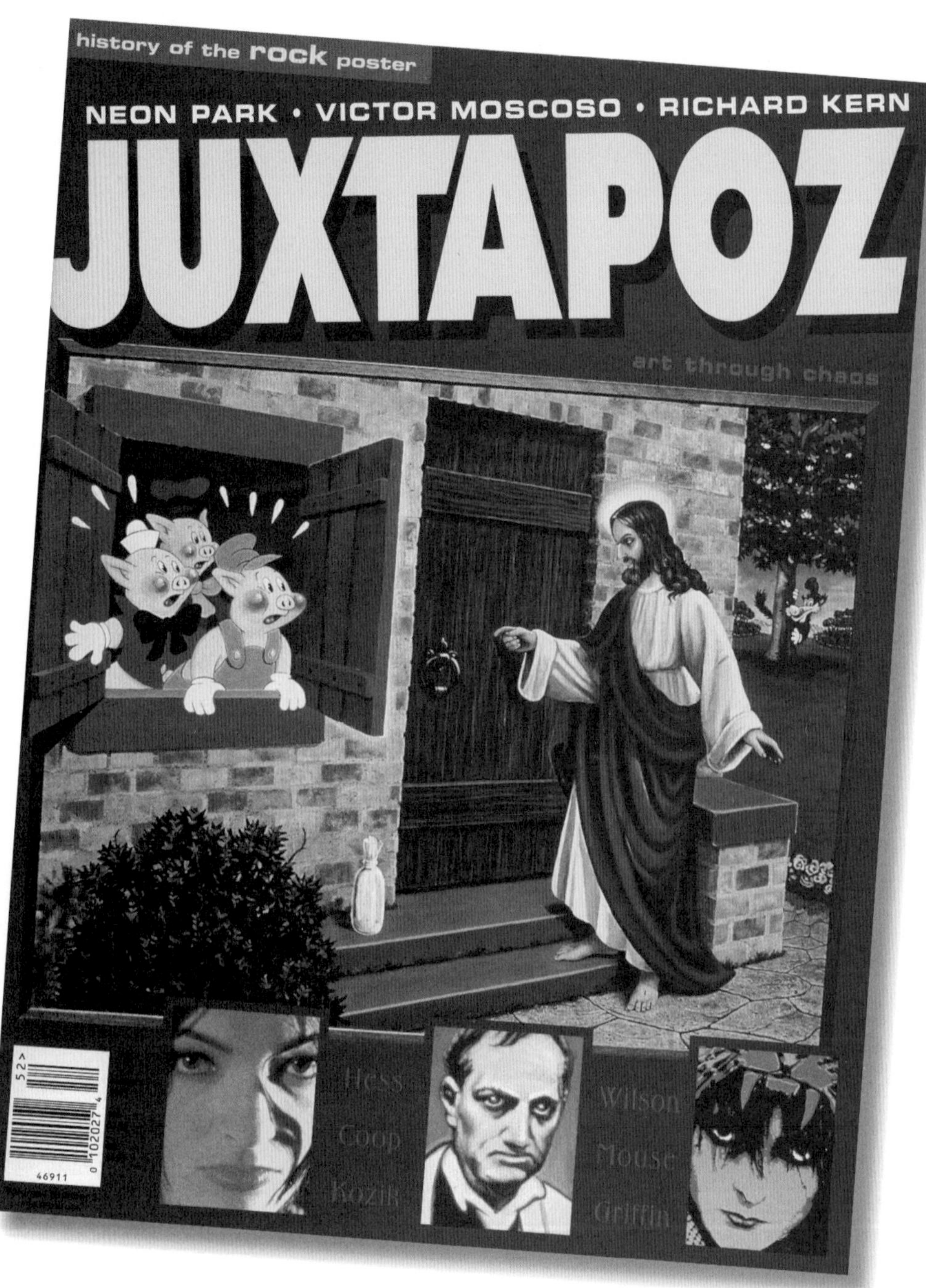

Cover art: Neon Park *Jesus and the Pigs*

Volume One Number Three Summer 1995 (#3)

One of the most important and spiritual elements associated with the arts is the belief in the "posthumous success fallacy." Artists feel that what they do and what they stand for might not gain acceptance in their lifetime, but they also think: "You'll see, after my death, my proper place in the panoply of great geniuses will be realized!"

Of course, art history is an aggregated accumulation of human struggles and endeavors that have caused enough influential waves to be passed down to us as "culture." Obviously, posthumous success does exist, but the captains of art industry have made far more of it than can ever be possible.

Now, I've always been a big fan of Van Gogh. He's one of my favorite artists. But the romantic line of bullshit that had been fostered by Post-Impressionist dealers and printmakers in the '30s, '40s, and 50s is shameful. The legends were part of a marketing ploy aimed at affluent middle-aged housewives to sell them prints. It is now believed that Van Gogh's work not only sold in his lifetime, but that he also had understudies. Museums are fearing that some of his work might have been done by these understudies.

OK, he was mentally ill. About as mentally ill as half the people you will find in Washington Square on any given Sunday. He was an alcoholic and a bisexual, and some say he gave his ear to a prostitute and that he was emotionally tortured! Yeah, he was tortured. That means every day was a Monday for him. He had to get up and try to get through the day like the rest of us. He had an ear cut off alright, but that isn't an open and shut case either.

Vincent Van Gogh associated with the French colonial troops known as the Zouaves. He painted portraits of Zouaves. These Algerian soldiers were reputed to have cut off enemy ears during the Franco Prussian War and World War I. American troops in the Vietnam War also took up the habit, apparently influenced by the French colonials who previously occupied Vietnam.

Do you judge Van Gogh the artist, or Van Gogh the art martyr? How many great artists have lived and died, done great work but failed to get bleeding heart press?

In my collection of art books I have the art bible of 1895, the English authority of the art world, called The Magazine of Art. It has thousands of the most renowned artists of that time. If you looked through this thick snobby book, I'd bet you wouldn't be able to identify more than five names!!! All of the bastards that got their names in the book thought they'd be known forever.

What I'm saying is that if you don't get it while you are here, you might not get it. I hope I'm full of shit, but that's been my observation.

In this issue of *Juxtapoz* we bring you more of what we think will stand the test of time. Whether you love it or hate it, rock 'n' roll music is the soul of the late twentieth century, and the greatest graphic incarnation of rock is the psychedelic rock poster, from its pathetic beginnings in 1965 to the third generation of punk and post-punk posters.

Although it might seem that I contradict myself about posthumous success, we offer you a look at the work of the late Neon Park, a brilliant painter, cartoonist, and album cover designer. Neon will be known deep into the next century because the group of artists he belongs to won't let him die. Popular art always outlasts academic art.

–Robert Williams

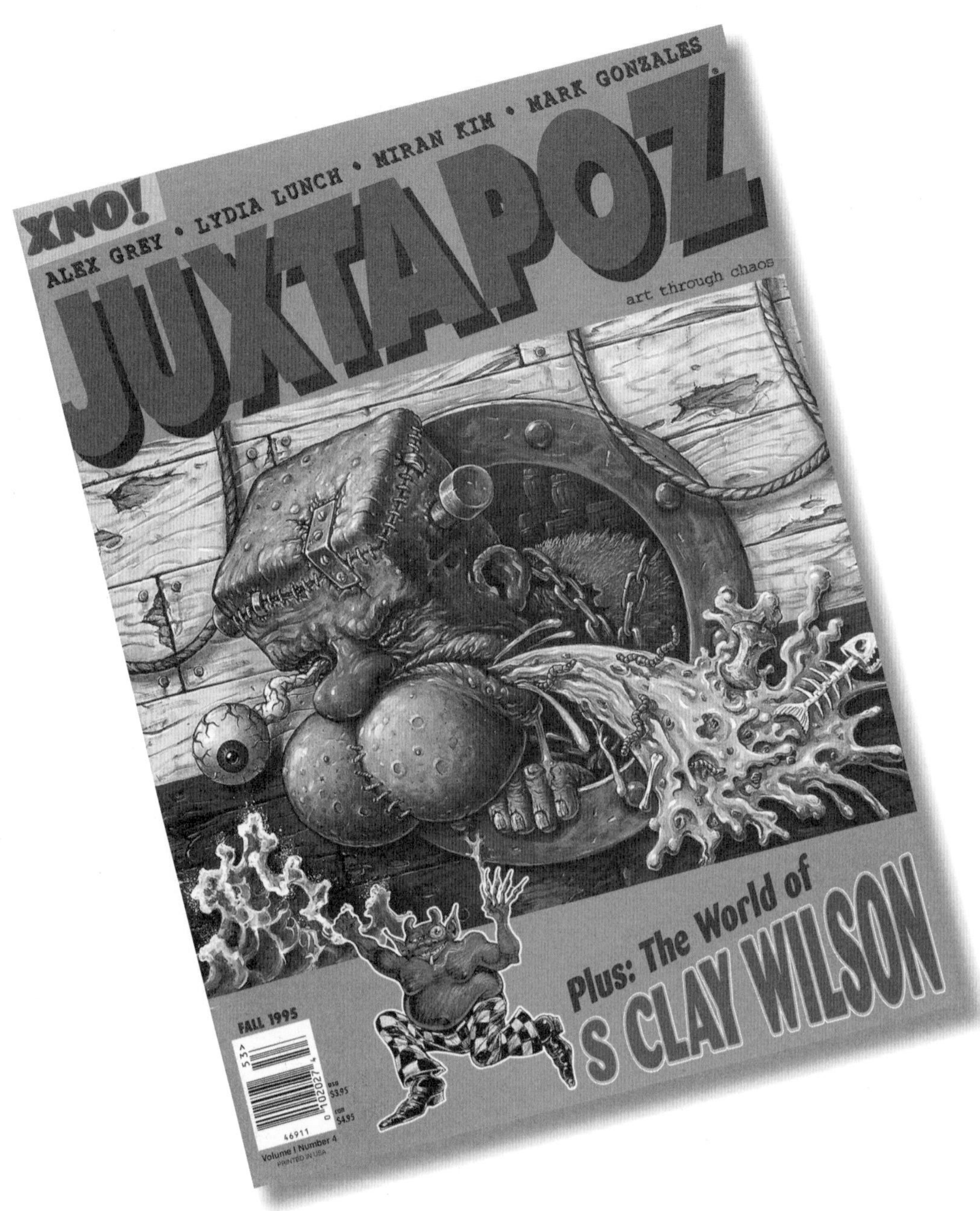

Cover art: XNO *Seasick FrankenPop*

In The Gutter

Back in my art school days, an old beatnik artist friend told me some interesting anecdotes about his struggles with bohemian poverty. He said it only fortified his resolve to create in the face of all obstacles. He and his girlfriend got thrown out of their studio for non-payment of rent. Prior to that he was embroiled in an 18 month court battle with the landlord over the bad conditions of the premises; conditions he and his girlfriend created by making their loft into one big shithole installation.

After the Chicago police bodily removed them and dumped their creations out on the street they left their masterpieces at curbside to let the weather, the garbage pickers and fate be the final administrators of their abandoned estate.

From this point they convinced a culturally starved old widow to move into an apartment and rent them her large brownstone house. By this time my artist friend and his skinny girlfriend had brought along some additional members of their entourage (their dope dealer and a few of her friends). So now they had what could only be called a free love hospice for convalescing cultural pioneers.

With no income, the colorful band did what they could. My friend wandered the streets and stole mayonnaise, ketchup, mustard and green relish from restaurants to use as paints. He would paint landscapes and nudes on pieces of cardboard and sell the multi-hued works to charitable passersby who would kinda get in the spirit of the "poverty is bliss" mood these works emanated. There was actually some notoriety stirred up over these paintings, but it was short-lived.

With still no income to speak of, he and his other "lust for lifers" sold the woman's furniture. They then got under the house and removed all of her plumbing which they sold for scrap–this brought their hygiene level down on a par with barnyard animals. My friend told me that they would sit on the toilet and, after wiping their asses, they'd slop the toilet paper on the wall to make a large collage.

Later, of course, the old widow lost the house and the happy band moved on. But where are they now? I don't know, but I'll tell you where they ain't. They ain't in the art world making any waves because I've heard many other stories of hip beat artists selling the landlord's plumbing and making turd collages on bathroom walls, later to leave the arts and melt into society.

There is one thing you have to remember; thirty years ago, in the arts, it was difficult, if not impossible, to make it as an artist. In 1965, one in one thousand artists could actually make a living by selling work through galleries. Today things are unbelievably better. Probably one hundred in a thousand can make a living in fine arts. I know you are thinking, "What about the other nine hundred?" Hey, they're written off as the "starve back factor." If there wasn't some deterrent to entering the arts, everybody would try to take up the smock and palette as an occupation.

Nonetheless, this magazine exists to help some of the more foolhardy to weather the storm. With XNO we have the epitome of a renegade cartoonist demanding a place in formal art. Also in this issue, we feature a number of very professional young artists. And, of course, we pay due honor to one of the forefathers of the American underground, S. Clay Wilson, who played such an important part in the direction which underground comix took. Without Wilson in the very beginning, alternative art would have developed into a weak, hippy-dippy and idyllic form of expression.

–Robert Williams

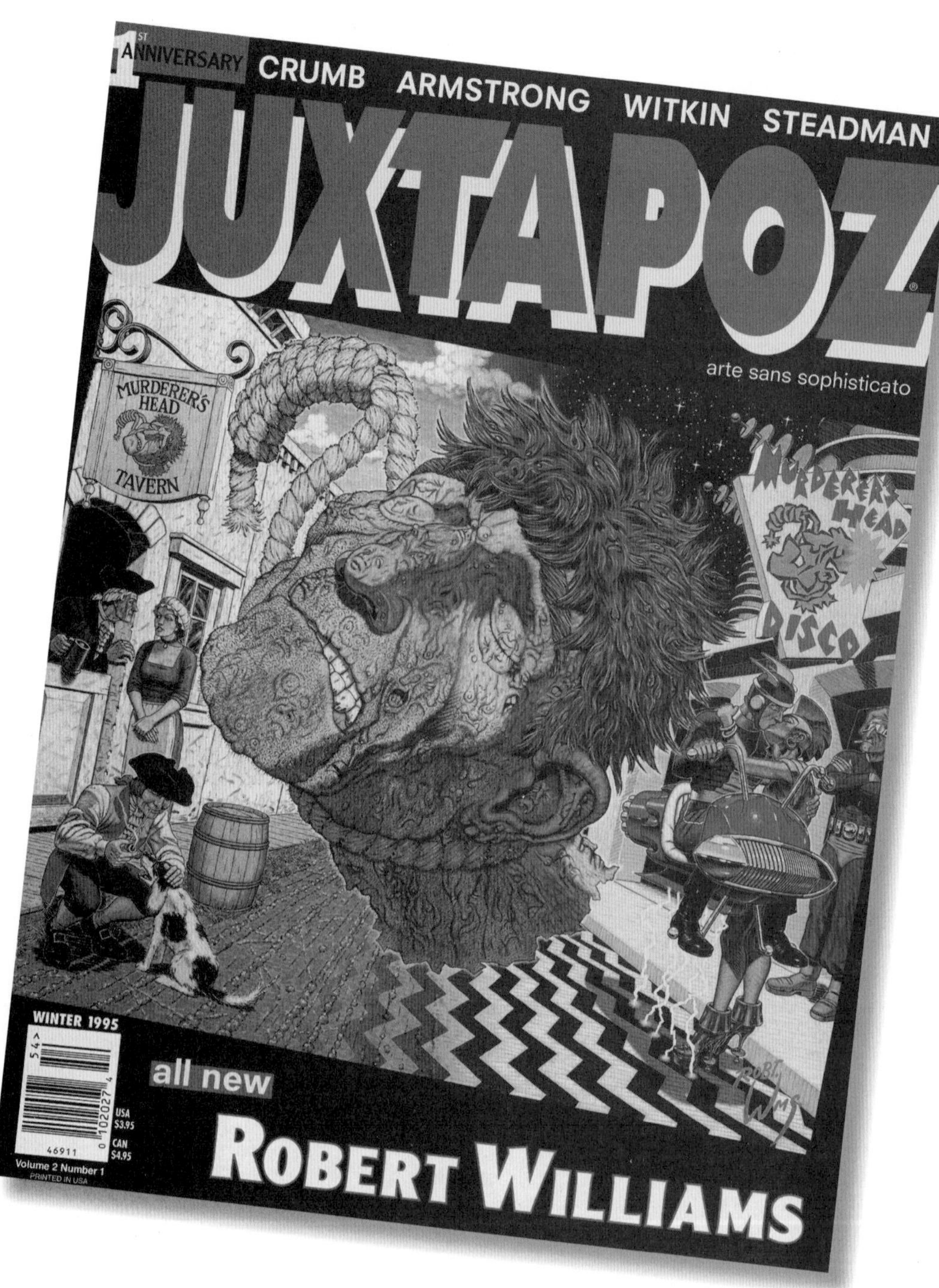

Cover art: Robert Williams *Murderer's Head Venerated*

The Elite Equation

Several years ago, I attended an art exhibition at a noted gallery in Los Angeles. It was a display of works by one of my favorite artists. At the opening, a friend of mine who has known the artist for years introduced me to him. The three of us were standing alone at the time and I shook his hand. I told him how much I appreciated his work and started to mention some points of his art that I enjoyed when he turned away, faced the wall and refused to talk to me. I turned to my friend in amazement and he said, "Don't look at me, you're on your own with this guy." My first impulse was to hit him upside the head to see if he would still ignore me, but fancying myself a liberal gentleman, I certainly wouldn't want to violate the canons of civil behavior. I was now left with the situation of my not liking him and him not liking me, but still, his artwork was a favorite of mine. I talked with other friends that knew him and they all concurred that this artist has a sizable impediment: his attitude. He tends to be enraptured by his own ego.

What I've described is a big social problem, especially in the arts. There seems to be an imaginary sophistication threshold that motivates ambitious people. They wish to separate themselves from others–in short, there is a "snob factor." We all suffer from it to some degree.

Elitism is as old as man and can also be seen in lower forms of life. With the decline of royalty, after the First World War, class distinction became something of a novelty reserved for the very famous and the very rich. The fraternity of the arts never lost its sense of snobship and still feeds off of it today. Remember, it was only through commerce, the military, or the arts that one could rise out of the lower classes.

The arts have always done the most to foster a sense of social aloofness. In the fifteenth century, the ability to ingratiate gained artists their way into court–acting with an air of educated specialty was their ticket. Before the Crusaders of 1096, the royal courts of Europe had no cultural interests or resident artists. It wasn't until the knights returned from the Holy Land, bringing influences from the Near East, that culture and chivalry entered the picture. Before 1096, the order of knights was little better than a motorcycle gang in service to a warlord, but by the thirteenth century most knights practiced courtly etiquette, were troubadours with skills in music and poetry, and spoke French (the language of all European courts). In the seventeenth and eighteenth centuries a knighthood had become a title of such arrogant eliteness that it had little to do with warfare. Even after a hundred years of art revolution and attempts to bring art to the common people, a false upper crust still reigns.

I know that you are thinking all of the above is propaganda for a regime of anti intellectuality, but you couldn't be more mistaken. Despite how offensive and arrogant aloof elitists can be, they make up a very interesting and varied segment of our population. A world of fake humility gets boring quick! Unfortunately, many of the more self-possessed sophisticates are technically helpless–only a small part of the art world actually does the work, but talking to art critics, gallery owners, and museum board members, one would get the idea that it's divine attitude that breeds the final product, rather than physical compulsion.

I have often thought about art being conceptualized to the point of sheer condensed ego. In other words, forget the art work, just credit the foundations of our modern culture on computer generated video flashes choreographed to the strutting and cocky rooster prancings of some artist refusing to accept adoration less than that of Moses, Mussolini or Michael Jackson.

Of course, I think "total asinine cocky" is great–where would we be without Oscar Wilde, Salvador Dali and Muhammad Ali?

–Robert Williams

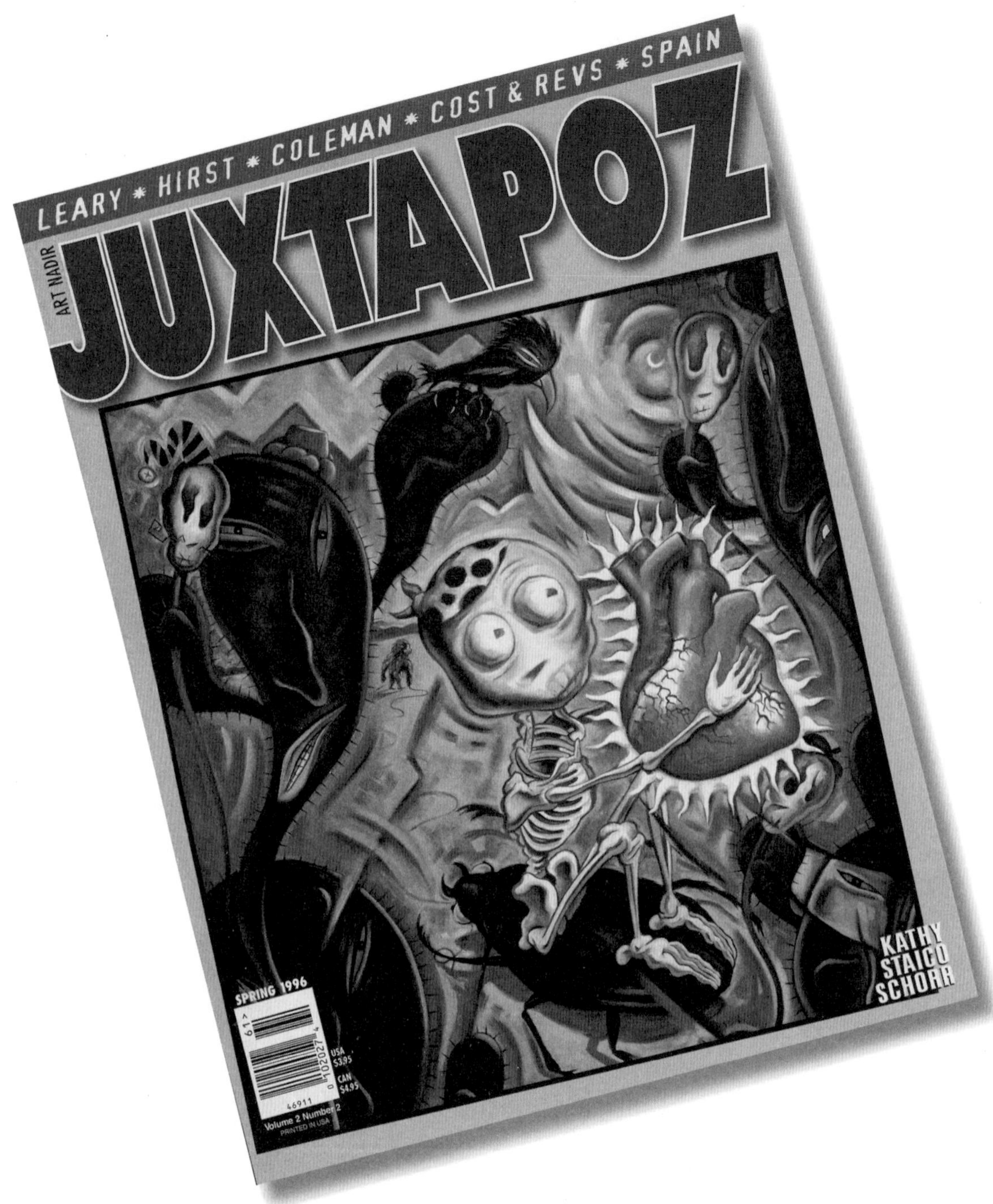

Cover art: Kathy Staico Schorr *Desert Ride*

Volume Two Number Two Spring 1996 (#6)

With this 6th issue of *Juxtapoz* we mark one-and-a-half years of production. Sales and distribution have climbed and so have subscriptions. The interest generated gives a good indication that there is a very valid need for a publication like *Juxtapoz.*

I think we have stayed very true to our original intent as set down in our first issue, to free ourselves from the styles and trends we have found ourselves subject to and produce an accessible art magazine highlighting the imaginations and skills of a large group of artists that are simply disenfranchised by the formal academic art authority. Along with relatively unknown and unseen work by new aspiring artists we have made available some of the most remarkable artists of our time, all are artists you would probably never see in standard flat-spine art publications.

We are truly cutting new territory into the art graphics field and because of this we bear the stigma of being confused with fanzines, Generation X magazines and a myriad of other assorted rock mags, comix and fly-by-night computer-puked-out rave 'zines. With this confusion *Juxtapoz* is sometimes found among some pretty goofy company on the newsstand. Nonetheless, *Juxtapoz* has a foothold and invariably the right people, those with the interest, do search it out.

The most gratifying response is the letters we receive from our readers who are artists themselves. It is obvious that *Juxtapoz* is being slipped into art schools. This must be disruptive to the dominant curricula and programming that has prevailed for the last ten years. We have heard stories of art teachers berating students for bringing *Juxtapoz* into class, but we have also been told of the positive effect that the magazine has had on art students and their teachers. Remember, *Juxtapoz* was embraced at the San Francisco Art Institute with a party last June.

The future looks bright. Soon, to keep up with the large flow of work we would like to publish, we plan to go bimonthly. Believe me, our aim continues to be to keep *Juxtapoz* from becoming a cliquish and "in group" sourpuss journal for a select group of yetis who converse only in language of international "art speak."

–Robert Williams

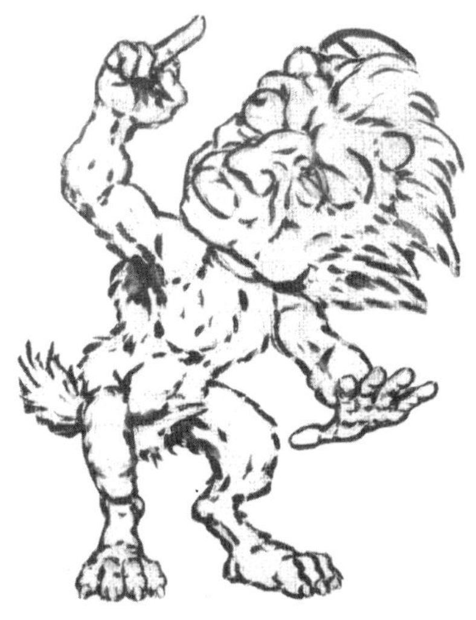

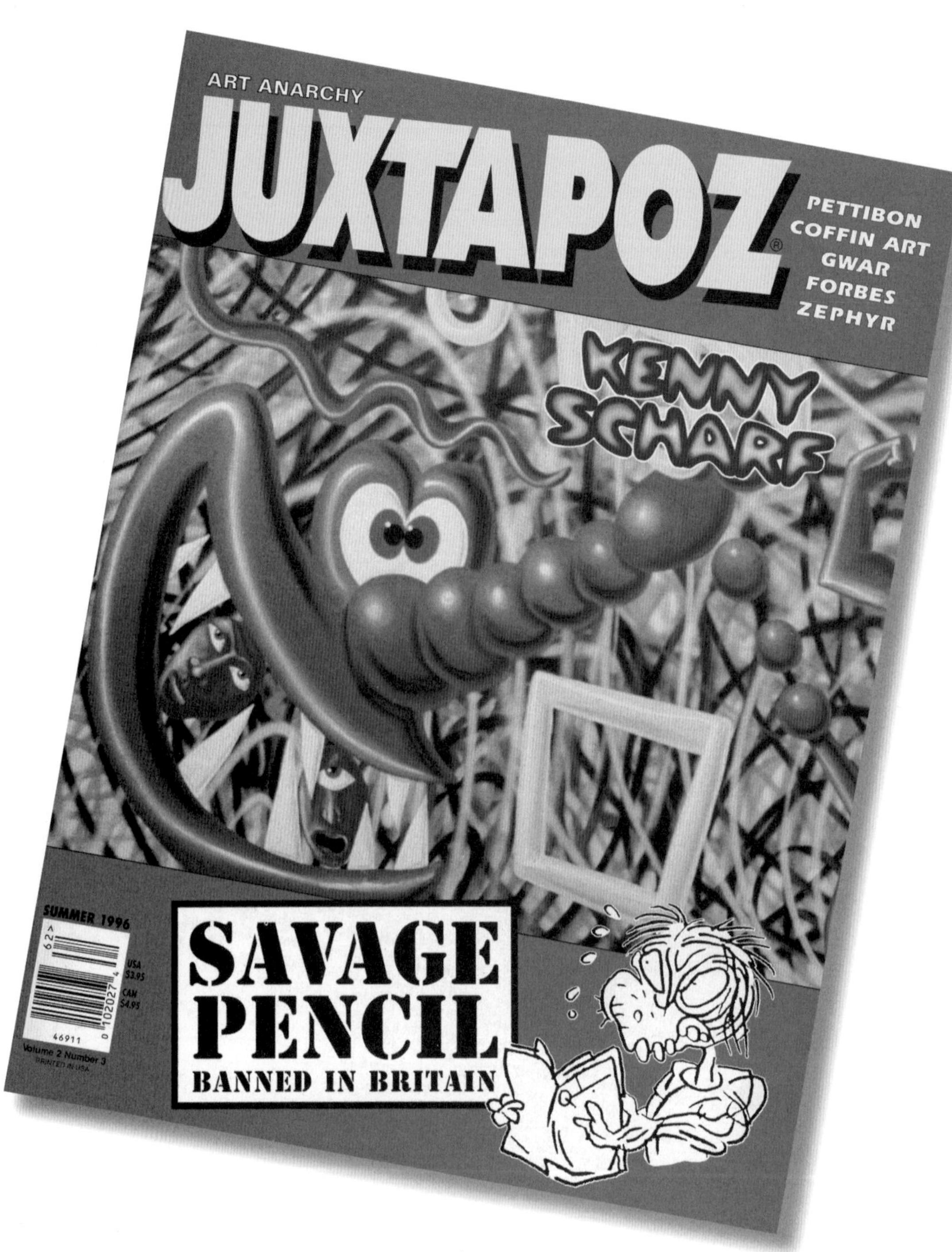

Cover art: Kenny Scharf *Do It Now*

Volume Two Number Three Summer 1996 (#7)

Is A Sinking Ship A Submarine? Is The Glass Half Full Or Half Empty?

Let *Juxtapoz* magazine once again explain relative value judgments that seem to be inexorably involved in finding work for this magazine. If you are a professional engineer, and you draw up the working plans for a mechanical device, and you have miscalculated the vectors, converging geometry, or tolerances of moving parts, the machinists that have to hone and cut these billets and castings and make a functional product will go nuts; your endeavor will not work.

Here, there is no question of right or wrong, good or bad. A 5/16"-24" nut will only fit on a 5/16"-24 bolt.

Right up to the beginning of this century, all art, music and performance was forced to adhere to this rather constipated credo of discipline. With the romantics of the early 1800s, freer art styles got a foothold. By the 1890s modern art had been firmly established. By 1915 Dadaists declared all art a sham and subject to the judgment of each artist.

It took the Dadaists until the 1970s for this anarchist philosophy to take control. Between the advent of Dada and the birth of pop art, minimal art and conceptual art, the old world of art regulations tried to hang on. Their power has exhorted over all modern art and is still preached to this day by what is left of a formal academic art authority.

Nobody! I say nobody wants the word out that art has reached the absolute totality of abstract anarchy. People who make their living in fine arts do not want the average rank-and-file plebeian on the street to know that everything is now declared art-his shoes, his house, his asshole, his feces, his urine, everything. It's all art!

Now here's where *Juxtapoz* comes in, "We don't care." It's not a matter of good or bad. "Good or bad" is over. It is now a matter of relative interests, the energy and pleasure (or pain) you get from interests relative to you. Whether you like it or not, we are all participants in a gaseous thought plasma of abstract modern art. How you react to it is all important, and you must understand that if you get depressed over the nebulous lack of structure in the modern art world, you haven't come to enjoy the freedoms that now exist in art. Just as it is now possible to declare body waste as art, there also exists a forum for very beautifully done meticulous works that can be free of otherwise liberal prejudices. All art is great–all art is shit. Don't let anybody try to tell you what's what.

Juxtapoz is simply trying to come up with art you won't see in a more policed environment. We will deal with art that is considered meretricious, tawdry, sleazy, and, commonly referred to by the name of one of the greatest architects of the 20th century, "Gaudy"! Is the glass half full or half empty, or is the outside of the glass the inside of the glass and it contains us all?

–Robert Williams

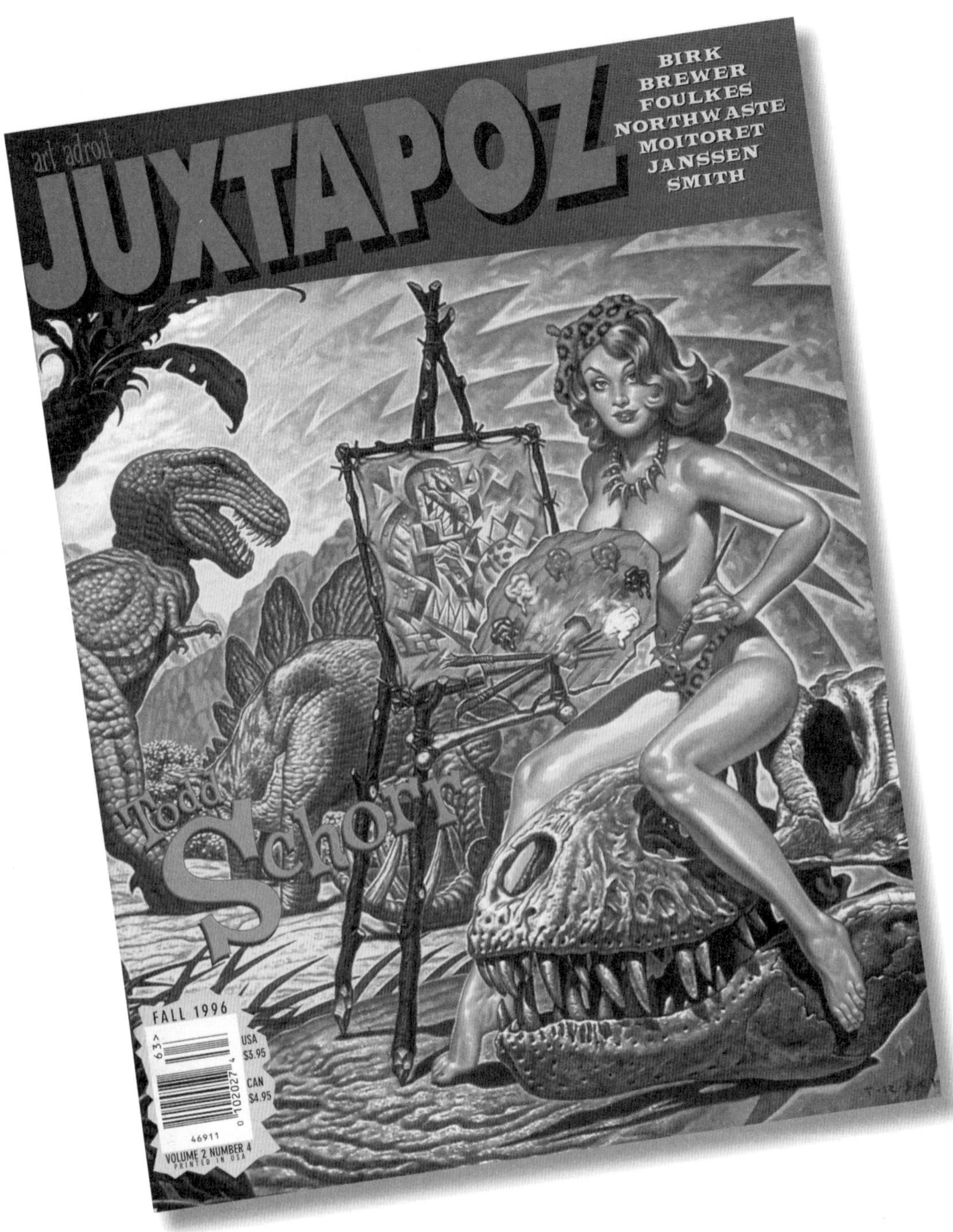

Cover art: Todd Schorr *Let's Paint Dinosaurs*

We're Only In It For The Frog Skins?!?

There have been a few accusations that this magazine is motivated by the want of legal tender, that we pander to advertisers, and we target a market that is susceptible to tawdry graphics. Well, yes, I guess if you look at it like that, you have stumbled in on a nest of self-seeking capitalists.

But let's talk about art and money, and let the chips fall where they may. First of all, if you get past the emotional implications of monetary exchange, you can understand that all currency is a form of solar energy. All living functions on this planet are caused by energy coming from the sun. Money is a way of storing this energy much the same as sugar has stored the solar power we get from flora. Sorry to get so elementary, but putting it in its most abstract context helps to realize what we're all sniveling over from day to day.

Now, let's say, just for the sake of making a point, that you are a genius artist. I mean, so brilliant that you live only to express your great ideals. You must do your art, if, for nothing else, than for the sake of future mankind who, by then, will have mentally evolved to the height of understanding your work. Things like getting a haircut, or paying rent, or dealing with financial problems are nuisances you shouldn't be subjugated to.

What I've just described is the view of about half of the people who currently see themselves as artists, and is a relatively modern outlook. This is the "idiot savant life application." You also see this with poets, writers, athletes, entertainers and aspiring rock musicians.

Before that, the resentment against money was focused on the old Bohemian concept that the bourgeois and upper-classes kept the masses enslaved financially and the true artist of the common people would fight money and the people who have it. This philosophy started just before the Napoleonic wars and gained its greatest proponents around 1848-50, with the revolutions that took place all over Europe. Karl Marx came out of this period.

Now, we all know what happens when starving artists get wealthy; they turn into demigod fops of the common people, as long as the common people are serving caviar with their truffles. The 1980s was a period in art when frenzy over conceptual-ism caused a financial conceptual-ism of spending. Things like a mannequin painted green with a beer bottle epoxied on its crotch for a dick would sell for $150,000. Three well-placed big wooden blocks brought as much as $250,000. Of the thousands of artists who did this form of conceptual-ism only one or two percent really reaped the big money.

And then it happened. On October 25, 1987, I was doing business with James Corcoran, one of the biggest gallery owners on the West Coast. He was really down in the mouth, and mentioned, "Did you see today's paper? The stock market has fallen." Little did I know how badly this would effect the art world. Within three years, the entire art market collapsed. New York and Los Angeles lost half their galleries. Art foundations tried to quietly liquidate their new art by offering it to museums for tax write-offs, but the museums were no longer accepting such generous gifts. Artwork that sold for $250,000 in 1986 was now worth $30,000, if they were lucky–pennies on the dollar. This hopefully, marked the end of bullshit art prices.

There is a logical way of pricing art. Just take out the factor that the artist is a god or a celebrity, and figure what it would cost to buy a piece of artwork that was done by a plumber with Einstein's brain, who charges by the hour, with time-and-a-half for overtime.

Remember, the same artists that have the gall to charge a quarter million dollars for art made of found objects are the same artists who feigned hatred for money before they found their first big, plump patron.

Not to look anti-intellectual, *Juxtapoz* endorses extravagant expenditures on what might seem like worthless objects d'art, and justifies this as the purchase itself acting as a participant in the concept of the art process. And, on the same token, we justify fleecing you for $3.95 for the privilege you will receive in being part of the conceptual interaction that makes this magazine.

–Robert Williams

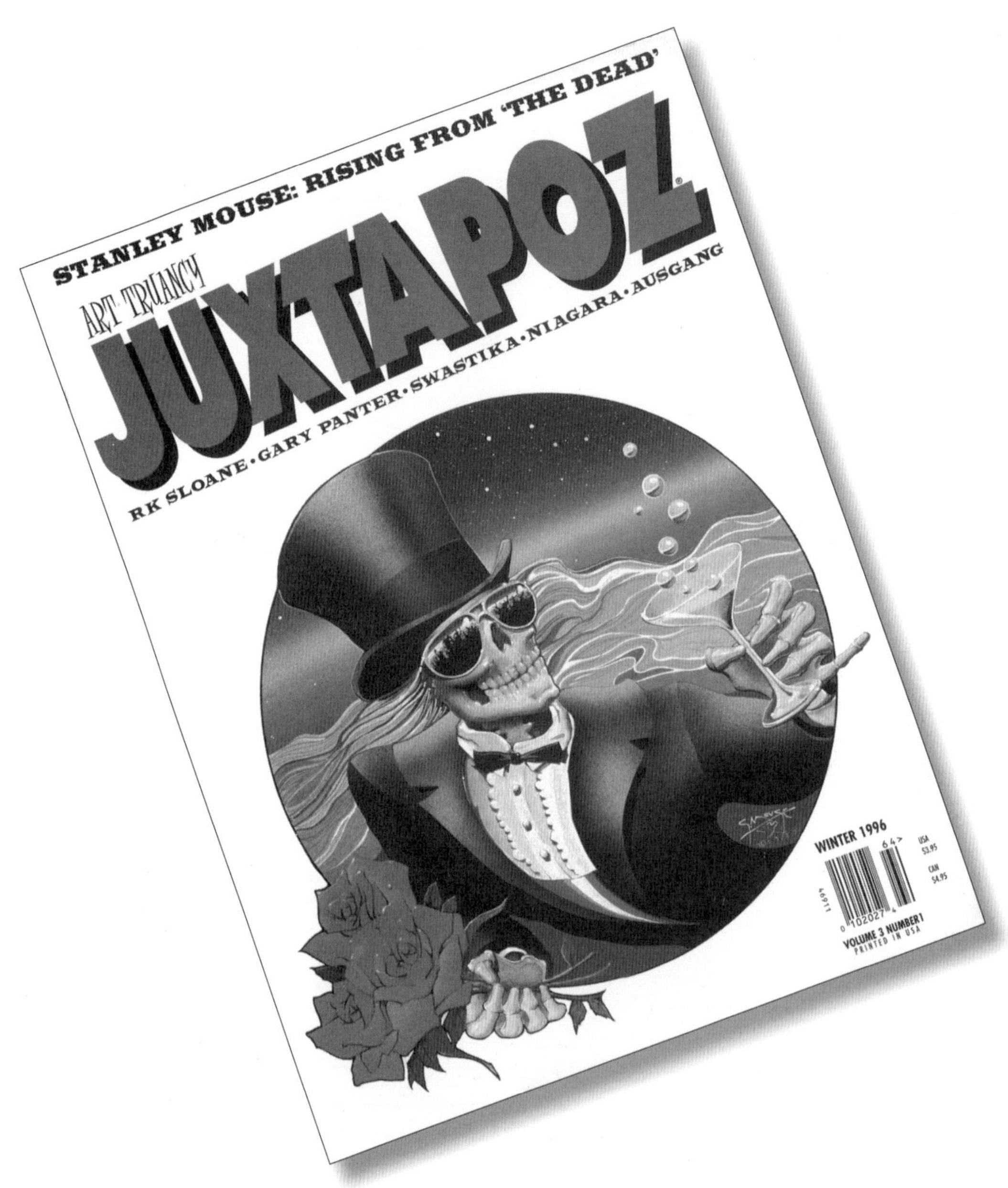

Cover art: Stanley Mouse *One More Saturday Night*

Volume Three Number One Winter 1996 (#9)

Half-Assed, Or Maybe Three-Quarter Assed

Being in a position to observe criticism hurled our way and in the direction of artists in the *Juxtapoz* vein of questionable art, I see our detractors sometimes really straining their linguistic hernias to pigeonhole this mode of ersatz pop creativity. Many names and titles have been devised for this name-eluding art. It's been referred to as: Underground Art, Outlaw Art, Lowbrow Art, Alternative Art, Bad Boy Art, Rat Fink Art, Cartoon Pop, Artoons, Cartoon Surrealism, Outsider

Art, Hot Rod Gothic, Veins & Eyeball Art, Melrose Primitive, Frozen Rock Music, Post-Horror Vacua, American Gnarly, and even Neo-Bodatious. All of these semantic chestnuts fail miserably to encapsulate a form of art that has spontaneously mushroomed up from popular culture. Existence of this magazine is a testimony to this outburst.

As I've said many times before, the one common thread that holds these diverse art forms together is the use of cartoon imagery. The cartoon idiom is the international graphic language of the 20th century and *Juxtapoz* has tried to create a forum to enlighten the art aficionado of this new proliferation.

Let me give you an example of how diverse, yet how united the different factions are that make up the subject matter in this magazine. In the last issue (Fall '96) we featured the work of Todd Schorr. Todd is one of the finest cartoon realists in the arts today. His technical virtuosity and rich imagination make it possible to vicariously experience his remarkable graphic apparitions. He abandoned a lucrative illustrating career, which he could have banked on for the rest of his life, to become a fine arts painter. He has totally made this commitment. As good as he is, he is not taken seriously by the powers that be.

Because of his slick and polished draftsmanship, Todd Schorr has come to represent one end of the pop cartoon spectrum. In this issue, *Juxtapoz* wants to make you aware of the opposite branch of this twisted tree.

The looser and freer side is headed up by Gary Panter. With the aid of his brash expressionistic cartoons, Gary was the first artist to bring together music and visual art since the abstract expressionists bonded their paintings with progressive jazz in the 1950s. Gary Panter had the distinction of being the forefather of punk rock art in the early '80s. Based in Los Angeles, Gary erupted onto the new wave scene with his comic strips appearing in *Slash Magazine.* From this seminal beginning, a graphic rage started all over the free world as young artists copied Gary's free-spirited style.

Although he was internationally recognized by art fans under the age of 25, he was virtually disregarded by the formal academic fine art authority. Even with the support of noted West Coast artists such as Ed Ruscha, Mike Kelley, and Bob Zoell, the imperious pissants that pulled LA art museum strings could not work him into their myopic agendas. So, Gary packed his bags for the Big Apple and the West Coast lost Gary Panter.

But while the Los Angeles art scene proved to be too constipated and constricted for Gary to move through, the New York counterpart seemed to have no asshole at all. Although Gary Panter had generated a gigantic New York audience through record album covers and Art Spiegelman's Raw Magazine in the '80s, he was not accepted by that trend-conscious fine art monster who just popularized the graffiti artists.

As different as they are, Panter has to share the same handicap that Todd Schorr labors under. Both of them have work that looks "too cartoony" to be passed off in an existing formal art category, say, like Pop Art. Gary is a virtual Picasso at what he does, but there is no tag for this type of art, and without a label, it's impossible to market it to art morons. It's reassuring to know that Gary Panter's name is far better known than 80% of the bozos who have shown at the Whitney.

Gary Panter, like Todd Schorr, is a consummate fine arts painter who, along with the other artists in *Juxtapoz*, belongs to an art movement that has been born spontaneously out of need–not contrived hype.

Unfortunately for the formal art dilettantes, cartoon means art for children, art that's almost art, a half art or demi art, half-assed, or, at best; three-quarter-assed.

–Robt Williams

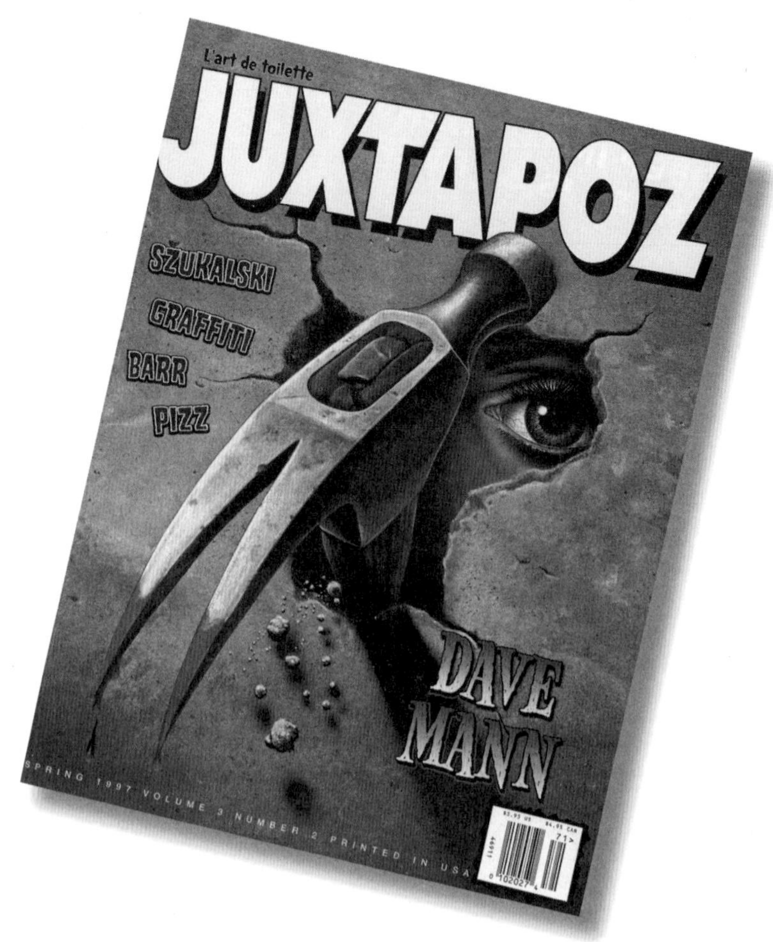

Cover art: Dave Mann *Clawhammer*

Volume Three Number Two Spring 1997 (#10)

If It Is In A Museum And It Doesn't Use Toilet Paper It Must Be Art!

In this issue of *Juxtapoz* we again examine two extremes of art that failed to gain blue blood "nose-up" validty from the cultural potentates on-high.

First we'll take on the question of graffiti. Photos of war-torn Berlin taken after World War II revealed enormous amounts of graffiti left by Russian soldiers on every municipal building. With this image in mind, the civilized world, after the 1940s, has come to think of defacement and vandalism as an indication of a collapsed society–a society that can no longer maintain or police its own appearance.

In 1987 I was commissioned by the city of Los Angeles to paint a very large mural in MacArthur Park at the corner of Alvarado and Wilshire. I was told that this area was, by police statistics, the most crime ridden location in LA and had the heaviest graffiti over any other spot. Well, it was obvious to me that a simple mural would be totally defaced and obliterated in two or three days. I decided on a pattern of boldly outrageous designs containing so much contrast and brutal angular geometry that common graffiti would just get lost in it. My designs remained virtually undefiled for three years. I won, but I left the city with a miasma of horrible patterns and colors that was probably worse than graffiti. Graffiti is an emotionally mixed situation. The artistic liberals who tout the bucolic aesthetics of unauthorized and impromptu wall graphics are the first to shit their pants when obscenities are spay painted on their garage door. Of course, the more adroit and enlightened advocates of graffiti can make a clear distinction between gross vandalism and the wholesome compulsion to create pleasing visual accents to an otherwise dismal and mediocre environment.

I myself see it this way: my neighborhood is starting to show more and more tagging. One year ago, 10 blocks from where I live, a home owner shot and killed a tagger. What this tells me is that if you are not cautious you might get your little creative ass shot off.

I am a big fan and supporter of well done and well thought out graffiti as many of us are. The use of color and abstraction of calligraphy rates as some of the top graphics of our time. But the matter of vandalistic tagging–well, it ain't that simple. I might hate it and it might be against the law, but it does fall within the perimeters of "art", and art is governed by a much higher set of principles that we must answer to (like religion).

Twenty-seven years ago a daring woman, in the dark of night, painted a rather funky looking large female nude on a cliff face above a highway tunnel in Malibu, California. The next morning the commuters and authorities experienced shock and embarrassment as a result of this uncommissioned Venus. After much publicity the city fathers had it removed (this was before graffiti became a household word) and I remember well how this artist became a local hero in the art community.

I had talked to many recognized graffiti artists and they say that they see themselves as muralists or "wall dogs" (large scale sign painters), but the taggers ruin it for them. I have also talked to one of the most famous taggers, CHAKA, and he says that he just wants to be a professional artist. I think crossing a busy freeway to climb a 60 foot steel pole covered with barbed wire to communicate with who the hell knows, rates higher than anything I've ever seen conceptualist do in any art museum.

Now, secondly, a subject that is a total antithesis to graffiti, the matter of the great polish sculptor, Stanislav Szukalski, or as the late Rick Griffin called him, "The Zuk." I have met many exceptional people in my life, but to be fortunate enough to cross paths with this eccentric prodigy tops them all. The art world after World War II was a lighthearted romp through the fresh possibilities of modern abstract art–just the place that would be hostile to Szukalski's hard-as-rock technical absolutism.

It is not by chance that a formal artist who was once world renounced, attended rigid art academies and enjoyed endowments from kings now graces the pages of *Juxtapoz* magazine, the literary refuge for black sheep. Szukalski faced indifference, disregard and derision from an art world that feared and frowned on unbridled imagination, a quality Szukalski was pregnant with. He gushed creative thought and originality. To be in his company was to be faced with a continual onslaught of verbal and visual expression. He was creatively incontinent. How much genius is "too genius"?

Szukalski confided in me that he had sexual intercourse with 60 women and remembered all of their names. I saw him measure the arms of a service station attendant to reveal if there was Yeti blood in his ancestry. But for all his eccentricities, he made it up with the most poetic, rhythmic and dynamic sculpture and design that I've ever found throughout the chronicles of modern art.

Ironically, and I can't stress this enough, Szukalski spent the last 15 years of his life in the company of cartoonists, comic book collectors and other disenfranchised artists 60 years his junior.

Szukalski stood with one foot in the late 19th century art academies and the other in the fertile soil of the outlaw fringe of 20th century art, and between these two steps languished thousands of lost artists, still trying to pry off the lids of their finger paint cans. He had enough imagination to upstage the entire contents of the fabled Disney library, but do you find him in the LA County Art Museum? Hell no.

–Robt Williams

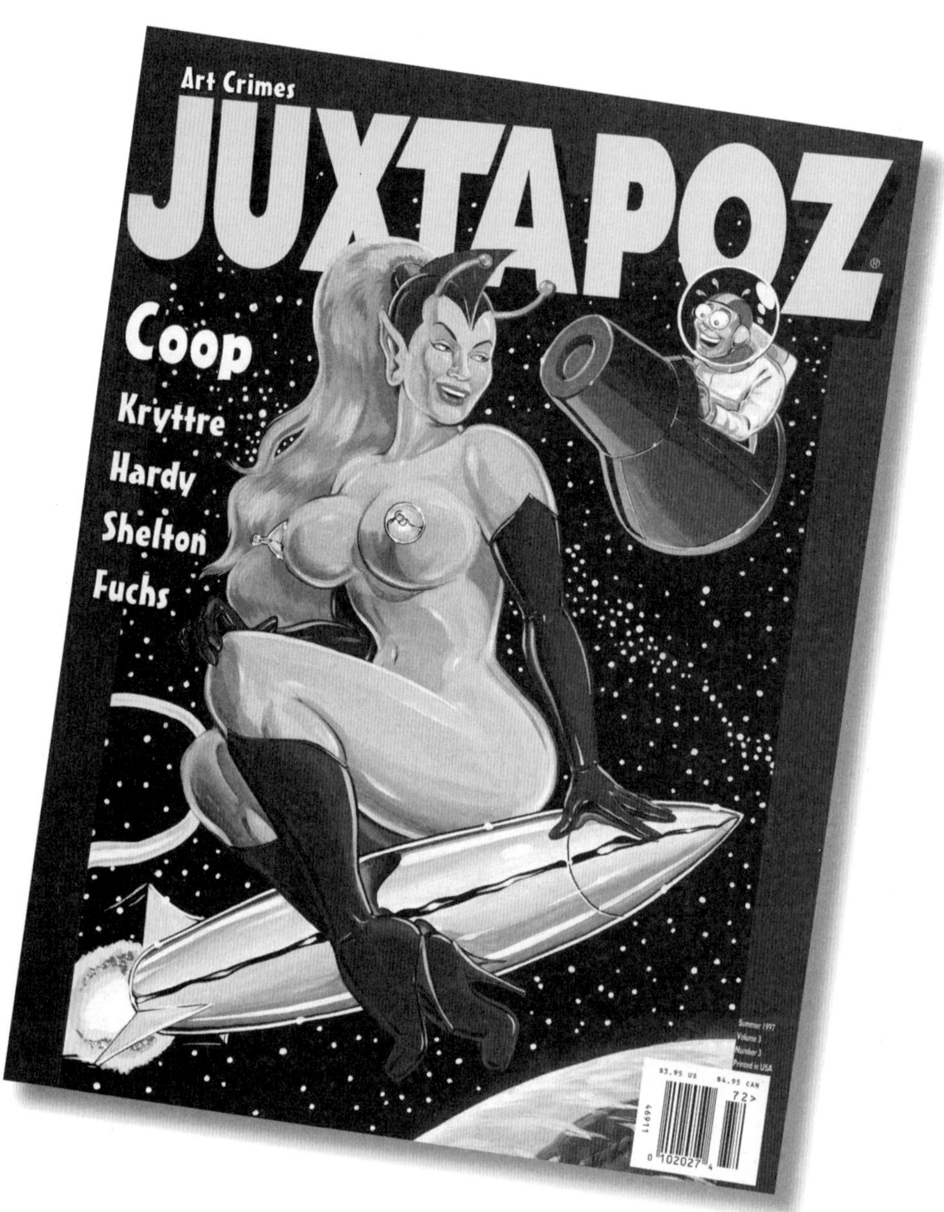

Cover art: Coop *Ground Control To Major Hard-On*

Volume Three Number Three Summer 1997 (#11)

Fashion Failure And The Magazine That Practices It

Several months ago, while interfacing with an old friend and one of New York's more respected art experts, I asked what kind of response he had gotten about *Juxtapoz* magazine within his circle of fashionable and erudite NYC art cronies. "Well," he said, "*Juxtapoz* is loved and looked forward to. But issue such and such had an article about what's his name and I don't know if you know it or not, but what's his name is over."

Now just a minute. What?!? "Such and such is over?!?" "Over," like the milk's gone bad? "Over," like being finished using the toilet?

New York is my favorite city and since the end of the Second World War, New York has certainly been the capital of the art world, but New York has a big problem. And that problem is that being the international metropolitan trendsetter, it has long been given to a bovine slavery to "voguelarities." For example, take notice of the life expectancy of its fashionable night clubs. I go to NYC every couple of years, and the hottest dance club in New York's history is out of business and barely remembered the next time I'm in NYC, replaced by the now hottest dance club in New York history. Fortunately, I'm always the guest of somebody with pull who gets me in the door. But I can't help but notice the poor club-goers lined up outside, hoping the doormen and bouncers will deem them cool enough to fit within the mysterious hip dress code they've delegated as the style for this period.

Now don't get me wrong–I know that this very form of fashion policing makes being a participant and getting accepted part of the thrill of being "now." That's OK, but what happened is that over the years this energy rush has lapped over into the timely mores of the art world. And what that means is no matter how good your artwork is, if you don't have the right look, you're "over." So be forewarned–a lot of stuff in *Juxtapoz* doesn't fit the dress code. How do you want your art, timely or timeless?

For this issue of *Juxtapoz*, we have some very interesting articles (some of which we've been trying to organize for a couple of years). After much communication and investigation, we bring you the compelling story of Salvador Dali's most logical successor, the noted Viennese surrealist, Ernst Fuchs. And it is written by one of the most colorful underground cartoon nouveau skallywags, England's Savage Pencil. Fuchs and his proteges Mati Klarwein, HR Giger and numerous other European artists make up an unbroken link to the Surrealist movement of the I930s, a remarkable continuity that's gone virtually unappreciated here in the States.

Also, it's our honor to reacquaint you with Gilbert Shelton, one of the founding fathers of underground cartooning, and probably the first underground comic book artist (since many of his earlier published works predate Mr Crumb).

In addition, we've dipped into that oblique world of outsider art to avail you to one of its superstars, artist-obscura, the late Henry Darger.

By the way, I'd like to mention ace editor, Kevin Thatcher, keeps Suzanne and I posted on the letters from readers. We very much appreciate and look forward to your correspondence. We receive a lot of mail, most it of very positive, some of it a little syrupy, but about one percent of it is out and out authentic hate mail. Now, I'm not making light of our readers, but the hate mail is always the most brutally poetic. With much of it too lewd to print. I don't want to go into details here, but believe me, if we could live up to some of these lurid accusations we'd be a much more kinky magazine.

–Robt Willliams

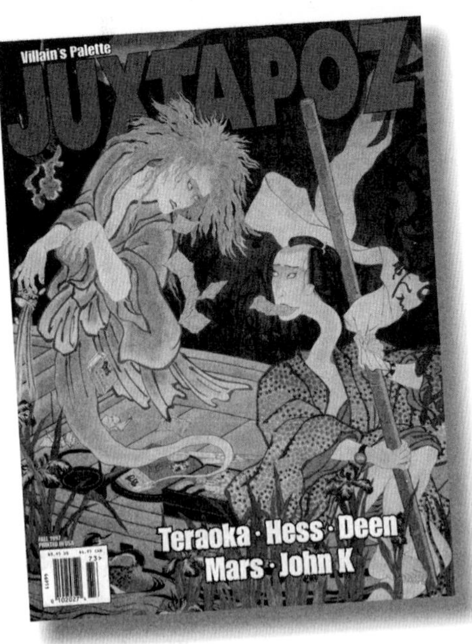

Cover art: Masami Tenaoka *Aids Series/Picnic at Iris Pond*

Volume Three Number Four Fall 1997 (#12)

Art Culpability For Our Imperfect World

Many people, including *Juxtapoz* management, have expressed the sentiment that we should be a lot more confrontational with the institutions that make up the art authority in this country. I agree. But why just attack? Why not analyze the situation.

Things seem to start at the educational level. When I was a young art school student it seemed that art institutes were a fugitive haven for helpless young dotes who were chronically sensitive and irredeemably technically inept. The teachers all seemed to be aging, failed journeymen artists who had to come slinking back to the schools for work because the real world would eat their spoiled asses. But, when I got older and became a guest teacher, over time lecturing to thousands of art students, I was the other side. I couldn't very well blame the art schools because they usually bring in whatever curriculum and teachers the students demanded. I'd say the schools, being generally adaptable to the student body's needs would be kinda off the hook.

The next villain in the chain of art functions would be galleries. Galleries dredge up a whole plethora of mercenary sins. I have long suspected that all art dealers have at one time secretly enrolled in a clandestine used car salesman's school as a prerequisite for operating an art gallery. I find, over years of observation, that roughly one third of all galleries fail to pay artists (usually only 50% of the retail sales price) for artwork selling in their gallery. Most artists (and collectors) have horror stories about galleries.

But now let's go back and look at the nuts and bolts of a gallery. To begin with, all artists want to show in famous and noted galleries in upscale neighborhoods. Galleries that will compliment and properly showcase the work. What this means is exorbitant overhead. Remember, when, as an artist, you've shot your wad and had your show, win, lose or draw you're out of there. The gallery's future existence is their problem. Consider that the gallery is also showing other geniuses like yourself and less than half of those shows make a profit. And I'm even talking about the top NY galleries. Many artists that show are floated by the artists who sell. The art gallery business is a very rough endeavor. Generally, they're run by good, well meaning people but they just don't survive long.

The art museum is who I see as our next big enemy. It has always seemed to me the place where politico-cultural malignancy most pompously manifests itself. If I told you but part of the sleazy tales of political manipulations and Machiavellian backroom maneuvers that go on to get shows in art museums I'd be subpoenaed into court. And as a result, these bastions of liberal "humanities" invariably turn out to be monumental mausoleums to stolidity (or temples of boredom). How do you get past the politically correct phlegmatic mummies that control these institutions? I'd rather peruse the girlie posters in a tattoo parlor restroom than waste a Sunday afternoon in a big, white room viewing badly created something or others, authored by hyper-sensitive academic supplicants, displayed in grand buildings that happen to be on the most expensive real estate in the country.

What I've just vented are my pent-up jealousies and frustrations from a lifetime of dealing with small and petty people in high places. That will never change, it's called human nature, and we all contribute to it. Museum directors are interested in one thing, public attendance. The museum will work for you when your art has the power to attract a big enough audience. Attendance generates badly needed financial interest from benefactors and corporations, which brings us to our next bad guys in the arts; big foundations.

Foundations have always seemed to me to be the vehicle overly wealthy corporate snakes use to get Uncle Sam out of their pockets while feigning the position of liberal cultural benefactor. And they always support and underwrite the most stoic and conformist drivel. Do you think Coca-Cola is going to finance an S. Clay Wilson show at the Met? But then again, if it wasn't for corporate sponsored foundations you wouldn't have any large art shows in the free world. You'd only have state sponsored foundations based on some form of propaganda. I'll stick with the capitalists.

The last culprit might be the most harmful and pathetic. It's the art collector. I have always thought that if the chain of events that makes the process of advanced and experimental aesthetics has a weak link, it is the collector. They come in three forms: do-gooder, speculator and interior decorator. I learned early, as a painter, that a far-out thought or idea, no matter how wild or abstract must always be reeled back a couple notches because it doesn't take very much to exceed the mental realm of your collectors. That's why so many successful galleries stick with the simplistically abbreviated abstraction of "simple is better." What this means is that they better be simple or the wealthy decorator sales will drop off significantly.

Of course, I have my observation for this. There are many intelligent and sympathetic collectors, and if it weren't for them I'd be driving a forklift or serving as a short order cook today (as would many other artists) and there might not be a *Juxtapoz* magazine.

Who is at fault for the pains of a dismal art world? Who can we hate? Who are these art shit-asses that we should ostracize? The fact is, with all the shortcomings an artist has to endure, it's still the artists themselves who are responsible for the character and nature of the art around us. For one to declare oneself an artist is to take extreme vows of personal application in the face of minimal reward. Real artists are usually miserable.

On the brighter side, in this issue *Juxtapoz* is pleased to feature the work of such artists as Masami Teraoka, Derek Hess, Tyree Guyton and Geoganne Deen, who, like many artists, is very familiar with my long-winded diatribe. She's someone that should be an inspiration to any young artist that doesn't see a clear path before them: Georganne Deen, with tenacity, skill and patience has established herself as a nationally known painter. And she's done this without piggybacking on any movement or ensconcing herself in the right crowd in order to coast along with the popular art tide that permeates the Los Angeles art milieu. She was one of the seminal figures in the punk rock art movement in the early '80s and rapidly rose above her underground roots to become an art star in a begrudging firmament.

–Robt Williams '97

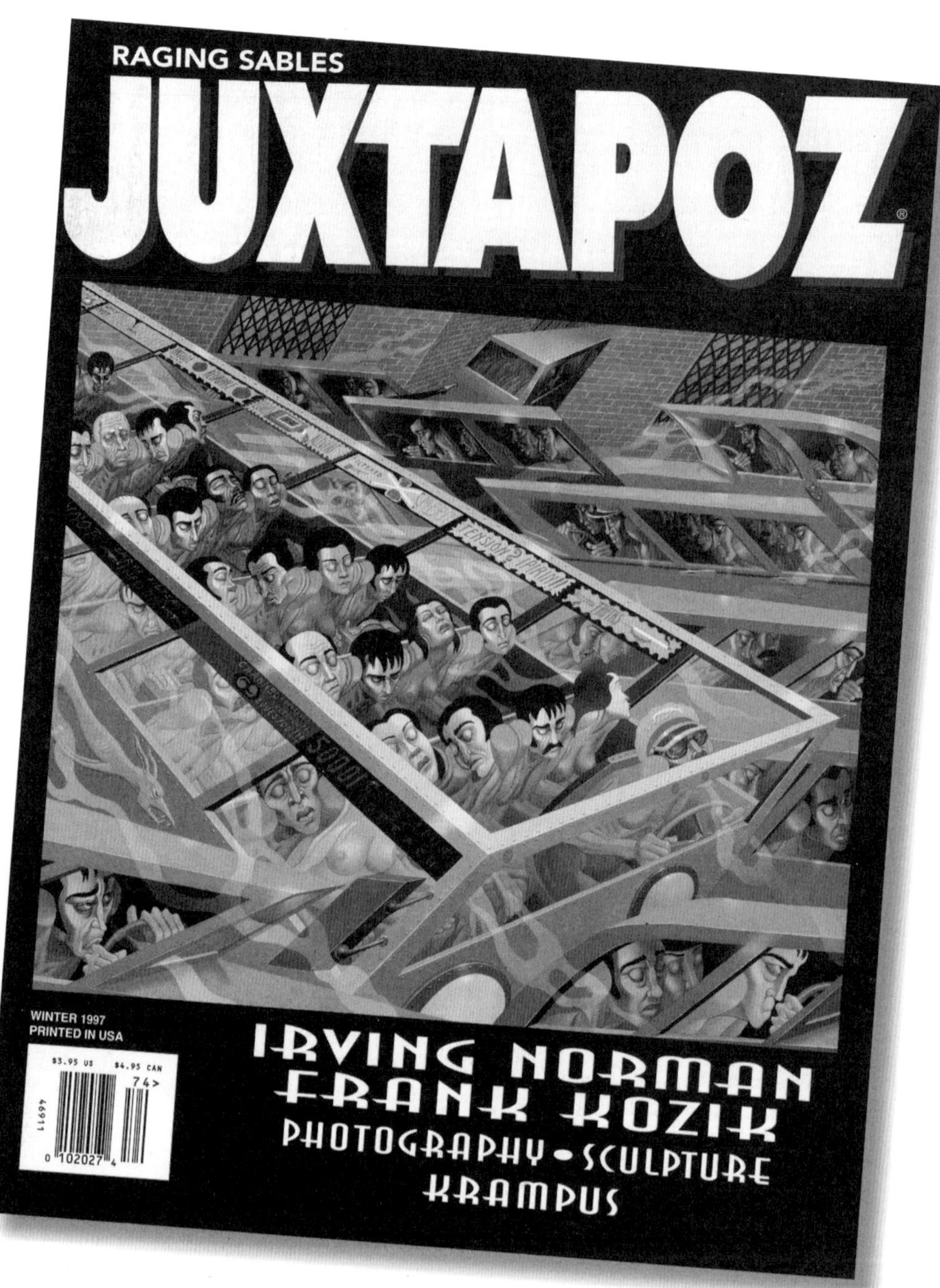

Cover art: Irving Norman (detail) *Truth Be Told*

Volume Four Number One Winter 1997 (#13)

Commercialism: Does Integrity Come With A Barcode?

A couple of questions have been addressed to me regarding where commercial art ends and fine art begins. What is selling out?

Let me put it like this, "fine art" wasn't even a concept until the late 1700s. All the great paintings and sculptures before that were monetary commissions. If you are an artist and have to survive, and can draw and paint, I would certainly seek out a graphic job before I'd tackle labor and agricultural vocations. But, there does come a time when you have to express thoughts that exceed everyday factionalism. If you are born with an investigative and abstract mind, and if you are not a fool completely deluding yourself, you might be an artist. If you are a fool that can support yourself and still try to be an artist, you are innocent. If you are a fool and can't support yourself, and are still determined to be an artist, well, you're on your own. Unfortunately, I find being pompous is a great aide to being technically inept.

As usual, we have a varied and diverse gaggle of articles this issue. *Juxtapoz* is proud to be featuring the near-obscure work of Irving Norman and the nationally-acclaimed efforts of poster artist Frank Kozik, plus a glimpse at the old German Christmas demon, Krampus, a fabled character of the repressed Teutonic psyche. Also, we've decided to treat our readers to a survey of thirteen works by artists who are familiar. This is not a pontifying endorsement of the greatest artists that have ever lived. A number of the artists have been excluded for use at another time so don't be hurt if you don't see work by Peter Max or Julian Schnabel at this time.

Let me end on a obituary note. It came to our attention, weeks after the fact, that early punk rock artist May Zone passed away. May Zone was one of the original artists and painters to burst on to the burgeoning punk storm that hit Los Angeles in the early '80s. May, along with Gary Panter, Raymond Pettibon, Bob Zoell and Georganne Deen, headed an energetic clan of new wave artists to have art shows that revitalized the otherwise stagnant West Coast art scene. Of them, May was the most brazen. Once, for a Saturday night show at the Zero One Gallery, she, in true punk rock tradition, didn't strike a lick until the afternoon of the show, when, on the way to the gallery, she searched all the alleys and garbage dumpsters along her path and started to gather up her "work". By seven o'clock that night, May with the use of day-glo paint and glitter, had entered the realm of the great conceptualists. She was a wonderful and innocent person. She died from brain cancer on May 9, twenty days before her 44th birthday. Good-bye May.

–Robt. Williams

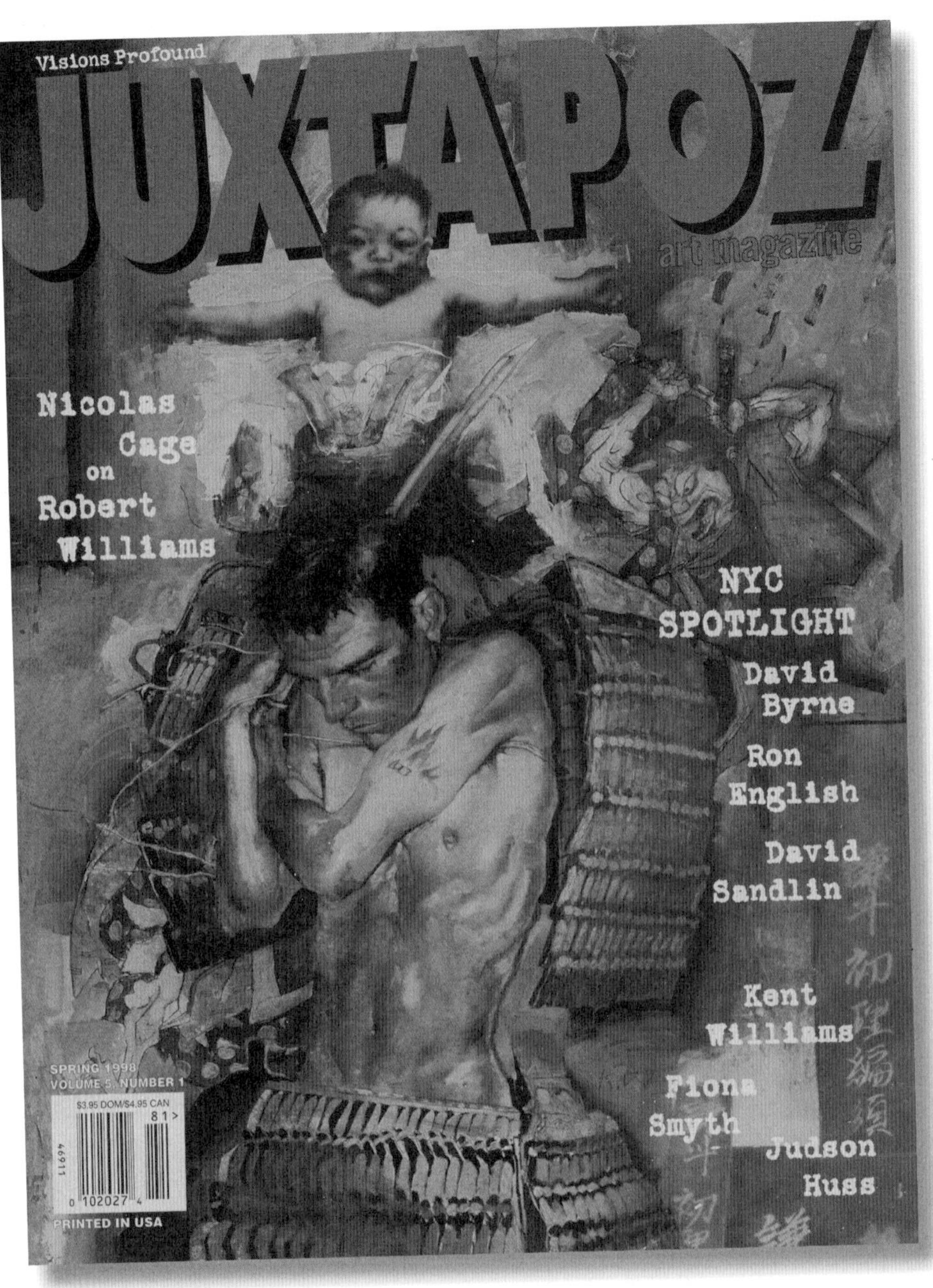

Cover art: Kent Williams *Kokoro*

New York, New York *Seen Through Philistine Eyes*

My first thoughts of NYC in an artistic context came about when I was taking art classes in high school in Albuquerque, New Mexico. A fellow student informed me that our teacher was of some relative importance in the big art world because he had an agent in New York. From that moment on NYC was for me an art Oz. New York City has maintained its reputation as the world art capitol since the end of World war II. In the '50s, Abstract Expressionism was the fresh direction that gave NYC the vitality to hold onto that title. And then in the early '60s, Pop Art once again reinforced the city's position. Graffiti art proved fashionable in the early '80s, but had to contend with much larger forces in New York and Europe. By the mid 1970s the theoretic aesthetics of Minimalism and Conceptualism had completely dominated all sectors of the fine arts authority, like Abstract Expressionism had a decade before. That's where New York art is today. Even after the big '87 stock market shake up, art galleries there still stick to the theoretical art formula of the '80s. New York remains my favorite city to show art, but it comes with its own set of problems. It has probably the highest per capita of failed artists on record. Guggenheim figures show the amount of artists in New York as over 100,000, but the amount of artists actually making a living is only a fraction. I remember in '92 at one point New York had only ten artists making a profit for their galleries.

But enough about the proper NYC art scene. Let me answer some remarks aimed at *Juxtapoz* about our supposed failure to cover the sub-art world there. To begin with, no matter what region we investigate, we're sure to neglect or piss off someone. I'm sure there's some farm boy in Kansas or some manicurist in Miami that has remarkable graphic talent, and that we've failed to recognize the scene they've generated locally. But, I don't think New York is one of our big neglects. If you want to investigate the East Coast's early undercurrents I suggest you find more on Mati Klarwein, as well as artists that were prevalent in the late '60s magazine, *Avant Garde*. From that point you might search out old copies of Art Spiegelman's *Raw* magazine for underground cartoonists. New York was not able to reach the height of underground comics of the West Coast because the New York mafia saw them as a form of pornography and thus subject to underworld control. *Raw* magazine superseded this problem with a more fashionable publication. Punk rock music's effect on NYC underground art was sized up in a book by Steve Hager titled *Art After Midnight*. This 1986 book gives a good idea of what's filtered down from the art youth movement in the last decade. Of course, Jacaeber Kastor's Phychedelic Solution Gallery continued the art traditions of CBGB's and Danceteria.

We don't pretend to know everything about the hidden New York art scene (or any other underground art scene) but we've brought to light a lot of material no other magazine would touch. This issue we've brought before you some of NYC's more ambitious artists. Besides Kent Williams, Ron English and David Sandlin, you'll see an article on David Byrne and a gallery showcase featuring some of the Big Apple's finest.

Juxtapoz is still the best art publication for *vox populi outré*!

–Robt. Williams

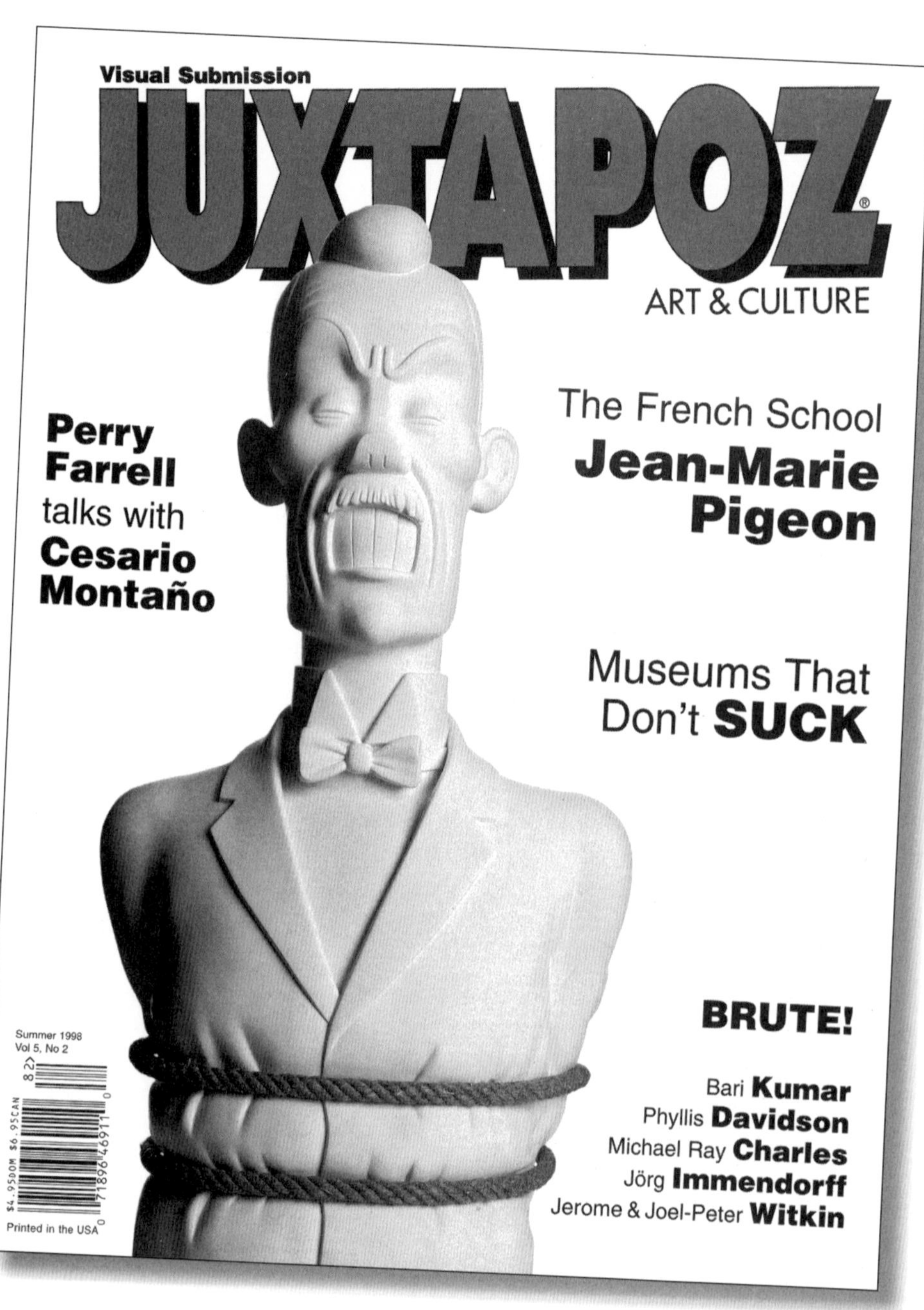

Cover art: Jean-Marie Pigeon, Mitsuhirato from *The Blue Lotus*

Volume Five Number Two Summer 1998 (#15)

An Impassioned Solicitation To The Discerning Collector

A few years ago an interested art buyer asked me if I had any paintings with the number six in them. Now, that sounds silly to me but if that is his point of entry into the art world, God bless him. He is what I would call a "tunnel vision connoisseur."

Many times other artists and myself hear requests for works with "lotsa tits & ass." While I would think of this buyer as a "libidinally-driven dilettante," this doesn't mean this patron is a nincompoop. This is just an honest way to appreciate the nude human figure in an art context and maybe shows a special proclivity for pin-up work (Olivia, Vargas, Kern, etc).

An art collector has to feel free to seek out what interests him without feeling foolish, and the artist has to be free to produce unorthodox, experimental and wild new work. However the artist is the fool if he does not try to make the work mentally accessible to his benefactors. Through the very act of purchasing the work the collector empowers him or herself as the endorser who validates the project.

In short, the collector is an intelligent participant in making art a reality. I cannot drivel on enough about their importance.

Juxtapoz magazine has done what it can with its ability to expose new artists and exciting artwork to an otherwise constricted modern culture. The collector has to pick up the reins and help us drive the art oxen into the next century.

One problem is that the artist lives in a dream world of whom his ideal underwriter should be. If you have lulled yourself into believing that trendy celebrities and wealthy captains of industry will seek out your work, wake up. We all envision that perfect buyer, "the Alpha collector," the young well-to-do *bon vivant* who can sense your genius and falls right in line with your program. Forget it.

And of course there is that old academic delusion of the sympathetic art foundation awaiting your application for a grant or fellowship handout. Good luck. Believe me, the artists who have success down this road have made a career out of it.

Oh, and don't think the right gallery is going to bail out the artist either. More and more large galleries expect the artists to bring their own following.

The artist alone has to learn how to cultivate a buying audience and form a personal covenant with them. And this can be done without depending on "decorator patrons." If an artist's work is intelligent style-wise, and worth its money, an advanced collector will understand that the work has more content than a mere wall decoration. And speaking of walls, the true art cognoscente buys much more art than that which will fit their walls. A great art collection is displayed in periodic rotation.

The noted paleoanthropologist Richard Leakey, while reflecting on the human nature of accumulating and hording special treasures that should be shared with the public, stated that collecting is a form of selfish psycho-materialism.

Well, if that should be the case, let me endorse this rampant psychosis. If an art devotee can reach the same degree of cogent enthusiasm the artist experiences in the creation of the work, the appearance of being psychotic and greedy is irrelevant. Invest in art.

This issue *Juxtapoz* is honored to feature the paintings of Jorg Immendorff, Jerome Witkin, Phyllis Davidson, Michael Ray Charles and Alonso Smith, alongside photography by Joel Peter Witkin, Cesario Montano "Block" and sculpture by cover artist Jean-Marie Pigeon. Enjoy.

–Robt. Williams

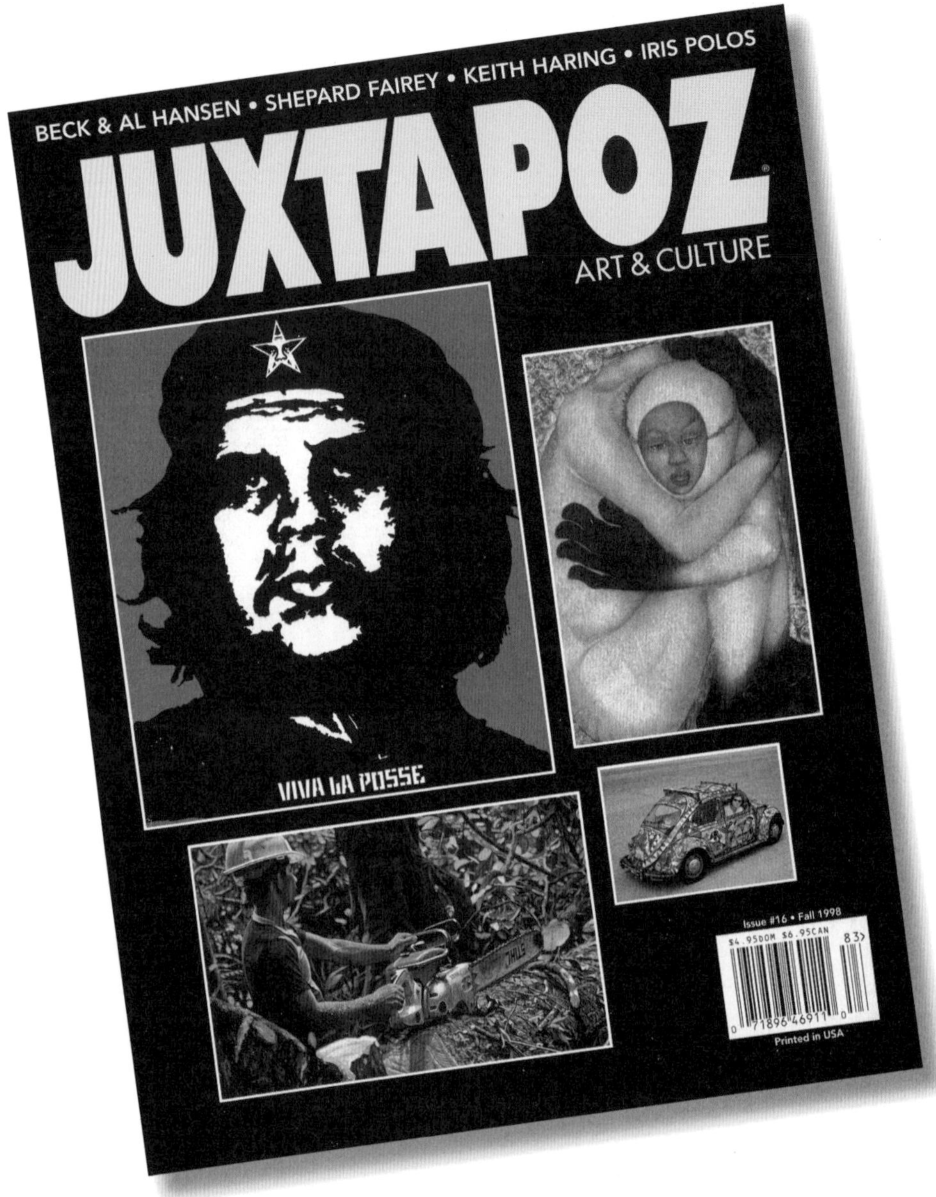

Cover art: (clockwise from top left) Shepard Fairey, Iris Polo, Ron Dolce, Paul Fortunato

Volume Five Number Three Fall 1998 #16

Speaking The Art Unspeakable

I have always given humble respect to the officially acknowledged institution called international art or fine arts. This aggregate of learned people and its academic establishment have, through a process of recognized merits, created a system of trends, styles, and isms that police the fine arts that we see today.

As a guideline for myself, I have perceived art as being the gratification received by the expression of ideas through abstract logic, which provides stimulus by either physically creating the work and/or mentally comprehending it.

But there is another facet–a big one. Art as we know it called "The Humanities" belongs to a branch of ideologies passed down from the ancient Greeks. It is here that a lot of people feel *Juxtapoz* magazine falls short of serving the artistic community.

The humanities means the generous and publicly responsible use of literature, philosophy and fine arts leading to democratic aid, charitable compassion for mankind, and the defense of the poor and downtrodden.

So, right there, by looking through *Juxtapoz*, you can see we're a little lean on crying Madonnas, mothers with child, starving urchins holding up empty food bowls, and grief-stricken minions at the bedsides of ill companions. Our charity, our compassion, and our tears are for the goddamned artists themselves.

Juxtapoz sells energy, imagination and blatant anxiety strained into oblique but legible communications–not utopia. We are not evil punk rock miscreants pimping a doctrine of "The Un-humanities."

Is morality a criteria for what is fine arts? Whose work is worthy enough to be considered humanitarian? If Mother Theresa left a stack of pencil doodles for her beneficiaries, how could Picasso's art compete? No matter how sensitive, caring and heart-wrenching the art's subject matter, is it not still some kind of propaganda?

"Alas, verily, are we not all liberal arts scoundrels?"

Nonetheless, in this issue, we offer you the works of Beck and his noted grandfather, Al Hansen, paintings by Joseph Bertiers, and the art of Shepard Fairey, plus our *Juxtapoz* Gallery and a feature on art cars. It's also our privilege to finally offer you a look at the work of Funkadelic album cover artist Pedro Bell. This article is long overdue.

On a sadder note, we regret the loss of one of *Juxtapoz's* good friends, Ms Pam Roberts. Pam was an imaginative painter who had developed a sizable following and had a wonderfully contagious personality. She lost her long battle with cancer as we went to press, and is survived by her daughter Ava. We'll miss you, Pam.

–Robt. Williams

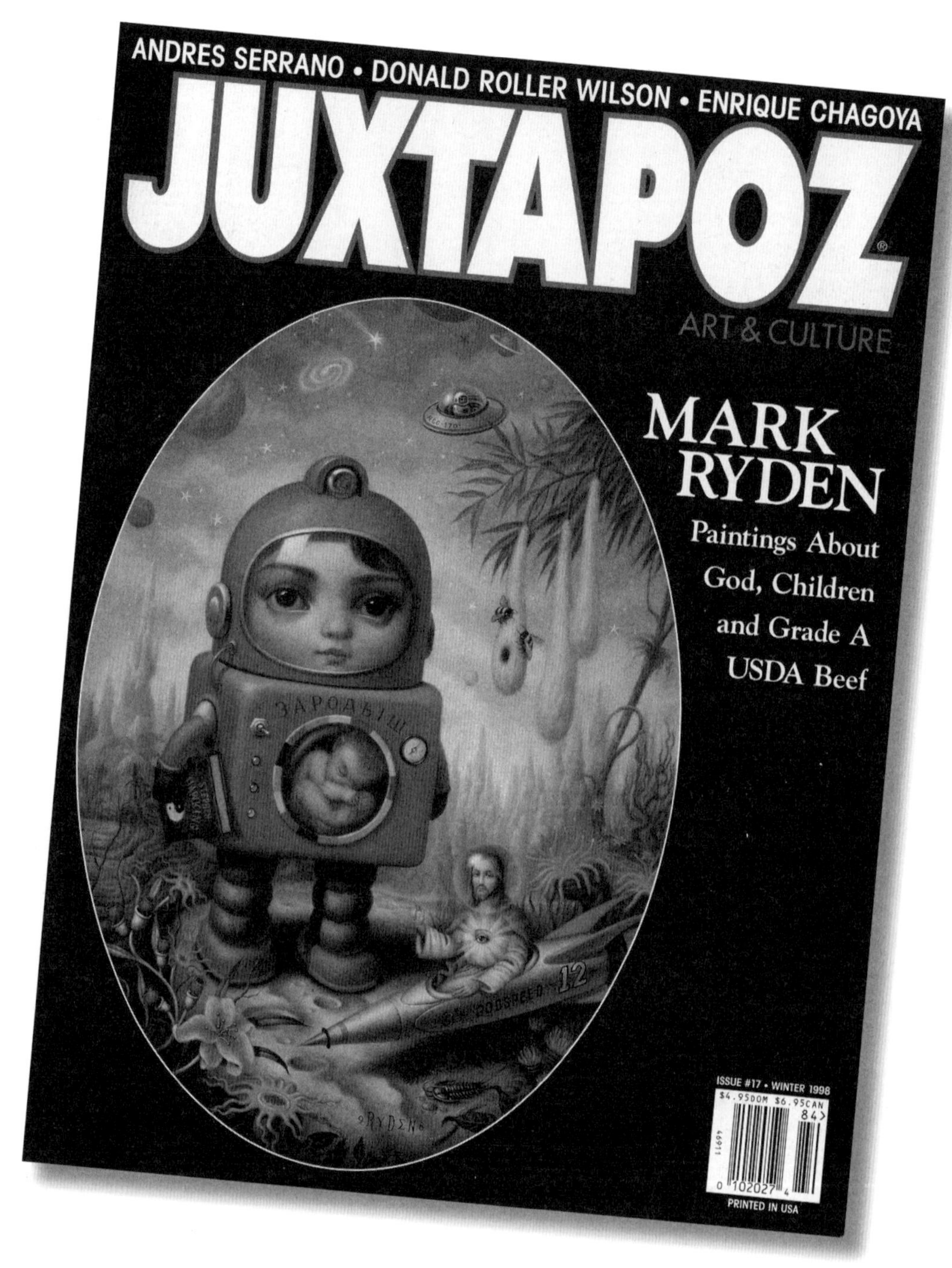

Cover art: Mark Ryden *Princess Sputnik*

Like A Turd On A Bottle Rocket

Juxtapoz and the art of *Juxtapoz* will eventually face an enemy disguised as success: ubiquity.

One day I was driving with my father and he pointed to a person walking along the road with his baseball cap on backwards. My dad said, "You know why that fellow has his hat on backwards?" I looked at this goofy guy with the bill of his hat jutting off the back of his head and I said, "No, why?" My father replied, "Because he wants to see where he's been, 'cause he sure as hell don't know where he's going!"

This once rare sight of a self-styled individualist has now become "ubiquitous." It's been ten years since the marginal rock star and front man for Guns and Roses, Axl Rose, popularized "the look" and now almost half of the baseball caps sold are worn inverted. Ubiquity's bastard son is mediocrity. That is when wearing your cap backwards is mandatory.

This happened when Robert Crumb's "Keep on Truckin'" image pervaded the decade of the 1970s. He now wears that cartoon like a milestone around his neck. It happened with the Clay Smith Cams decal of a woodpecker smoking a cigar, although nobody remembers. Clay Smith. It also happened with Rick Griffin's flying eyeball (an image that he lifted from Von Dutch). And of course, the all-time grand ubiquity, the yellow "Happy Face," for which people are fighting for the title of original creator as we speak.

Many artists search for a catch-image like "Keep on Truckin'" or "Happy Face" in hopes of graphic fame. But with that kind of cheesy recognition comes a giant superficial audience, with its inevitable guarantee for mediocrity. And, of course, most of this audience will never remember the artist's name.

Juxtapoz showcases a lot of emblem-flashing hotshot artists whose work lends itself to catch-image cliches. I guess that includes me as well. But for me personally, mediocrity is a crime that rates with public defecation and child molestation. My rule of thumb is, when your work ends up on a refrigerator magnet, you're over.

–Robt. Williams

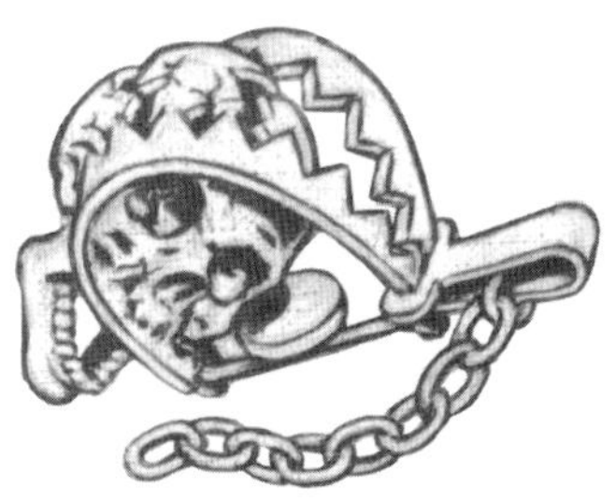

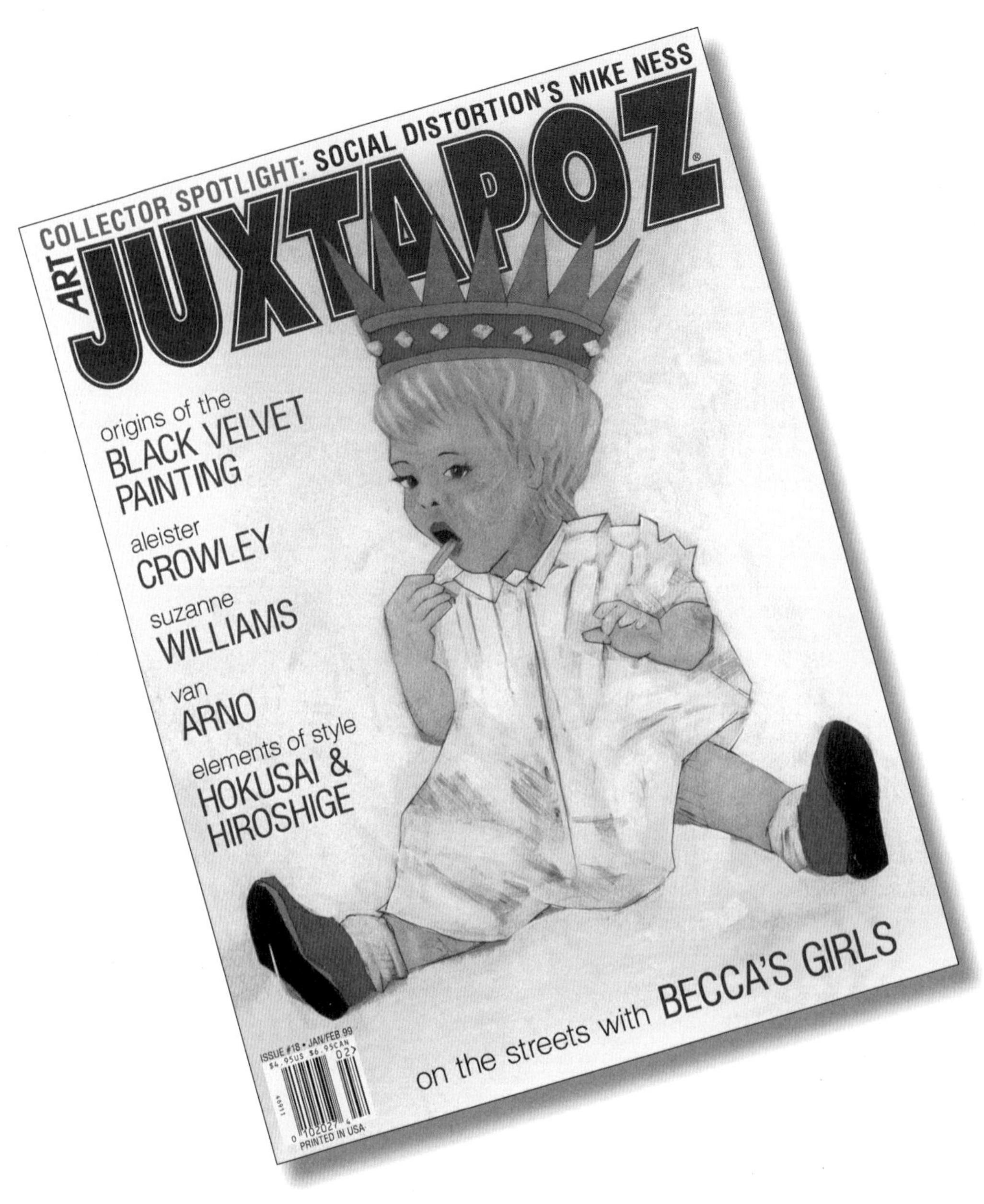

Cover art: Becca *Untitled*

The Rebuttal Of Rebuttals

The last issue of *Juxtapoz*, and especially my introduction addressing the overexposure of certain imagery, caused a great deal of consternation. Well, it's good that a number of readers responded with letters and e-mail.

Let me come to my own defense about any prologue titled, "Like a turd on a bottle rocket." I am going to have to take full responsibility for not clarifying the thrust of my remarks. I certainly had no intentions of casting snide aspersions on any artist who works the commercial side of the arts.

Posters, decals, stickers, album covers, and yes, refrigerator magnets are all noble fixtures to emblematic art–all of which I use as marketing devices myself, and are certainly not below my dignity. What I failed to get across is that with some of these catch-images it can backfire in one's face.

Let me give you one example: In 1974, I licensed a t-shirt design called "Sworn to Fun, Loyal to None," to the largest t-shirt design company in the world at the time. The sales were enormous, soon lifting it to the largest selling t-shirt design known (only to be topped later by sales of promo shirts for the movie *ET*). The shirt design brought me good royalties for ten years, but the design started to come back to haunt me. The image was brutally exploited and misused by unlicensed swindlers. What I was trying to achieve with a career in art was compromised by what I did for commerce. Don't get me wrong; I love money, and I don't mean to sound like a snob. I was satisfied with the shirt design, but not the unexpected response. It became a heraldic device to make a statement that in some small way I agreed with, but not something that I wanted to be branded with. I'm not alone; other artists have prodigal art work they later find themselves trying to hide from.

The other matter that distressed some of our readers was the article on bull-fighting. Boy, is this a sensitive issue. But in reality both sides are right. I can foresee that eventually the animal rights faction will extinguish gladiatorial/bovine combat to the death. Thank goodness public viewing in slaughterhouses isn't open to the general citizenry, or we'd all be eating veggie burgers. I have enjoyed bullfighting but I did wonder what happened to the animal after it was dispatched; after all, it is food. If you outlaw bullfighting, is boxing next? Boxing grew out of Roman coliseum spectacles also. And then what other areas would this protective banning slip into?

On a sad note, I need to mention the passing of a good friend and loyal art supporter in the Los Angeles area. Robert Weiss, killed in an auto accident on Halloween Day, was a champion to the art underdog.

–Robt Williams

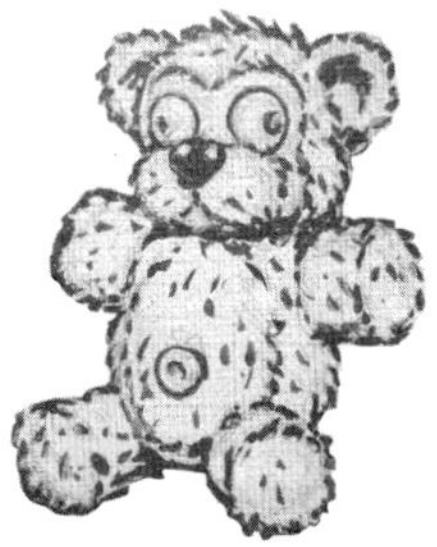

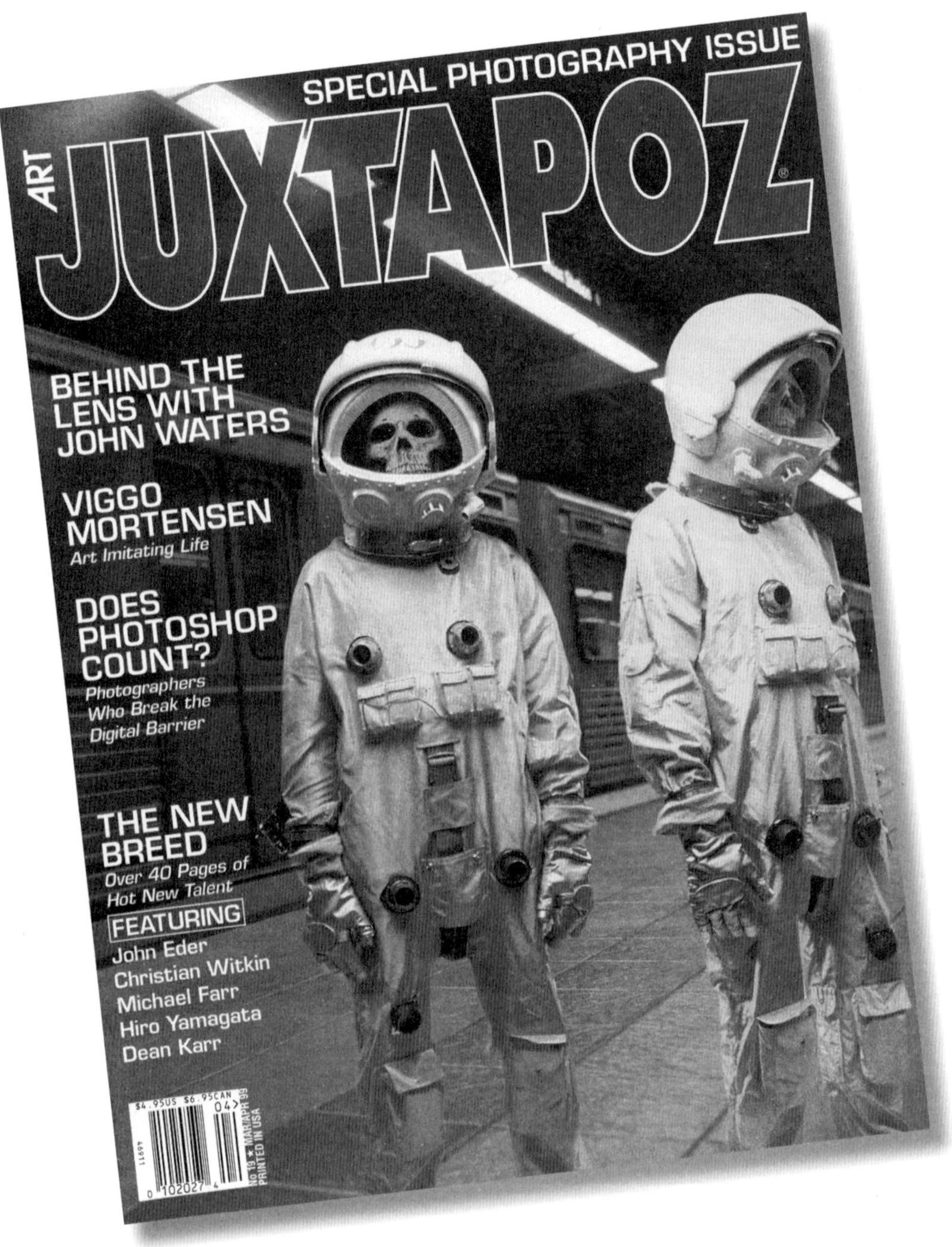

Cover art: John Eder *Cover Photo*

PHOTOGRAPHY Science, Art, Or Metaphysics?

In this special photography issue of *Juxtapoz*, I would like to make a few observations about photography as an aesthetic expression, including mood and mystery.

Besides the obvious, fine arts photography, the camera played an unseen role in art. There is no doubt about its effect on the world of drawing and painting. Consider any painting or drawing created after 1840 to be affected by the possible presence of the camera, as artists immediately started to copy photos. Prior to the advent of light sensitive copper, plated and treated with mercury vapor (early Daguerre photos), artists who wished to use technical viewing devices for copying and studies were greatly limited. However, there were a few primitive ocular inventions that artists used, some of which led to the development of the camera itself.

The first device, called the "black mirror" (circa 1600s), was simply a piece of glass painted black on one side. It caused a subject reflected in it to reveal only its sharpest contrast (a striking black/white chiaroscuro), breaking down lights and darks for the artist to copy.

The second invention was the "camera lucida" (circa 1700s), or the first cousin to our modern opaque projector. This instrument was made up of a simple prism, or angled mirror. With this, the artist had to completely cover himself and the paper or canvas he was working on with a blanket (achieving complete darkness), allowing the little mirror to be aimed out at the subject and then be reflected back onto the drawing surface.

This led to the third invention, the ancestor of our modern camera, the "camera obscura" (circa 1800s). This copying device was an entire light-free room with a hole and simple lens in one wall which projected the outside imagery onto the opposite wall.

I don't mean to bore you with technical history, but the point I am making is that all these gizmos were once the sole domain of artists. In fact, Louis JM Daguerre (progenitor of the first daguerreotypes) was an artist. He designed stage sets.

What I'm alluding to is that photography has always been in the hands of individuals with protracted and abstract minds, not merely self-seeking opportunists fulfilling the need people had to have photos of themselves.

There is one notion I would like to challenge: the claim that the selfless camera is impartial and unassumingly tells it like it is. I might be stepping out on thin ice here, but I think I should bring this up. Over the years, I noticed an odd characteristic about very old photos, and although I never brought it up, over time I've heard one or two other artists mention it. There is something different about a photo from the past. I don't mean clothes, vehicles, or architecture. Robert Crumb himself said, "There is something different between people today and people in old tintypes." Of course, that sounds like the most ridiculous remark a student of physical anthropology could make. How in the hell can human characteristics or physical evolution change in just five or six generations?

At the risk of sounding superstitious or ghost-prone, I do feel that the camera has an innate personality of its own. I don't mean older cameras simply took old-timey pictures, but more like there is some unexplained element causing a camera to "over-express." I would avoid casting an occult veil over fine arts photography, but it is obvious to me that some photographers have an intuition about this and try to use it. With that said, I hope you will enjoy our first special photography issue of *Juxtapoz.*

–Robt. Williams

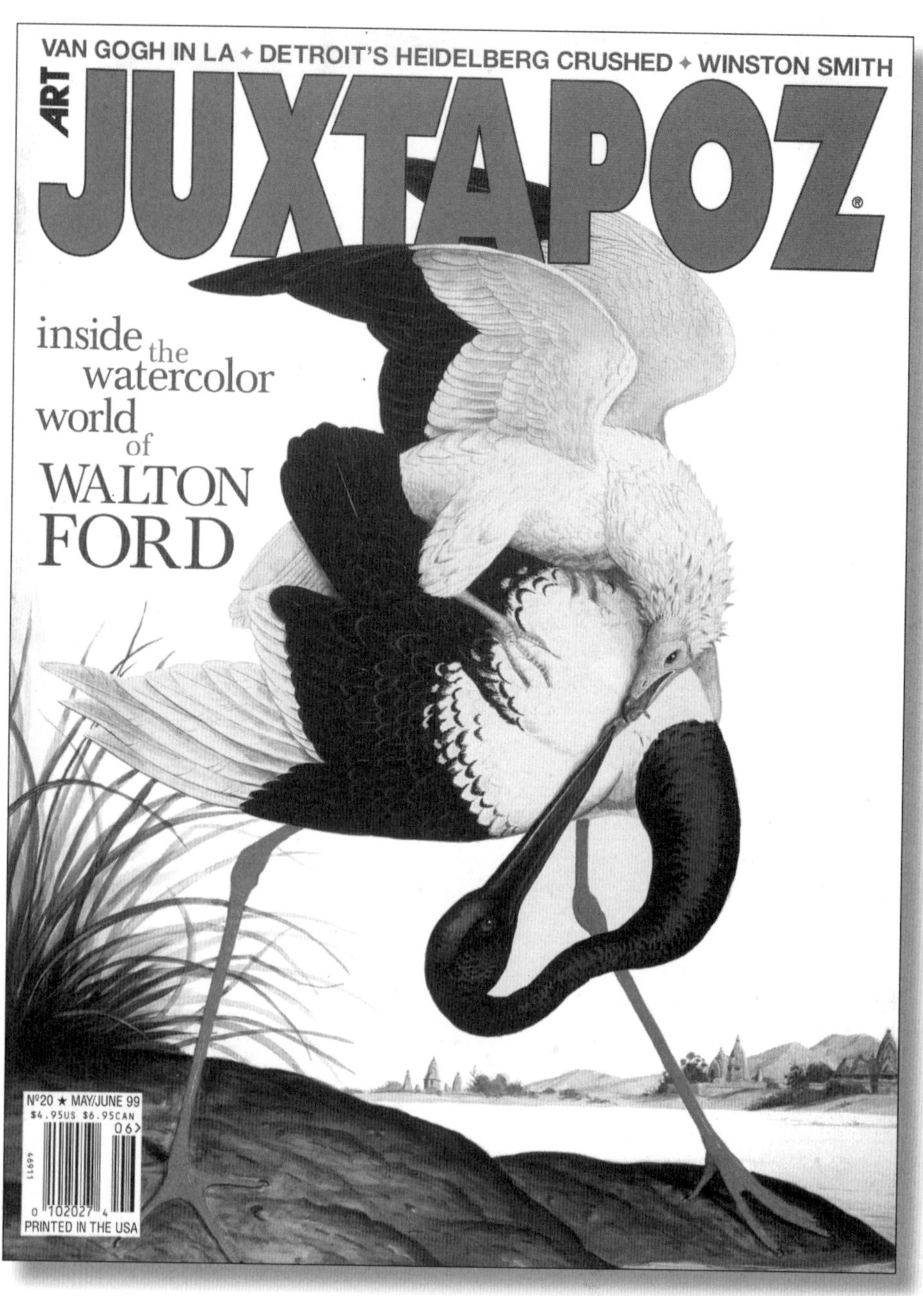

Cover art: Walton Ford *Avatars–The Birds of India*

Volume Six Number Three May/June 1999 #20

Five Years Of Cultural Erosion

IT DOESN'T SEEM THAT LONG, but this fall it will be five years since our questionable little art periodical has been eroding the Styrofoam bedrock out from underneath the great formal arts monolith that seems to dominate independent artists like a nuclear winter.

The majority of our readers and contributors have only been attracted to *Juxtapoz* within the last couple of years–after we had gotten a firm foothold. This being the case, let me reemphasize what the original premise of the magazine was.

The tenets for *Juxtapoz* were simple. In a cold and pedantic academic art world, a fixed system of rights and wrongs has been inadvertently established by an authoritarian consensus of museum directors, funding boards, special interest galleries, bias art critics, conforming artists, and a bovine buying market in general. Art purveyance has become (and in most cases always was) a political network, controlling sacred museum real estate and what goes in it. The current attitude of international modern art has shown its favoritism towards artists who practice the doctrine of theoretical assemblage over emotional and technical physically produced expression. Consequently, artists with hands-on ability and imagination have long ago been encouraged to seek expression in the un-arts (commercial art).

Juxtapoz magazine espouses that it would be in the best interest of the big ol' constipated art world to make concessions to imaginative and skillful artists who don't particularly bear sympathies for dadaist-inspired theorist art movements, minimalism, and conceptualism. "Can't we all just get along?" Rodney King, 1992.

During our five years of publishing, *Juxtapoz* has made a gradual evolution. The circulation has increased dramatically and the magazine has gone from quarterly to bimonthly. Because of *Juxtapoz*, a number of academic hierarchy, who determine what shall be sanctified formal art, have come to realize that there is a growing loose-knit "second world" of art that has a voice, and this magazine is one of its pronouncements.

Recently the staff of *Juxtapoz* has adapted to the needs of a much more diverse art community. Gone are the days of conjuring up the spirit of the old underground. Our editor, Jamie O'Shea, and his trusty aide *de* camp, Jordan Alexander, are continually traveling and investigating the cultural mine fields that the more erudite art rags find outre. Five years, and not once have we let our meat "loaf!"

This venerable issue is honored with the works of cover artist Walton Ford, brothers Rob and Christian Clayton, montage artist Winston Smith, the demolition of the Heidelberg Project, and much more.

–Robt. Williams

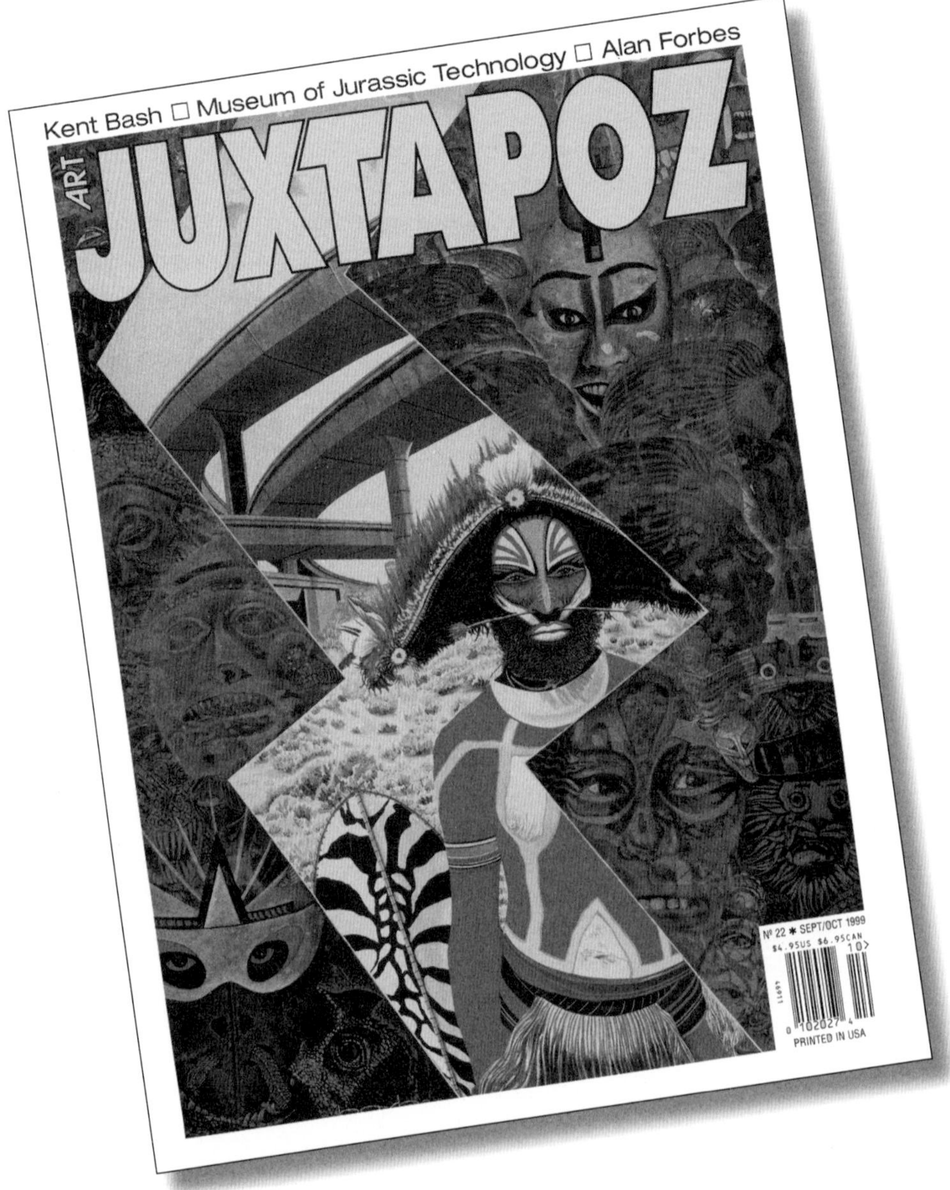

Cover art: Kent Bash *the Function of Dream Sleep*

Repudiation And Renunciation Of Repudiation

This has no bearing on any one instance, but I have long been stymied by people who repudiate their past actions. I don't mean just repent or ask forgiveness for their misjudgments. I am talking about a schizophrenic mind-change by someone who has conducted himself with all the appearances of self-control and then all of a sudden does a 180° about-face and renounces their past and usually all the people in it. You see this a lot in old people, bikers, ex-criminals, drunks, prostitutes, porn stars, and elderly souls who claim to have wisdom that can save you after they no longer have the energy or inclination to get in trouble themselves.

In the arts it can be accepted as a creative direction change. The well-known French artist Jacques Louis David, who was court painter to Louis XVI, had no qualms about the king losing his head after deserting him for his revolutionary cronies, only to have to re-repudiate his association with the revolution and Napoleon years later.

I have met and known many young artists who have gained great personal solace by later renouncing the type of art they do or all in general. Art is not a tangible thing or occupation like being a short-order cook or topless dancer. It is philosophy with a knot in it. I can cut a fart, pronounce this to be art, and then a month later slander those kind and caring people who endorsed my action as participants in a fraud. Disciples seem to always disavow something they have blindly eaten with a shovel and then fail at.

Maybe mood swings make up part of this self-imposed insanity we call art. I believe the primary characteristic of art is the cloak of emotional compulsion that hides fixation, hysteria, and arrested development. You see how people of responsibility, in more lucid moments, would repudiate segments of the arts.

I love that lost gossamer never-never land of art. I plan to buy property there. Maybe I'll build an ivory tower on a cloudy vanilla bluff, and then I can send messengers down to reality to tell everybody how fucked it is.

Although my ramblings may get a little convoluted, the artists we have in this issue are rather straightforward. We are pleased to host the work of Kent Bash (ace hot rod, slash, Surrealist) Greg Jezewski (Zero One alumni), Moira Hahn (watercolor virtuoso), Alan Forbes (sculptures by San Fran's jack-of-all mediums), along with painters Jorge Santos, Timothy Cummings, Brian Clarke and a special visit to LA's legendary bastion of abstract philosophical thought, the Museum of Jurassic Technology.

–Robt Williams

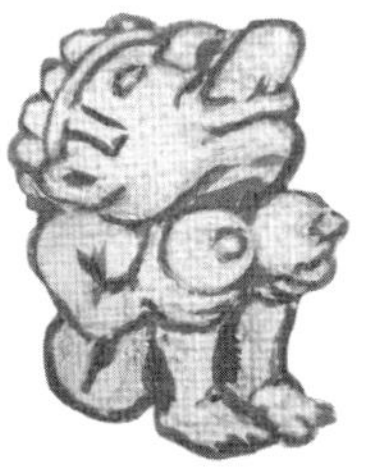

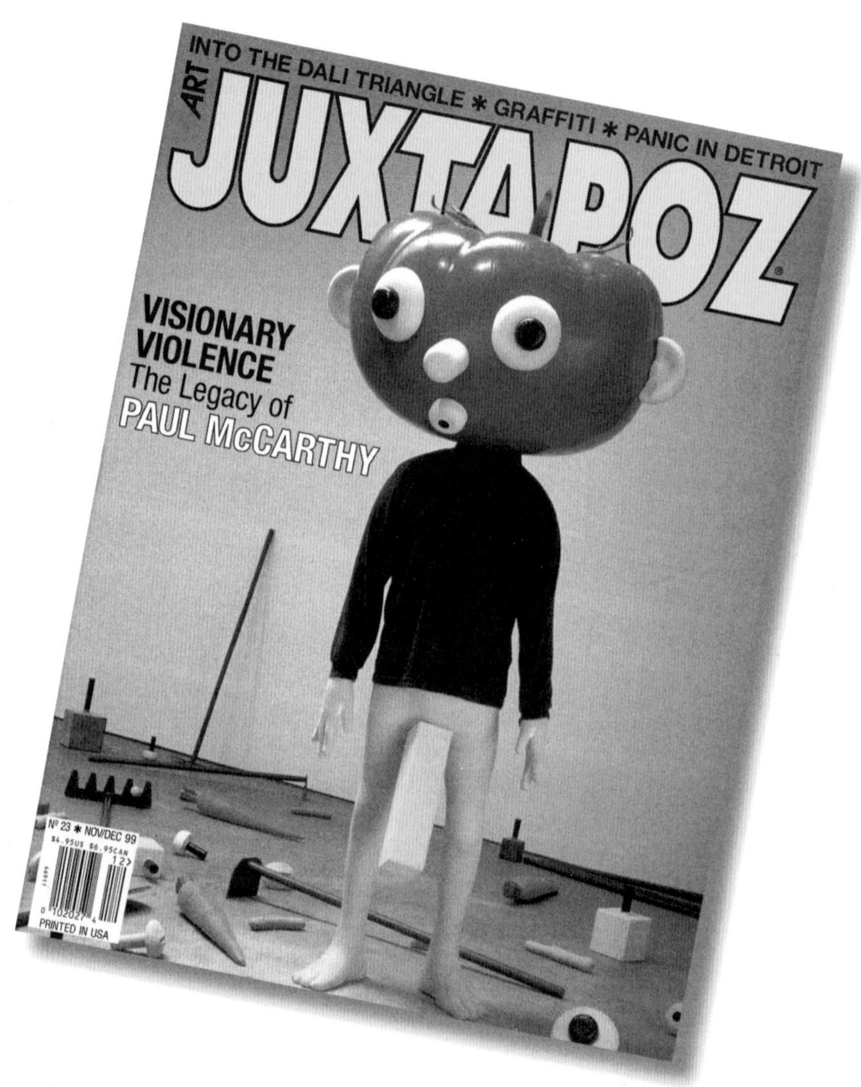

Cover art: paul McCarthy *(detail) Tomato Head*

Volume Six Number Six Nov/Dec 1999 #23

Change, Where Art Thou Sting?

ARE THINGS CHANGING US, or are things standing still while we move like rabid bats flying through an abandoned theme park? What I'm getting at is that if you have developed your education and art interest in the last three or four years you sense no change, but if you have been a participant in the visual arts for 10 or 15 years, you have watched a growing tolerance for new ideas–a tolerance going well beyond the mind expansion hyperboles of installation and found item art that was so important in the '80s.

Traditional painting and sculpture is actually showing up in galleries again. But in what direction are the works going? The established art critics writing for our popular newspapers and publications are the people most in the dark. Even the brightest among them can only categorize all modern art into about four groups. They still bandy about tired appellations such as expressionism, neo, pre or post, conceptualism with a vague connotation of minimalism, or vice versa, or both, with a mixture of pop. Sometimes they use a combination of all the categories, perhaps describing a resulting catharsis or the characteristics of being kitschy, even sub or retro kitsch. As you can see, I'm not a big defender of art-speak.

However, my criticism of the four dominant isms of our time doesn't go unchallenged. My good friend, artist Mike Kelley, has suggested that I quit denigrating minimalism and conceptualism, it now being considered somewhat old-hat and actually overshadowed by a very decorative form of pop art that has revealed itself in the last three or four years in major museum shows. Kind of a happy Doris Day, Mr Rogers pop.

Nonetheless, let me come to the defense of conceptualism. The theory of conceptual art is a very worthy form of intellectual expression which focuses on the importance of the idea over the physical existence of the object. However, modern conceptualism has never been able to throw off its old dadaist fomat of "the shittier it looks, the more intelligent it must be." Doing a bitchin' job on a project is just as valid and artistically orthodox as expressing your intellectual hatred for the physical valuelessness of "art."

A change seems to be at hand. And, within curatorial powers in our museums, there are now beginnings of acceptance for undefinable artwork without foisting it off as simply "outsider art," art done by an uninitiate (or brilliant simpleton).

OTHER MATTERS: At the end of September, Jaimie O'Shea, a number of artists, Suzanne, and myself attended the grand opening of the new C-Pop Gallery in Detroit. This 2 million dollar establisment is without question the most elegant venue in the country, dedicating itself primarily to the promotion and sale of alternative and underground art, and is definitely worth a visit.

This will be our last issue of the 20th century. To take us deep into the 21st century, we wish to avail you of the work of modern artists that you will come to respect in the future: Paul McCarthy, venerable master of sculpture, installation, and performance art; figurative prodigy Eric White; painter of Asian pop culture, Saiman Chow; graffitist Doze Green; and artistic jack of all trades, Craig Stecyk.

From all of us at *Juxtapoz*, see ya next century.

–Robt. Williams

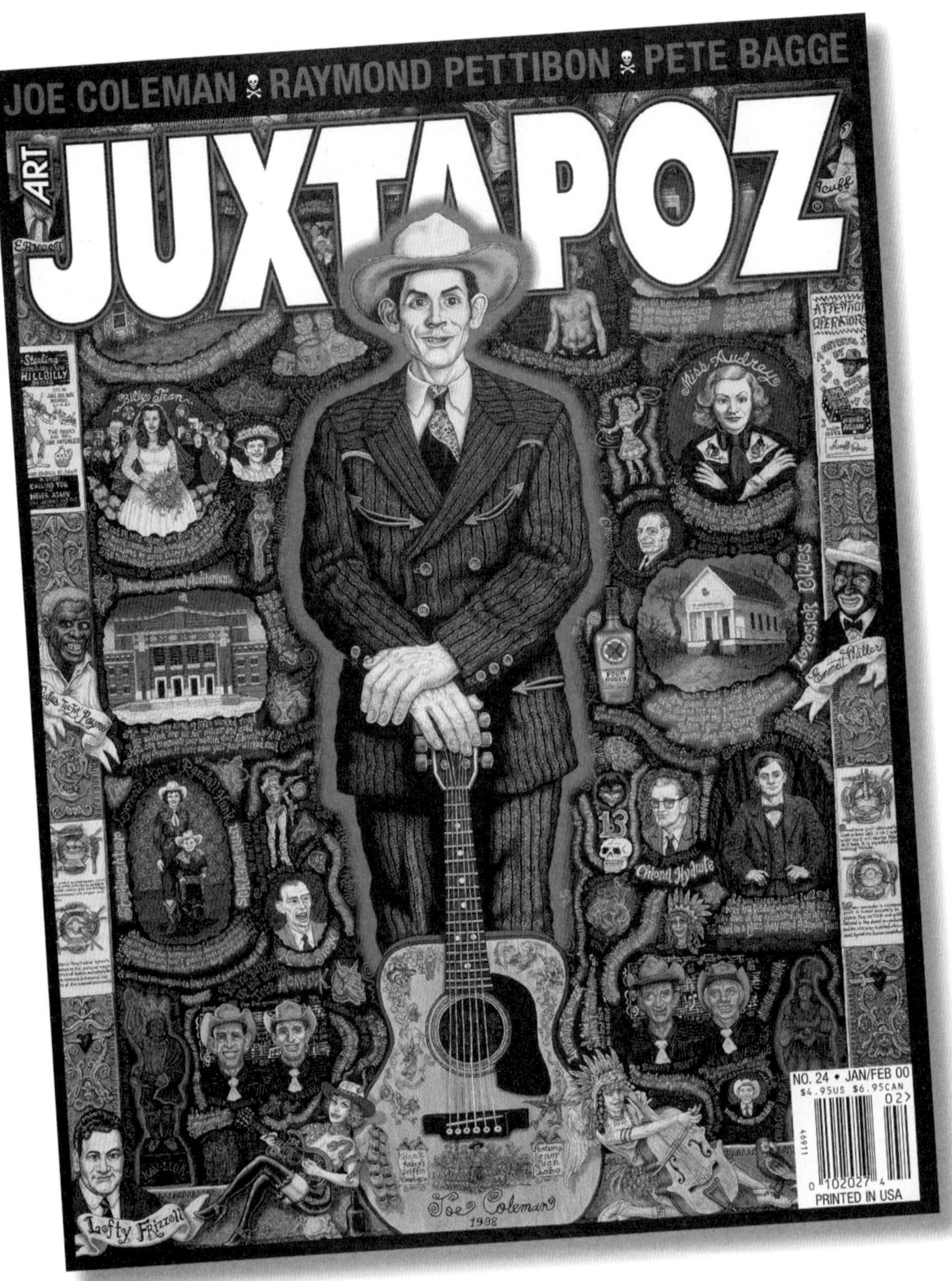

Cover art: Joe Coleman *A Picture From Life's Other Side*

There's Somebody At The Door And I Think It's The Future

Or should I say the cathode ray tube age? Remember, more than half the world's population has their faces in computer monitors or television sets. Everyone will soon be subject to all the same input and information. In less than 50 years, the global village will be so omnipresent that cultural customs and ethnic costumes will only appear for holiday pageants. This means everybody will have their baseball hats on backward.

What about the Arts? Well, I see the same old group of academic morlocks flogging the ghosts of Dadaist heroes for at least another 15 years, or until the last of the wrecking yards and city dumps are depleted of all their "ready-made" treasures. I think it has already been determined, in the late 20th century, that anyone with the faculty to "cut the cheese" is a master artist.

But believe me, the future is so goddamned bright. A hundred years ago, less than 20 percent of the educated population was privy to the very guarded and elite sphere of fine arts, although abstract notions of art thought were barely starting to appear.

A thousand years ago, art wasn't even considered an entity unto itself. It was strictly a device to promote religion or an innocent form of decoration. Granted, another thousand years earlier, the GrecoRoman culture embodied an appreciation of the applied visual arts, but sculpture and painting never strayed from under the safe wing of Greek and Roman religion and philosophy.

Today, not only is art free, but it has become religion and philosophy. Enjoy your art future; a lot of people have gone to a lot of trouble to make it as diverse as you want it to be.

We here at *Juxtapoz* are always glad to receive mail from our readers, whether it be just a friendly hello or a biting criticism. You can send us syrupy salutations or vent your rudest hostilities against the art we present on these pages. Please feel free to write us, but keep this in mind: art is not science or physics. If it is not done correctly, it does not mean 1500 fucking people are going down in the North Atlantic. Art is simply opinion, and what might taste like *creme de menthe* to the lounge lizard might taste like feces to an ordained minister. There are only two kinds of art: pleasurable art and mis-appreciated art.

I don't generally like to prattle on about an artist, but in this case I can make a good point. The painter Joe Coleman has carved a niche in the American art world that is now indelible in our psyches. Whether you like his work or it nauseates you, it's obvious that he speaks in a clear and lucid language, revealing a person with a wide variety of interests and a firm poetic grip on history and legends.

Joe and I are old friends. We were both involved in underground comix and we share the colorful experience of having worked for traveling carnivals during our youth, but we have had our differences. The striking thing about Mr. Coleman is his career. In an art world that is absolutely flush with namby-pamby sensitivos, politically correct ethics enforcers, and pipe cleaner-spined civilization directors, Joe has cut his own swath through the bleeding hearts and menstrual fluid savers. He has persevered in spite of polite art convention. He should be an example to all young artists. If you have skill, imagination tenacity, and guts, you will flourish.

–Robt. Williams

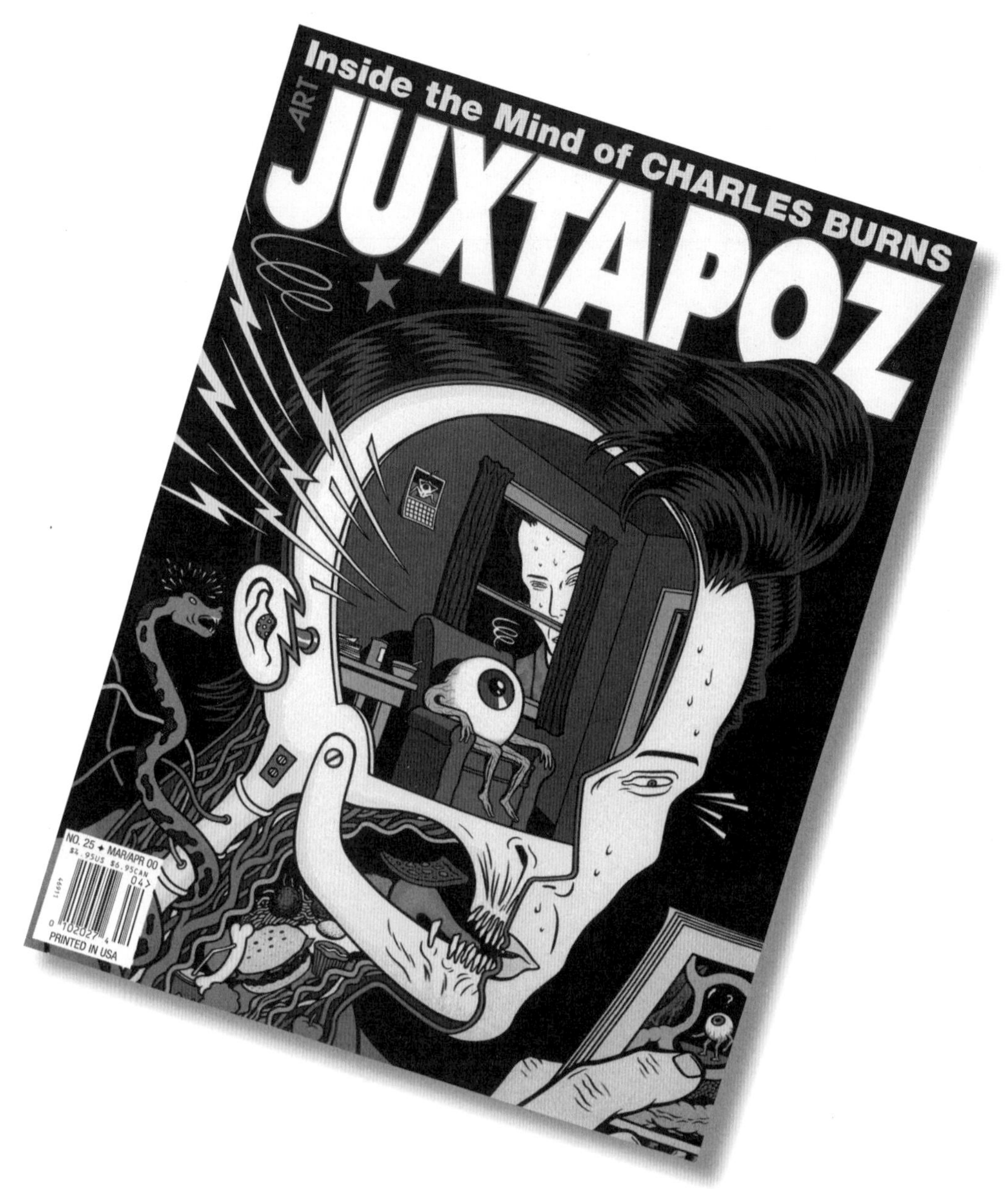

Cover art: Charles Burns *Comix Addict*

Volume Seven Number Two Mar/Apr 2000 #25

A Tan Balloon By Any Other Name

WHAT IS IN A NAME? Apparently everything, when it comes to scholars and museum administrators and their acceptance of new and unauthorized art movements. If you have been reading *Juxtapoz* magazine for the past few years, you will understand the vicissitudes that most artists in *Juxtapoz* face in attempting to fit into respectable classifications and categories. It is obvious to all but the most myopic that a sizable amount of disenfranchised artists–all from the demi-mode or unacceptable realm of "not-quite-art"–are uniting, and emerging slowly and spontaneously into the fine arts arena.

However, this is no longer a pathetic patchwork of underground cartoonists, sign painters, and other misguided art miscreants. The only thing that seems to restrict our barbarian federation from swamping the world fine arts cognoscenti is not having an intelligent art movement designation or title.

Critics, academics, and historians almost insist on having an authorized appellation to hang their nuts on. The problem is that if you don't have a scholastically sanctioned manifesto espousing a trick name, these shortsighted pipe-cleaner spines will give this movement one of their own. And believe me, it will probably be so embarrassing and dippy that it will make you want to go back to your day job.

This fringe movement to which I belong, and with which I presume most of the *Juxtapoz* readership exercises flirtations, has, over the past 20 years, faced such pigeonholing names as: Underground Art, Lowbrow Art, *L'Art de Toilette*, Pop Surrealism, Cartoon Surrealism, Outlaw Art, Bad Boy Art, Alternative Art, Rat Fink Art, Cartoon Pop, Artoons, Outsider Art, Hot Rod Gothic, Melrose Primitive, Horror Vacua, "Rod, Surf n' Skate," Vox Populi Outre, Wrist Lizards, Facilities, Art Nadir, Lounge 'n' Tiki Retro, Veins & Eyeballs Moderne, Artista Non Grata, "That Kinda Art You Guys Do," and a few more I can't bring to mind.

So, I can imagine that with monikers like these, stuffy, self-lauding art blusterers would rather delete these phrases from their cocktail party chatter.

But to arrive at a name, let me explore some other common word usages to see how something distasteful will adjust naturally to being a comfortable colloquialism. If you can completely disregard what people think and allow abstraction to precede moral decency, titles will find themselves.

Let me paint you this picture. You are walking along and looking in the street. You chance upon a recently used condom lying in the gutter in front of a neighbor's house. You are, of course, repulsed by the sight of this filthy object, but in your unrefined mind's eye, you describe verbally to yourself its physical appearance. "I see a sun-bleached, dehydrated, used fucking rubber, kinked up in flattened stacks and pasted in slime-dried coils, that still gives evidence to the presence of about three thimbles-full of semi-viscous semen bacteriafying in the noonday sun. This is accented with nauseous pubic hairs festooning the opening like whiskers on a banana slug." The only saving grace for this vile sight is that it is hopefully a sign that there will be one less asshole on the freeways with you in 20 years. Now let us verbalize this image as pedantically as a nuclear physicist would.

"There before me, in a northeasterly direction at 13:26 o'clock, lying at an oblique angle to the street, is a recently jettisoned prophylactic, and by the obvious contents, which I assume to be the male ejaculent sperm, it is deduced to have been the product of a successful sexual congress, hopefully an emotionally rewarding coitus for both participants involved. However, the surreptitious lovers have greatly impacted their likelihood of siring a future president of the United States in this particular liaison.

Now, let us weigh the remarks of my neighbor, who lives near this scene. I say, "Henry, look at this trashy thing I found in your gutter." Henry walks over to the curb and, after looking down at it, says, "Oh, we saw those all the time in New York. We call them Coney Island whitefish!"

Okay, you think about it. Do you think the doyen masters who operate the world's great art museums can work "Coney Island whitefish" into their prattle? We have no title, and maybe that's for the best.

For this issue we present to you some outstanding artists and articles such as: Charles Burns, draftsman par excellence; the young poster master, Emek; the mistress of stained glass, Judith Schaechter; a look at the quickly growing tiki phenomenon; and other artists and well-known collectors.

–Robt. Williams

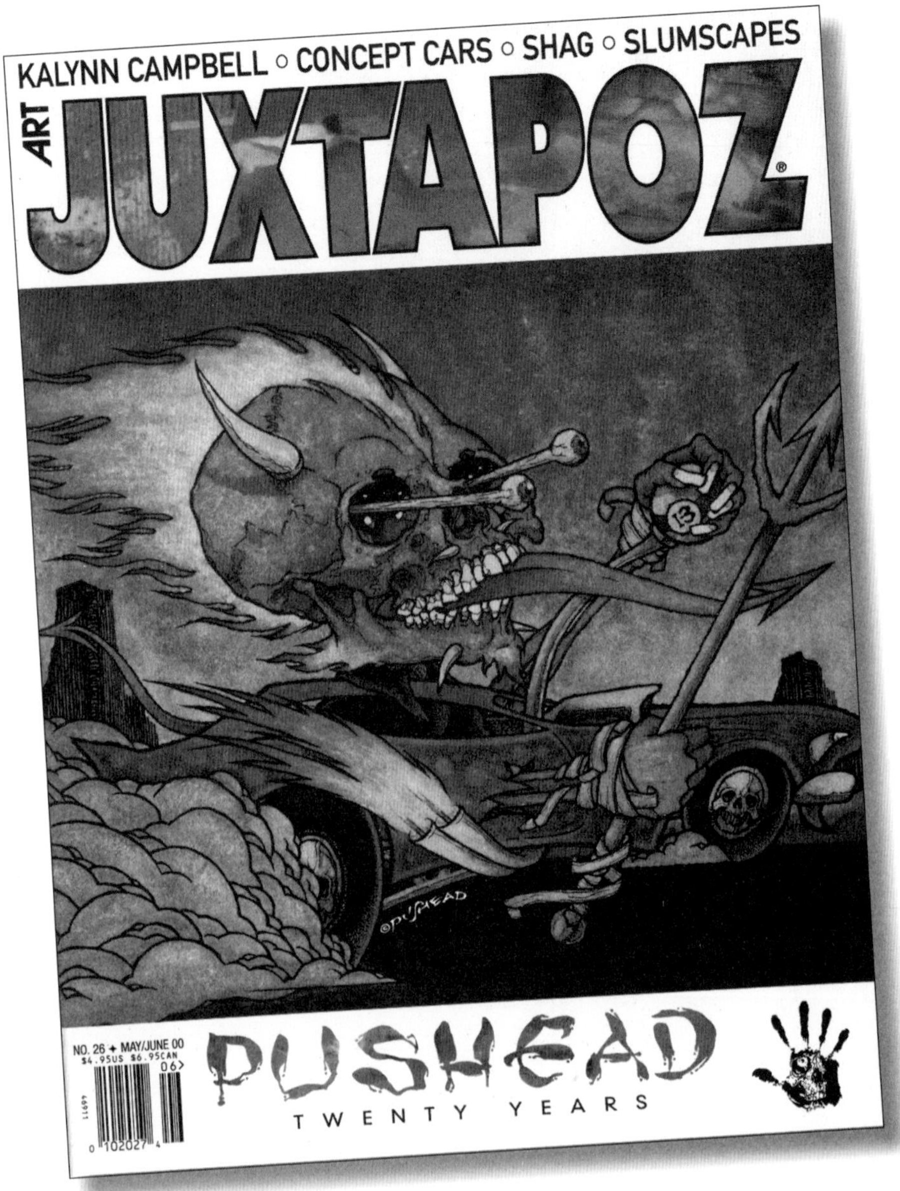

Cover art: Pushead *Hand of Fear*

Volume Seven Number Three May/June 2000 #26

Disrespectful To Authorized Criticism? You Betcha

In Volume One, Number Two (Spring 1995) of *Juxtapoz*, I went into a long-winded prattle about the worth and use of art critics. But now I feel a need to readdress the subject (possibly even overstep my bounds) and say a few things about them that I think will probably come back to haunt me. If you are a young artist and have a pronounced and clear-cut talent, and your style is not in harmony with other aspiring artists, your uphill battle may be met with an obstacle you never concerned yourself with much until you find yourself confronted with it.

To many wild and self-liberated young people who live in that half art/half decal, T-shirt, record album, graffiti, hot rod paint job, cartoon limbo, the thought of some snide, dissociated, typewriter-bound columnist denigrating you is only cause for amusement. But after years of cultivating a following and competing with more respected artists, you might find what these self-infested critics say is taken quite seriously by the public. In fact, most of these Carpal Tunnel Syndrome goofballs in big newspapers have put themselves in positions of real power.

Allow me to dissect the personae of these opinion-wielders. The vast majority of art critics have degrees in fine arts but usually have failed in their applied, hands-on art careers, have thus swung with their consolation aptitude into a foray of "man o' letters" writing and journalism, and then see themselves as *bon mot* aces of grand art theory. Theory is something they can manipulate–they sure as hell can't manipulate paint.

Art critics have role models with whom they vicariously associate themselves. The most famous is the writer John Ruskin, who brought to light the great painter William Turner in the mid-19th century. The other primary demigod for critics is Oscar Wilde.

However, as guardians of aesthetics, both these men had serious shortcomings. After defaming the well-known painter James Whistler, Ruskin found himself embroiled in a notorious trial for libel. After losing the much-publicized lawsuit, he consequently suffered a mental breakdown. With Wilde, the *faux pas* was more common. Wilde, being the outspoken art maven that he was, declared Oriental art (Japanese art in particular) of no importance, this in the 1880s when Eastern art influence was just about to explode onto the European art scene. In later years he had to completely regurgitate that conviction.

If I sound bitter, it's because I am. I attract journalist detractors like pathologists to a tumor. Yet still I feel that my personal opinion is not insular or closed-minded. I think that there are two factions of writers–art critics and art reviewers–and a reviewer is more objective. An open-minded newspaper writer is a necessity. He can open new avenues to explore, not just criticize, or lead a marginally disinterested public in a direction that would benefit the writer's own bullshit interest.

There are some very well-educated and impartial writers who add a great service to the art community: Carlo McCormick in New York and Peter Frank in Los Angeles, to name two. Without good writers, the connection between artist and public would wither, and diverse sources of idea input would become polarized and completely isolated. It is *Juxtapoz* magazine's responsibility to foster these idea exchanges in an open forum.

Speaking of critics, in the Florida press last month, the show *Lowbrow Art: Up from the Underground* received mixed reviews, and unfortunately it seemed as though it was generally misunderstood. This Hollywood, Florida exhibition was held at the Art and Culture Center of Florida and presented by its director, Lawrence Pamer, with the help of L.A.s Doug Nason. More than 30 outlaw artists were represented. I have been told that this show was an outstanding presentation at a wonderful venue. I feel that the most important factor about this exhibit is that it happened at a respected community museum and will be seen as the first museum underground art show. Congratulations.

In this issue we offer you the work of Kalynn Campbell, Pushead, Shag, Simon Larbalestier, and Carlee Fernandez, plus concept car art and the collection of Long Gone John.

–Robt. Williams

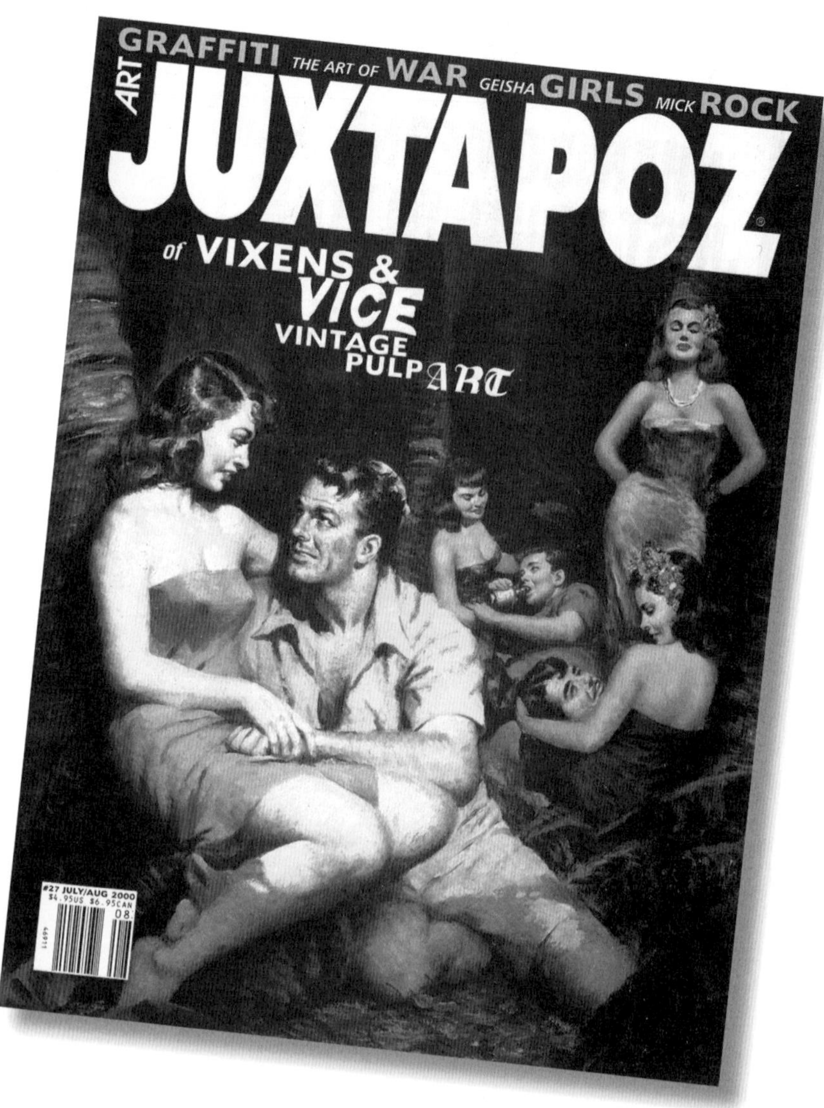

Cover art: Raymond Johnson *Vintage Pulp Illustration*

Volume Seven Number Four July/Aug 2000 #27

A Question of Intelligent Intent

A NEW TERM has been emerging that art critics like to use concerning works of art that fall outside the parameters of their interest. The expression is "dumbing down." And here's how it's being used: "It seems that some museum art exhibits are dumbing down."

What they are referring to is artwork that has been slipped into art shows and that lacks the usual stoic, bromide dullness that makes so much of what is called high art such a yawner. Intelligence has nothing to do with it–their judgment is driven by emotion.

It would be simple to write off the bulk of *Juxtapoz* artists as graphic cretins who dabble in the most obvious cartoon elements: devil decals, skull T-shirts, monster hot rod ogres, skateboard and surfboard heraldry, large mammaried pin-ups, tiki and toy cliches, and a slew of other visual mantras that would thrill a barroom full of auto re-possessors. But there's much more intended than a quick scan might suggest.

Fundamentally, in art there lie two very serious driving forces: Number one, there is the artist who relies on emotion and spontaneity to speak in a very fresh and urgent honesty–the quick artist. Secondly, there is the methodical artist who wants total control of a personal language and takes complete responsibility for the finished product by polishing ideas, using notes and sketches to make sure the end result is a finely tuned piece of poetry.

However, with respect to "dumbing down," we're forced to perceive a third type, the theoretical explorer who surrenders completely to representational abstraction. These Robinson Crusoes, who know that if they look hard enough on this barren island called art they will find a secret form of expression that will cut a dry path through the ocean of mental endeavor and allow them to go anywhere they want, have visions so broad that they force the rest of the art world to be a little, marooned group of dullards on a likewise deserted island.

Let me clarify what I mean. What do you think was the most popular piece of artwork to come out of the 19th century in America? Winslow Homer's *Gulf Stream*? Gilbert Stuart's half-finished portrait of George Washington? Albert Bierstadt's famous landscape of the Yosemite Valley? No, the most well known single American image was a rather vulgar rendition of Custer's Last Stand by an unknown artist, rendered as an advertising print for Anheuser Busch in the 1880s. The elementally drawn color print portrayed the entire battle of the Little Big Horn, complete with dismemberments, scalpings, beheadings, and other atrocities. This work was framed and dispensed to almost every bar, barber shop, hardware store, and public school, where it hung prominently for nearly 40 years.

Many famous illustrators and painters of the '20s and '30s have made reference to this bloodthirsty print as a source of influence. It would be virtually impossible to publicly display this print today, but its abstract soul has been passed down to us in other forms.

Unfortunately, the word "cartoon" has come to mean comic. Cartoons are a very valid language that absolutely depends upon abstract thought. A cartoon that is not made up of protracted and oblique imagination is not a cartoon but a lifeless, exact image fitting more accurately within the category of a mimicked photograph.

The basically unexplored mental playing field of a cartoon syntax is a visual idiom that would befuddle even the stodgiest art authority, and for that reason we'd like to think that *Juxtapoz* magazine is, in reality, dumbing "up!"

In this issue, we're joyously offering you the works of painters F. Scott Hess, Aaron Marshall, and Steve Galloway; the rock photos of Mick Rock; a look at pulp magazine art; and World War II combat art.

–Robt. Williams

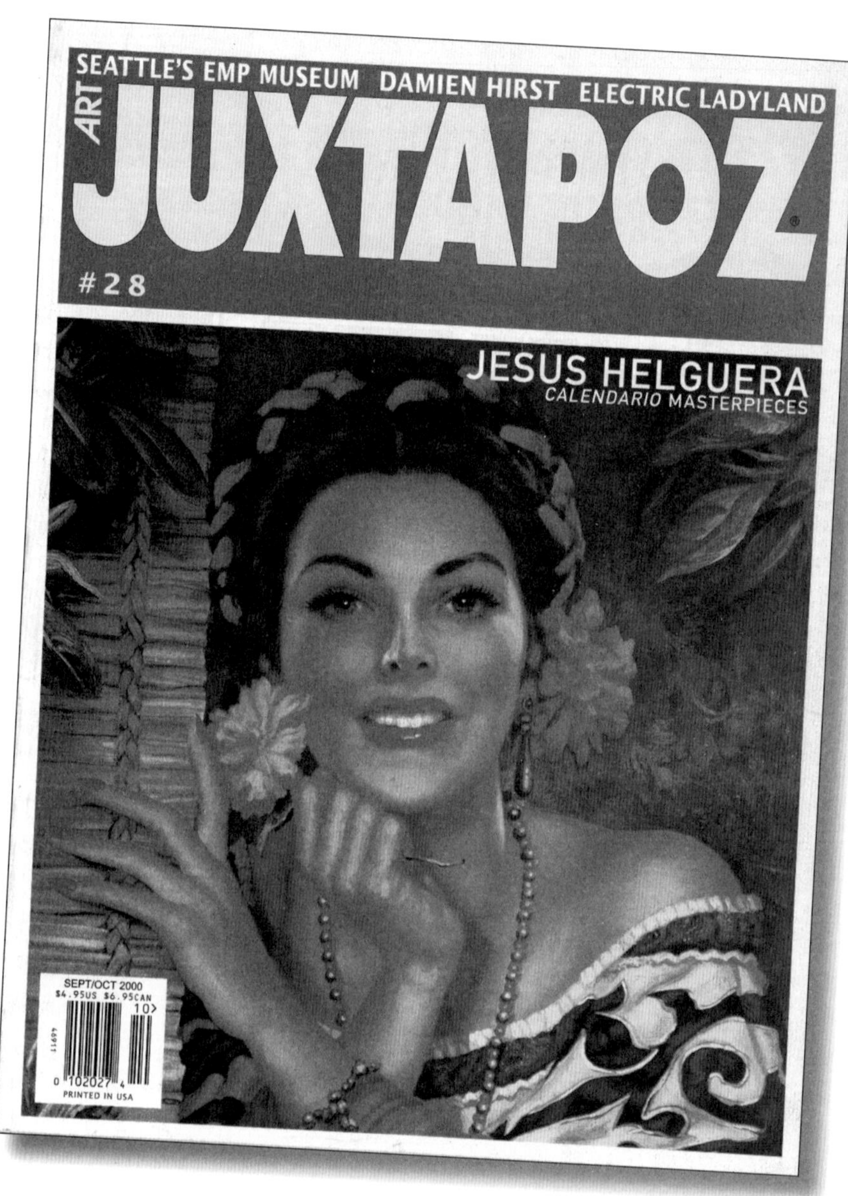

Cover art: Jesus Helguera *Portrait*

Volume Seven Number Five Sept/Oct 2000 #28

If Only I Could Be That Sensitive

In the last couple of years, we have experienced a benign temperament shift into more gentile imagery, somewhere between the delicate reveries of '50s retro and the blossoming of a sparrow hearted, saccharine second childhood. A caring Pat Booneishness seems to be developing in alternative art.

Let me express my feelings on this direction by focusing on the artistic tribulations of one well known, tender individual of the past. Ninety years ago this young fellow faced rejection after rejection while attempting enrollment in art schools around Europe.

As a sympathetic person, he would bring no harm to any living thing. He was a vegetarian and personally bore the burden of the atrocities inflicted on the animal world as an indictment of inhumanity. He refused to hunt with his friends in a time when this was a norm of manhood. He allowed himself to be drawn into a horrible world war and witnessed the deaths of many of his fellow soldiers, which affected him for the rest of his life.

This artist's work affectionately glowed with the brush's gentle kiss, much like today's genius Thomas Kinkade, but with far more lugubriousness, and it was bathed in lights and darks that poetically hinted of melancholy, forgotten long-agos. I myself have to reel in my emotions when I cast a gaze on this artist's effortless souffle of gossamer watercolors, which bespeaks of warm earth hues against cold cobalt skies.

I guess by now you've figured out who this asshole is that I'm talking about–it is Adolf Hitler. If only I could have been his Wendy, and he my Peter Pan, I'd a' shot that son of a bitch back in 1923!

Well, enough for my abstract diatribe. In this issue we have some great artists: one of my favorites, and a well-loved master in the Latino culture, Mexican calendar artist Jesus Helguera; Sandow Birk, who has just gained more notoriety with his *War of the Californias* series; and the works of surfing and South Seas defamer Kevin Ancell.

As a footnote to our posthumous tribute to beloved LA painter Mark Gash, I would like to mention my association with him. In the early '80s in San Francisco, the poster artists Alton Kelley and Stanley Mouse instituted a renegade underground artists' club named The Artistas. To join, all that was required was to buy an expensive, full-color jacket. In a short time, this club became the province of rock celebrities and high-society coke dealers who had little to do with art.

To right that, me, Suzanne and Ray Zone started a similar club in Los Angeles. It was called the LA Art Boyz. And to join, your only obligation was to purchase a 10-dollar T-shirt. We threw some pretty weird art shows that embodied the spirit of punk rock art during that time. Many now-famous artists participated: Gary Panter, Matt Groening, Mike Kelley, and Jim Shaw, to mention a few. Mark Gash was instrumental in hosting some of the insane theme exhibits, such as the "Ugly Madonna Contest." This brother Art Boy will be missed.

–Robt. Williams

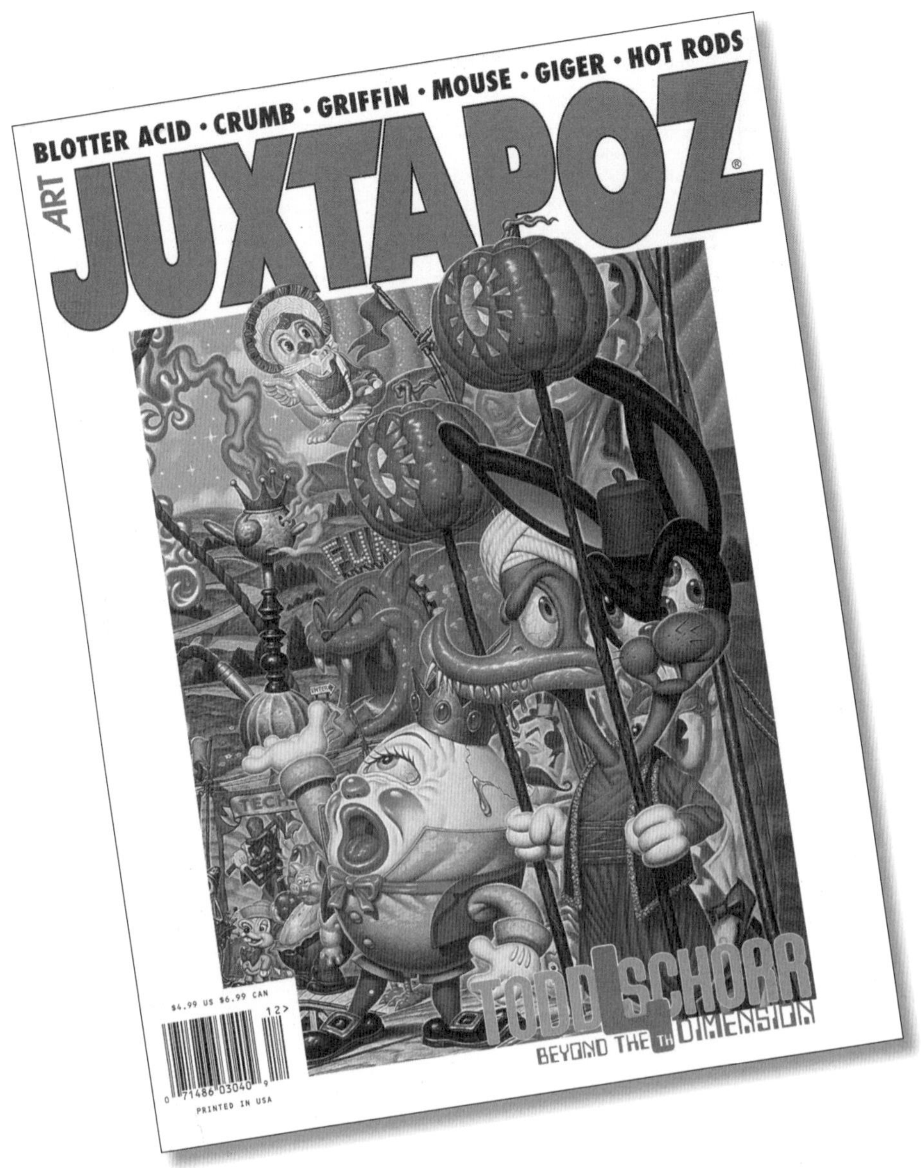

Cover art: Todd Schoor (detail) *The Spectre of Cartoon Appeal*

Volume Eight Number Six Nov/Dec 2000 #29

Chunks Of Tiger In The Dung Of Lamb

I WOULD PRESUME that many (if not most) of the readers of *Juxtapoz* see themselves as aspiring artists who have no qualms about accepting commissioned projects as long as they can remain independent and self-employed. I enjoyed this philosophy in my early career and would revert back to it if the situation required it.

Do keep in mind that commercial and professionally solicited illustration and design are always predicated on the largest possible market base, which will in turn provide the greatest chance of financial gain. The layman's market, as a whole, has about the same degree of abstract comprehension as lawn furniture. In reality, the purest form of this creative science is something along the lines of preparing pamphlet illustrations for Wal-Mart.

Now, I know you are thinking that my remarks are too simplistic and I twist them to make my idealistic point, although there is obviously a large range of commercial art that is very exciting and requires a wild imagination, such as rock art, tattoos, TV and movie work, surfboard art, and so on. And that's great. *Juxtapoz* magazine recognizes this art and caters to it. But a full-on realm of fine art does exist, and it offers absolutely limitless uncharted wildernesses of mental investigation.

If you have a rapacious and prehensile imagination, submitting sketches to a mordant art director for some rather uninspiring product is like being stifled. Sure, you can be the greatest shoe illustrator Payless Shoe Source has ever seen, but it's probably only as spiritually gratifying as leaky Depends undergarments.

To openly cast your lot in the "art for art's sake" world is far rougher than pursuing the corporate favors of a sportswear company looking for a good tiki artist to design their fall line. As cold and snobby and shitty as the formal art establishment can be, this is the only art drag strip to run your mental top fuel imagination. However, it's not an easy thing to enter a cultural sphere where realistic or controlled abstract form is not particularly welcomed. When any academic discussion comes up regarding the use and revival of representational and geometric configurations, modernists brush technical skills aside and ape the old mantra about painting and drawing being dead. However, keep in mind that there hasn't been a serious attempt to reintroduce representational graphics and sculpture since the surrealist movement of the late '30s. There was a brief flirtation with recognizable imagery in the pop art movement during the '60s, but that was only in the most condescending form of rendered witticism.

The only artists that have conscientiously tried to progress the graphic syntax of hand-drawn art are comic book artists and animators. Consequently, the legacy that's been with us since the paleolithic cave painters has been in the hands of so-called lowbrow artists for the last 50 years.

What do you think would happen if the responsibility of this neglected gift was again in the hands of credited and capable artists in the present art world? This magazine is in some ways a testimony to this. Artists like Todd Schorr, Joe Coleman, Sue Coe, and Mark Ryden make it evident that a visual language of pictures is an area that has gone virtually unexplored in the current age.

Once a viewing audience has accustomed themselves to search out a changing visual abstraction, then the object of their visual gratification can protract or compound itself, and facets of interests can be further amplified. This is akin to taking a common chicken and raising it to the glory of a Macy's parade balloon with the cackling skills of Lily Pons and the reverse egg-laying function of a black hole in space. I believe that the imaginatorial possibilities in art have hardly been scratched.

And as I euphemistically alluded to at the beginning, on close examination even the stool biopsies of pastoral sheep will provide evidence of a diet of Great White Shark.

–Robt Williams

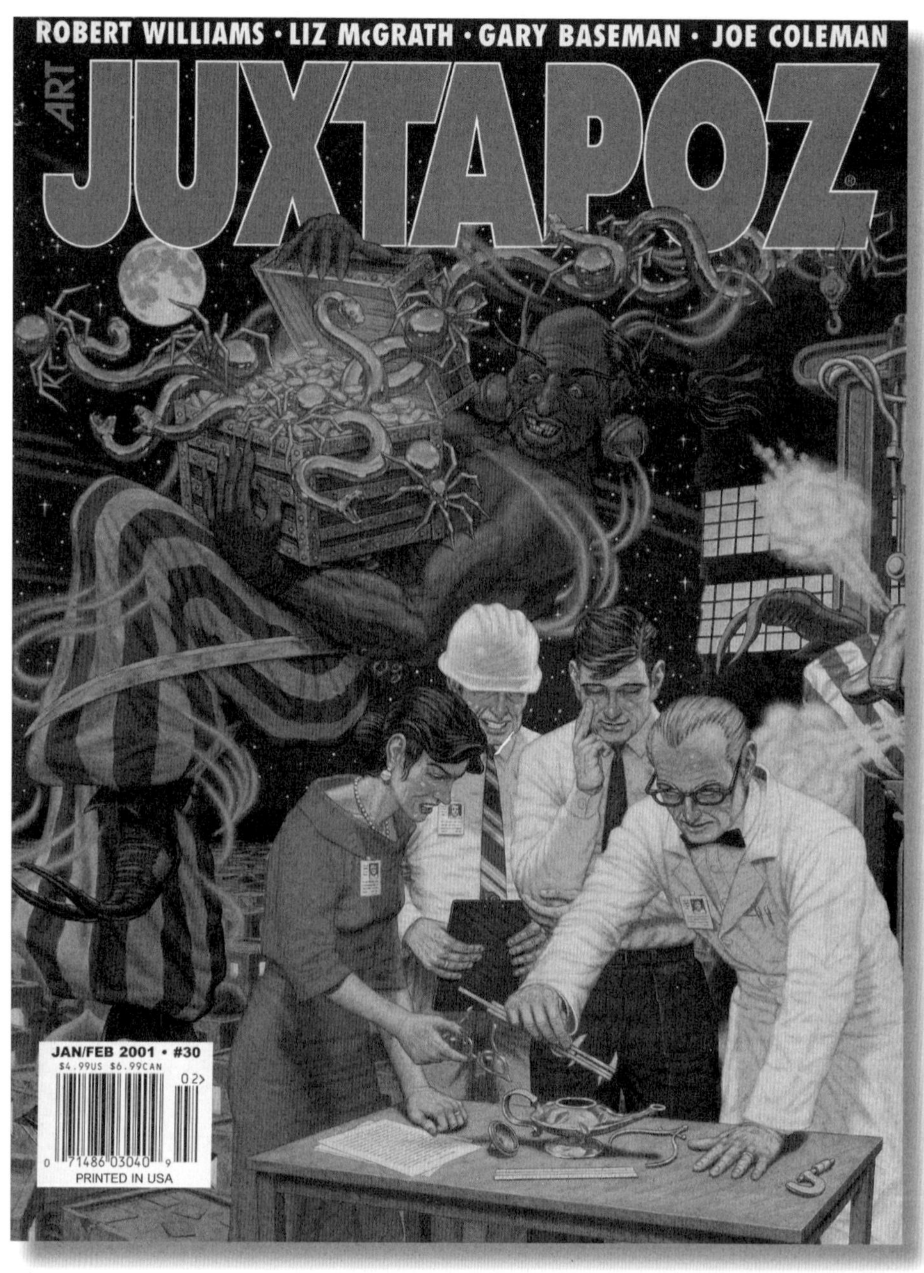

Cover art: Robert Williams (detail) *Puitting The Genie Back In The Bottle*

A Return To "Too Many Jujubes"

A NUMBER OF YEARS AGO I attended a comic book convention with S. Clay Wilson. A pair of seemingly out-of-place housewives passed our booth, and one stopped long enough to glance at a page of Wilson's complex ink drawings. She whispered a comment to her friend, "This is too busy." Fortunately for her and her friend, their investigative skills were lax and saved them the experience of viewing cartoon characters in assorted acts of sodomy, replete with bodily fluids and dialogue.

These women saw art exactly the way most modern art has been taught to be viewed–with detached peripheral interest, working on the assumption that if it takes more than 45 seconds to examine, something is amiss. Contemporary art has completely stripped away anything that might be considered superfluous detail or minutiae.

In fact, there is even a clinical, psychiatric word for art that is lavishly over-embellished. The term is "horror vacua," or fear of an unoccupied area. The minimalist movement of the 1980s formally ended all hopes of the generous use of labor in paintings, drawings, and sculpture. The artistic tradition of a thoroughly hand-wrought intricacy goes way back in time, and until 150 years ago, rich, lushly involved paintings and sculpture were testimonials to a well-orchestrated composition. Two thousand years ago the Celts wound every design they did into compulsive knots, as did the Chinese, the Japanese, and the Aztecs in later centuries. Gothic and baroque art also found harmony in clutter, and later, art nouveau would foster a rebirth of poetic convolution.

However, after the First World War, intricate compositions were put on a par with county-fair filigree or bad wallpaper. Then, in the early 1950s, a strange graphic phenomenon surfaced in comic book art. A number of cartoonists who contributed to the controversial EC Comics put together a new comic called *MAD*. One of the primary characteristics of this comic book was its use of psychosis. And, of course, one of its most powerful visual effects was overusing the space in the cartoon picture plane–or again, simply "horror vacua."

These crowded comic strips energetically screamed with visual interest and are still graphic milestones in American culture. Artists like Jack Davis, Wallace Wood, and Harvey Kurtzman inflicted untold mental damage on artists like me and a lot of my contemporaries. Fortunately, compositionally intense artwork is beginning to find new supporters. And hopefully the day of the art connoisseur with the attention span of a paramecium is over.

–Robt Williams

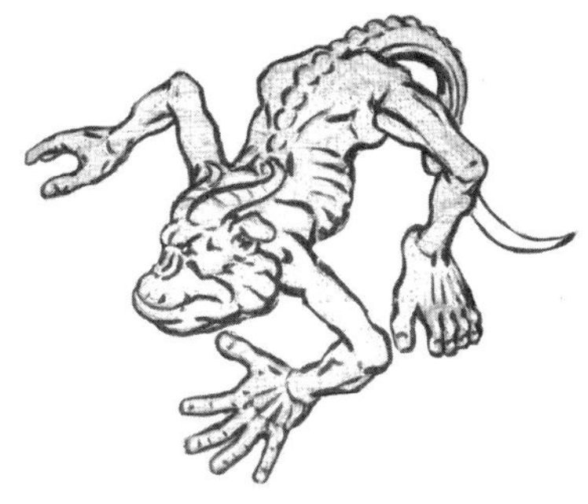

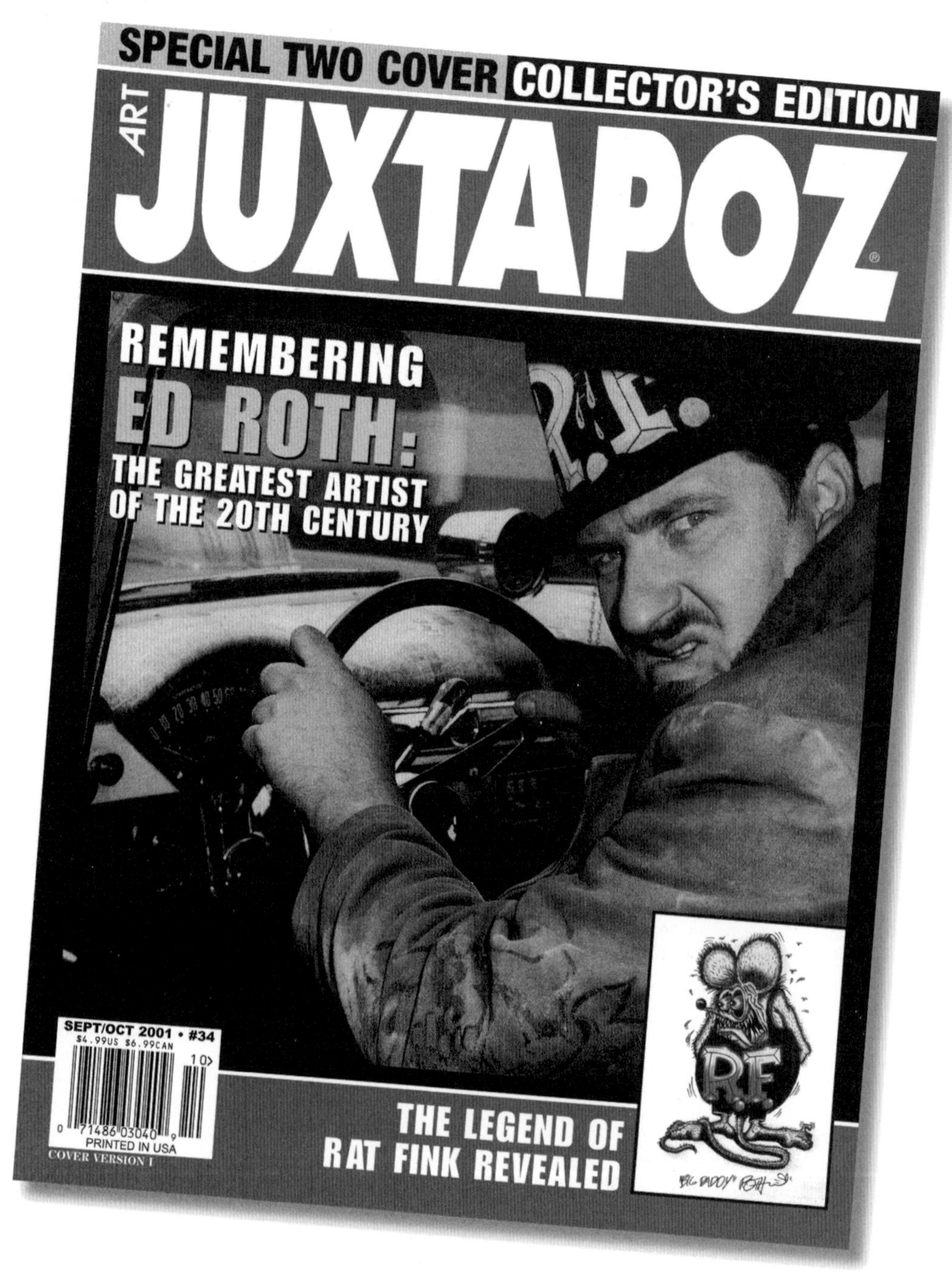

Cover art: Photo of Ed Roth behind the wheel of his '55 Chevy

Abstract Art vs Abstract Thought

I GENERALLY REFRAIN from responding to letters and email sent to *Juxtapoz*, because the bulk of it is compulsive opinions that kinda answer themselves, and I tend to put my foot in my mouth. But in the July/August issue, I found a letter that an art student sent that seemed to get right to the crux of the very reason *Juxtapoz* came into existence.

Wayne Huang wrote a poignant note explaining his observations in art school regarding abstract art versus representational art. In his letter, entitled "Abstract Thought," Wayne brings up a point. Students in his school have differing opinions about abstract art in relation to recognizable or three-dimensional suggestive realism in painting and sculpture. Furthermore, some of the instructors resent representational renditions of art done by their students.

This attitude was already entrenched in art academia when I was an art student (in 1963) during the heyday of abstract expressionism. Their logic was about as simple as it is today: if you can draw and paint you are an illustrator. But if you are too mentally gifted to be burdened with actually developing a style and technique, you belong to the select few who have the cerebral powers to speak in the elite language of theory. Hence, we poor bastards that can actually draw belong to that pathetic group which is doomed to eternal, menial knave-hood.

Well, evidently there's enough self-affirming draftsmen out there to warrant a magazine: this magazine, *Juxtapoz*.

Defining the word "abstract" becomes a confusing question because the term "abstract" is abstract. First of all, there is a problem with semantics. The dictionary definition doesn't seem to encompass all of the meanings that we think "abstract" means. In the art world, there are two different modes of abstraction.

Number one, there is the most common form: something that has been altered to a point of taking on a new persona or essence. This can also mean a type of abstraction that is non-objective in content, has not evolved from a parent or host form, and owes nothing to its free-form shape but imagination.

And then there is number two. This form of abstraction is abstract thought. This deals with oblique or protracted avenues of thought that can visualize violations of time and space. The perversing of perversity to a point that the rational becomes perverse, and the development of nonsense becomes a codified language–or, put quite simply, anything you can think up.

You say, "Gee, that sure sounds like theory oriented or conceptual art." Well, you are right, but modern conceptual art doesn't have a language. The only voice minimal and conceptual art has is that which is produced by art critics who write ponderous art-speak and by artists who create statements of intent with hopes of giving their projects credence. The artist that can draw and paint does have the language, they just need to develop a vocabulary.

The most obvious form of art language is the much-maligned cartoon. Many ask, "Why worry about being in the art world at all?" Simple; you're in it already. *Juxtapoz* has always been a cheap excuse for an art manifesto. By purchasing this magazine, you are an accomplice. If a person has inadvertently fostered some kind of art philosophy, they become an accessory to whatever art action they contemplate.

The Taliban in Afghanistan, who destroy giant Buddhist statues, are indirectly conceptual artists. Definition and opinion aside, there is no bad art.

–Robt Williams

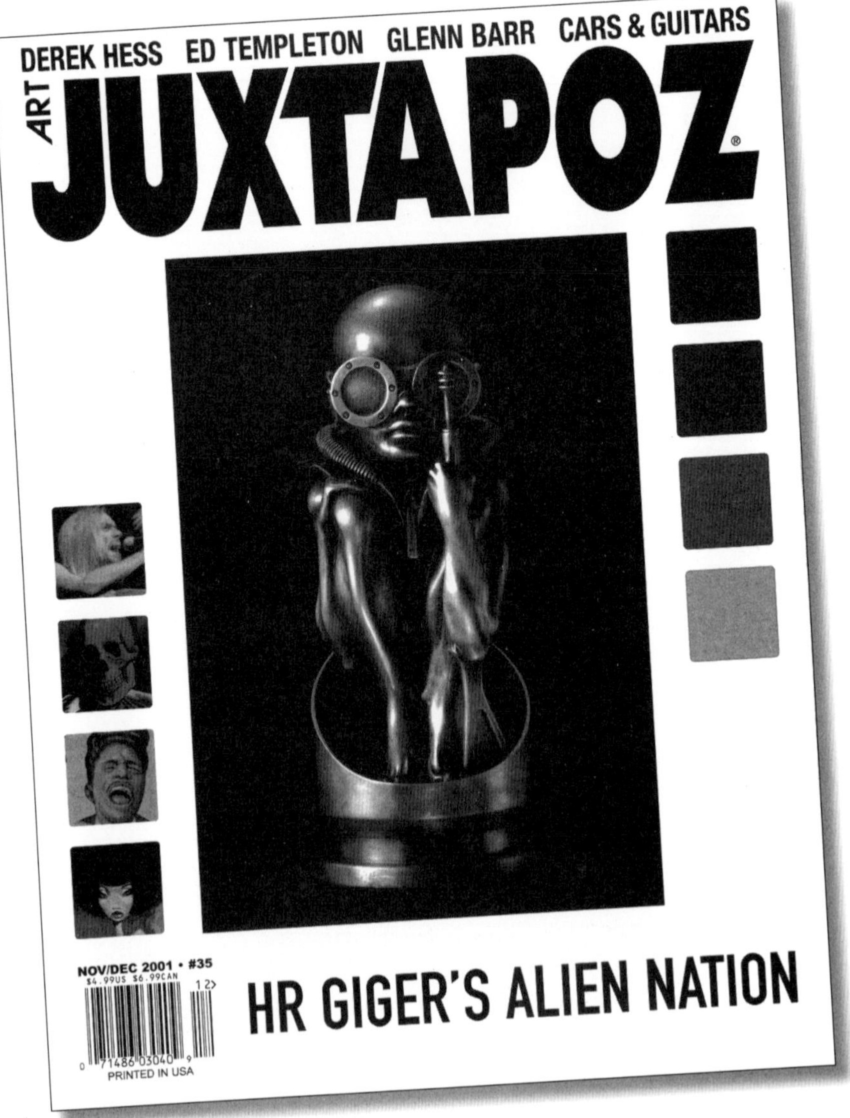

Cover art: HR Giger *Birth Machine Baby*

Volume Nine Number Six Nov/Dec 2001 #35

Two And Two Is Five

... WHAT KIND OF BULLSHIT is that? Simple: all numbers move in progression even if they are out of numerical sequence. By adding or subtracting numbers, the figures still move through theoretic time. And any movement has momentum or inertia. Numbers will advance and compound themselves until they slow to a stop or they are declared stopped.

Sounds silly, huh? Because in this example physics has slipped into art.

Allow me to bring this storm of nonsense into focus by citing a parable out of the old book *Zen Flesh and Zen Bones.*

A fellow was being pursued by a tiger through the jungle. In his panic he ran off a cliff. In his fall he, by chance, grabbed a vine and pulled himself to the face of the cliff. As he started to let himself down he noticed another tiger waiting below. He looked up and saw the original tiger above waiting for him. While looking up, he noticed the vine he was clinging to was beginning to break. He looked to the side and saw a berry growing on vegetation in the rocks. He reached over and picked the berry and then ate it. He thought to himself, "This is the best berry 1 have ever eaten." That extremely significant berry, in the eyes of a theoretic romantic, is "art."

I am going to be so bold as to say that all modern art since the dadaist movement in the earlier part of the 20th century could be conceptualized into that berry. And further classifying the idea that "everything is art" is basically "Zen."

Now, I am sure serious Zen Buddhists will resent that remark, but I have another direction here. If the past century was Zen, I am going to point out how the art of the future 21st century will be influenced by quantum mechanics.

Quantum theory deals with the workings of the physical universe and is, in many cases, far more absurd than kookie religions, flying-saucer cults, or metaphysical humbug. Hydrogen bombs, black holes in space, and parallel universes are the fruits of quantum mechanics.

Let me use this old analogy: "For the optimist the glass is half full. For the pessimist the glass is half empty." But for the quantum mechanic the surface volume on the inside of the glass is the same surface space as on the outside. Consequently, the glass, in theory, contains the whole universe. It is relative to what you call inside and outside–the glass doesn't know.

Therefore, judging the contents of the glass is, we reason, if not science, then art. Explaining that in writing or painting is the physical art.

Zen, which I credit with defining "everything is art," is superseded by quantum mechanics, which defines art as "everything around a given subject that has been declared art, at a particular time, is the vacuum that is not art." Art is where "not art" isn't.

I know as a *Juxtapoz* reader you are asking yourself what in the hell does this have to do with lowbrow art, devil-girl decals, tattoo flash, tiki napkin rings, skateboard graphics, and gang graffiti? Well, individually maybe little, but collectively, everything.

Juxtapoz is made up of every loose nut and bolt that has fallen through the cracks of the formal art establishment and if you look through the pages of this magazine you will find everything from sticker peddlers to cigarette-lighter salesmen, pinstripers to pornographers, high-strung illustrators to wall defacers.

What we are short on is conformity. Progressive art theory and half-cocked art precepts are just as valid as the rest of the unsavory retinue that populates this magazine. With our most rudimentary subjects we still endorse the contents of our publication as infinitely profound.

This issue of *Juxtapoz* marks our seventh anniversary. Not bad for a questionable little art gazette.

–Robt Williams,

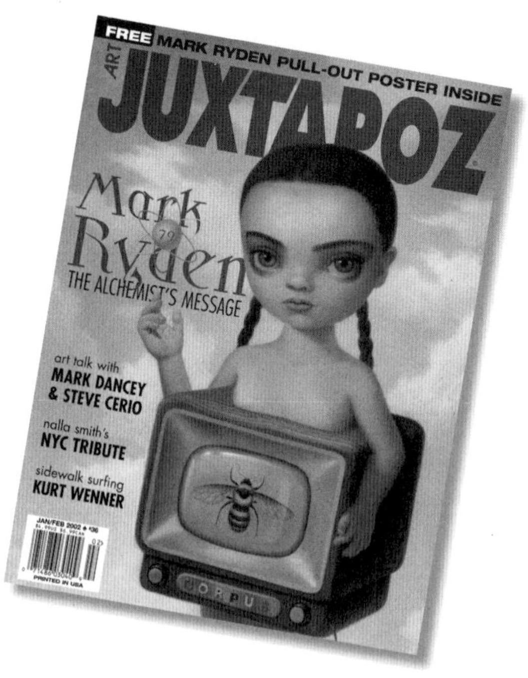

Cover art: Mark Ryden *Puella Animo Aureo*

Volume Ten Number One Jan/Feb 2002 #36

Wars And Rumors Of War

THREE MONTHS AGO, in one of my earlier editorials, I made reference to the Afghanistan Taliban for their barbaric destruction of Buddhist statues in that country. Evidently, very few of our readers knew or understood who I was talking about. After the events that took place in New York City on the morning of September 11, I feel fairly confident that everybody has quickly worked the term "Taliban" into their vocabulary.

I say "term" in discussing the Taliban because I feel that is exactly what they will become. Over the last 200 years, the pejorative expression for a crude, unartly dipshit has become "Philistine," referring to the ungainly brutes of the Old Testament who ravaged the Holy Land three millennia ago. However, recent archaeological evidence has come to prove the contrary. These invading Greeks, called Philistines, were quite sensitive to art and craftsmanship and culturally exceeded the peoples they vanquished. I think "Taliban" is a much more fitting term.

On that fateful Tuesday morning this September, our world instantly changed, and none of us will know to what extent for a long while.

If this terrorist round-up develops into a large-scale war, over an extended period of time, the arts will be affected. Even though familiar artists who enjoy our alternative philosophies are somewhat removed from the larger art world, the changing world events will cause emotional and creative reactions that will show up in future artworks. The established art market must surely be bracing itself for the worst–and probably for good reason. Because of the anemic nature of art as a crucial necessity, the arts are always the most reliable barometer for bad times. Granted, during periods of financial instability when currency and stocks and bonds become volatile, historic, old-master paintings and sculpture become fairly sound commodities, while newer, more experimental art quickly starts edging toward questionable worth. And similarly, the art that appears in *Juxtapoz* magazine, even in good times, hardly makes a blip on the screen of the high financing world of premium art. This is why we actually stand a better chance of survival than the recent blue-chip artists who have sold their souls to the big auction houses.

I'm not trying to say that "when you are on the bottom, the only way is up." I am simply pointing out that nouveau-riche artists who have acquired their laurels in the last five or ten years, purchased big homes, and gotten accustomed to opulent lifestyles might have their ears trimmed back by slow auction sales, whereas artists of our ilk can usually weather the worst storms.

Using the past as a guideline, it is easy to see that most great cultural trends are spawned from repercussions of major national conflicts. I'm not going into a long-winded dissertation about the effects of war and the art movements that have arisen from them, but just a look at the Vietnam War, for example, will demonstrate how a sharp left turn in the arts developed after 1965.

If our current conflict does protract into a major conflagration dragging on for years, the temperament of the country will change, and this will be reflected, most obviously in the arts. The disposition of the nation, as I present this writing, is as patriotic as I have ever seen. And from what I've been told, even more so than when it was when the Japanese bombed Pearl Harbor or when Pancho Villa attacked Columbus, New Mexico. I was surprised to find a certain nationalistic spirit in my fellow artists, something I had never seen before. Of course, I still have artist friends who feel that the terrorist attack on the World Trade Center is the fruits of our imperialist greed coming home to roost.

I have acquaintances in the arts who bear the millstones of all mankind and won't be happy until we are all wearing hair shirts and pulling, like draft animals in the hot sun, the stone testimonies of our malicious disregard for those less fortunate.

Putting all politics aside, let me bring to mind what might be the consequences of an Islamic, pro-terrorist war on the forms of art you see in *Juxtapoz* magazine, and maybe on art in general.

During the long, drawn-out struggle that could be before us, two things seem possible.

One: because of the horribly repressive nature of our adversaries, the arts, and indeed the whole nation, could go into a liberating expression of vocal and visual freedom the likes of which the free world has never dreamed.

Or, number two: this country, and the free world, could withdraw into an inhibited, controlled regression of arts and science, in sympathy with the Muslim world, to show empathy and our new face of charitable humility. This kind of situation could bring on social mores that would return us back 600 years, as with the Taliban. Remember, there are already religious and political elements in this country that have been trying for years to do just that.

If, for some reason, our government loses sight of our basic goals of freedom and uses this crisis, in years to come, to reform our society, I am afraid the new reformers might find the die has too long been cast. For sensitive art humanitarians who find fault everywhere but in the hands of the terrorists, I suggest that you imagine yourself on the streets of Kabul, in better days, and wonder how long your ass would last if you attempted your artistic trade. Being caught with one nude sketch would probably mean a summary trial for a capital offense. You might counter me and, in your gentle, re-conciliating voice, you would say, "But you can't judge an entire innocent people for the actions of a misguided few."

Yes I can. If the whole of the American people are held responsible for every action that takes place, then all people are all guilty for every action everywhere.

What stands out in my mind is the horrible fate of those poor souls that were burnt, crushed, and ground to death in the two collapsing skyscrapers and the Pentagon. The word "innocent" doesn't seem to apply to any of us anymore, and this may show up in the expression of the arts.

Whether the graphic arts become more benign, infantile, timid and innocuous, or extend themselves even further into the gratuitous realm of sex and violence, *Juxtapoz* magazine will be there, Osama bin Laden or not.

–Robt. Williams

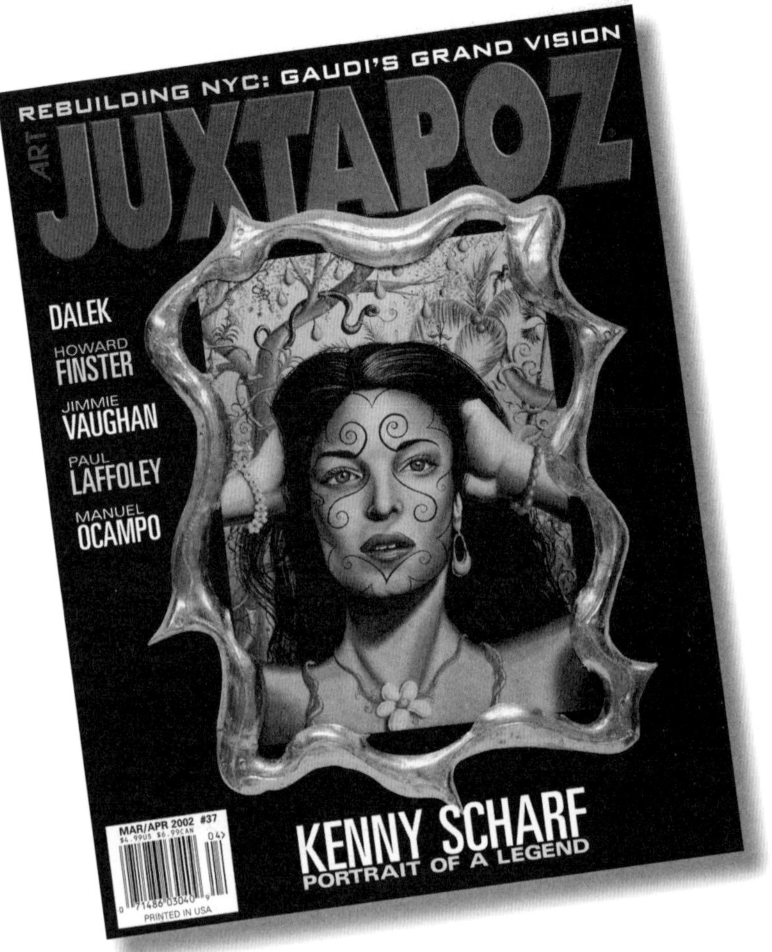

Cover art: Kenny Scharf *Amazon Woman (Stephanie Seymour)*

Volume Ten Number Two Mar/Apr 2002 #37

A Few Rambling Notes About Our Flaccid Economy

THREE DAYS AGO, our financial experts informed us that we are now officially in a recession, something I think everyone recognized even before the events of 9/11. So now we can fault a financial downturn for the interruption in our successful destiny. However, being a little older, I've seen a number of these economic slowdowns and I don't think they've had much effect on my personal aspirations–although I haven't set the world on fire even in the best of times.

There have been a number of artists who have risen from the ashes even during the worst of times. And those artists have one factor going for them: publicity. Promotion and hype are, unfortunately, 60 percent of art recognition and accomplishment.

I seriously believe that Jackson Pollock would be unheard of today if it weren't for a large article about him appearing in Life magazine during the mid-'50s.

Salvador Dali's entire career was a testimony to overt, sometimes ridiculous publicity escapades. Dali followed, and improved on, an already successful attention getting ploy, the "bohemian mad genius" ruse, which originated with the overwhelming acclaim given unfortunate mental patient Vincent van Gogh long after his death.

Later, in the mid-'20s, "crazy genius" was the basic persona for anarchistic dadaists, and it was only natural that the fruitcake pretense would be passed on through the Freud-oriented surrealist movement. In fact, the vast majority of noted artists prior to World War Two alluded to some type of latent, brilliant psychosis.

Although Dali was one of the most remarkable artists of our time (and one of my favorites) his asinine antics ended up casting a shadow over his art. As a dashing young Catalonian surrealist during the 1920s, he soon saw the advantages of publicity and transformed himself into a pedantic hybrid, somewhere between Oscar Wilde and Baron Munchausen. His embarrassing and aloof alter ego had long before cost him his surrealist friends and a serious place in the annals of art history, but his showmanship did achieve its ends. He became second only to Picasso and very wealthy (for a time, anyway).

Once, while promoting himself, he attended a lecture wearing a deep-sea-diving suit to illustrate symbolically how he could delve deeply into the human subconscious. As he entered the lecture hall, he tripped on the diving suit air line, fell to the floor, and damn near suffocated before the audience realized he wasn't joking and someone took action to save him.

Dali's shameless self-promotion made pop artist Claes Oldenburg and conceptual artist Christo world renowned. In fact, the question comes up: is their conceptual art really their publicity? Is true art the art of stirring up success and the applied gestures of producing art (paintings, sculptures, etc) an insignificant formality to reach the objective of being some kind of cheesy luminary?

It's always interesting to watch artists seek out fame. Years ago, one of my friends tried a short cut and simply declared himself famous. He spent thousands of dollars promoting himself through ads in expensive art magazines but eventually ran out of money.

Traditionally, publicity for an artist is usually rationed out in newspapers by art critics, but believe me, that's politics in its most merciless form.

In any economy, good or bad, promoting oneself is the answer to success. I have noticed that the very people who hype themselves the hardest are the ones who are the most impatient if their self-promotion doesn't quickly bear fruit. They generally become disillusioned and apply their impetus drive in other directions, like maybe becoming art directors, set designers, or something else art oriented.

I find, and this from years of observation, that any artist who can hang in there for years and years without jumping around and changing their style too drastically will become fairly well known and successful. I would call this accumulative publicity. Compare René Magritte to Salvador Dalí both with the same surrealist origins. Magritte, with almost no promotion, is now as well known as Dali by just hanging in there and developing the best kind of publicity: word of mouth.

Juxtapoz magazine is seven years old. Where will the artists in these current issues be in another seven years? I'm sure of one thing: *Juxtapoz* magazine will be there to see.

–Robt Williams

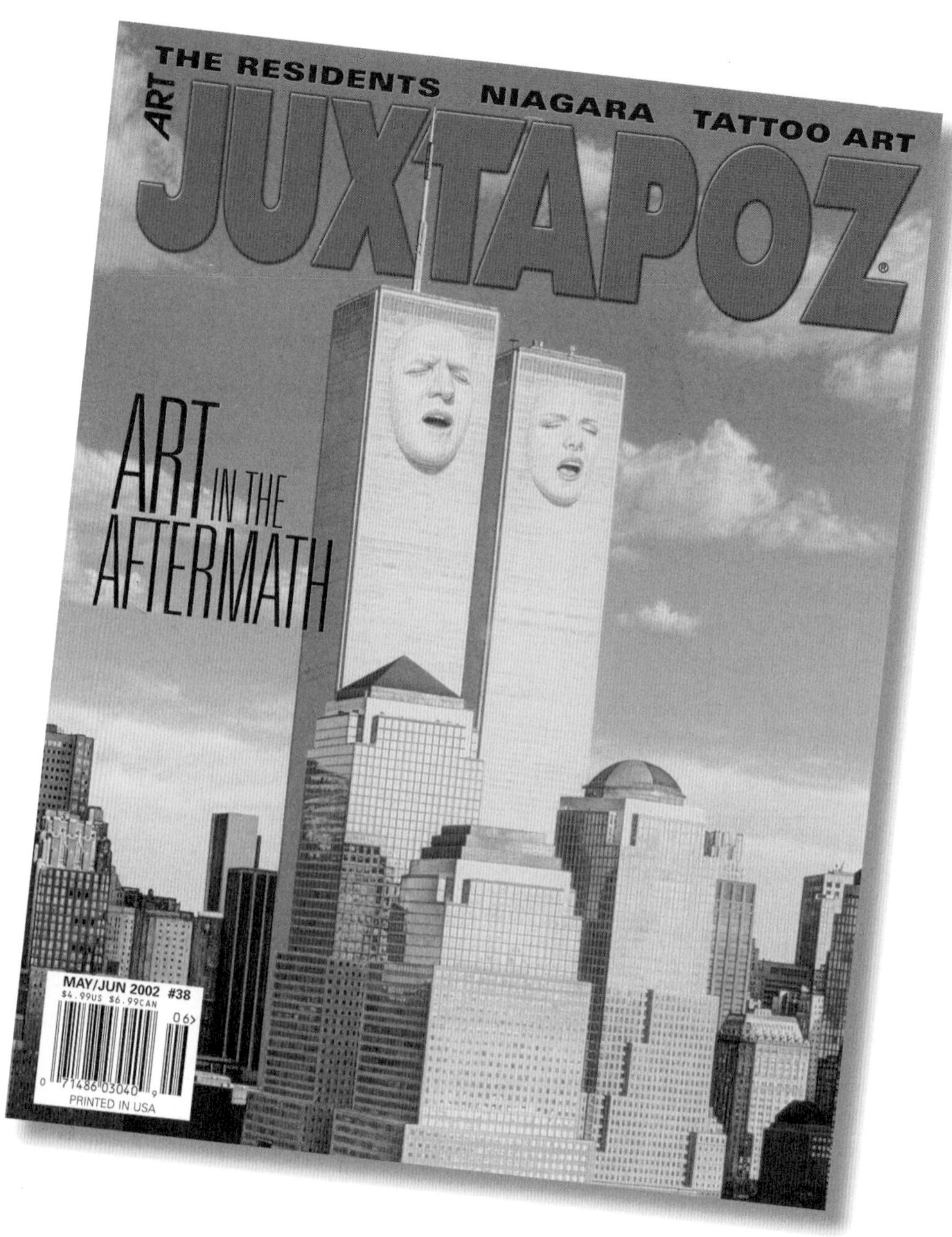

Cover art: Doug Web *S.O.S.*

The Most Liberal Use Of The Word "Art"

I AND OTHER MEMBERS of *Juxtapoz*, as you can well imagine, have long been devotees of girly magazines. This can best be attested to by our former sister magazine, *Erotica*. And this curious association is not by chance. Girly mags (or spread magazines) have always been a very accurate barometer to how liberal the general public is and just what the courts will tolerate. Allow me to elaborate.

Although erotic photography was probably born within months of the invention of the camera, published material didn't appear until much later. The first nudie photo portfolios seemed to surface around 1880 and were only accepted in cultivated society, which allowed them to be privately disseminated under the strictest definition of fine art (I'm not including pornography and French postcards; they were always contraband). What we know as girlie magazines supposedly started out as artists' photographic anatomy references in the early '20s. This phony "art" format carried over into the first burlesque magazines when these publications were able to worm their way onto magazine racks in the 1940s.

Remember, the premier masturbatorial picture material for young men up until that time had been women's underwear catalogs and movie-star magazines.

Artists had always been at the forefront of sexually questionable material until Hugh Hefner produced *Playboy* magazine. This magazine shrouded itself in a new cloak of culture by presenting an "urban sophisticate" philosophy to justify its display of tits and ass. But it was *Playboy*, in 1970, that was first to publish an article about the artists in underground comix (*Zap*, etc). Hugh Hefner, or at least the people who worked for him, realized that there was an arcane underground world of very talented people worthy of mentioning.

Since those times, many more skin magazines have run articles about alternative art and their artists. From very early on, the one magazine that has always been conscious of this art and supported it is Larry Flynt's *Hustler* magazine. For at least 10 or 15 years, many noted underground artists have graced the pages of *Hustler*, with S. Clay Wilson, Peter Bagge, Dan Clowes, Georgeanne Deen, the Pizz, Coop, and Gary Panter, just to mention a few. These artists and cartoonists have boldly illustrated stories and deprecated themselves in the name of visual pleasure, myself included. *Hustler's* editorial director Allan MacDonell, seems to be the force that has long encouraged Flynt Publishing to periodically use artists from this imagination pool.

The symbolic connection between artists and girlie mags goes far deeper in our culture than just making a buck, and I think a lot of artists are grateful.

–Robt Williams

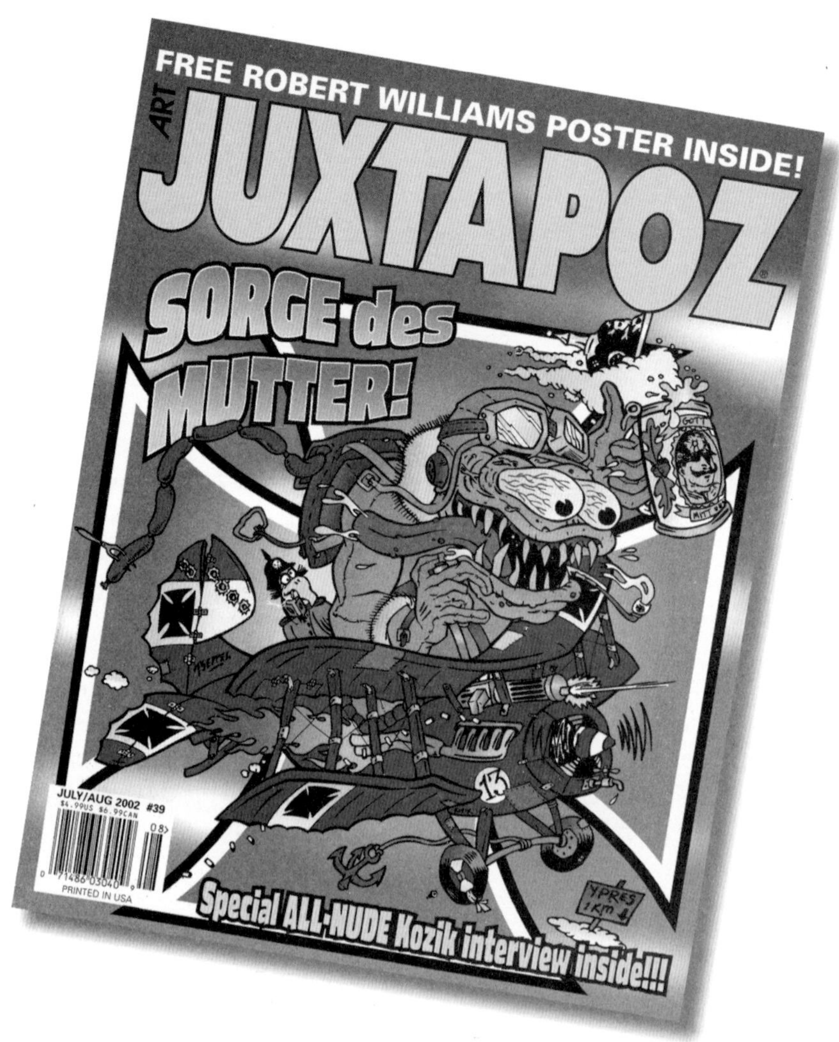

Cover art: Frank Kozik *Fokkers Eat Sopwiths*

Volume Ten Number Four July/Aug 2002 #39

Imagination Is Bad Taste

IF YOU ARE AN ARTIST or involved in the arts, you hear this phrase frequently: "I don't know anything about art; I just know what I like."

Gee, no more profound words have ever been spoken. To just honestly see and judge, speak freely from the hip like the sincere voice of the "average Joe." This is the genuine audacity that *Juxtapoz* magazine would like to foster and regard as our reading audience.

This sounds down to earth, but honestly, unencumbered good taste isn't quite this simple. The matter of taste and artistic judgment, at best, is a complex and convoluted combination of already predetermined preferences and prejudices. When judging art, our pure and unadulterated opinions are loaded with poison. In fact, our ability to be unbiased when evaluating the merits of a given piece of art is flush with emotional discrimination.

The first opinionated hurdle art has to climb over is collective public opinion: What will other people think? Will it be acceptable to rank-and-file strangers? Will the art be suitable for families, children, religious elders, people with limited attention spans, and individuals who feel indignation about anything provocative? This requires that art projects be simple and non-engaging (trite).

Secondly, because of my art, "will I lose favor with my peer group (friends and acquaintances)?" Since peer pressure must be served, and embarrassment avoided, this means whatever project you produce or collect has to be sanctified by your respective cronies.

The last factor in judging art is that timely matter of fashion. Unfortunately art, more than anything else, is held hostage by its shelf life and by how it makes both creator and buyer feel the excitement of being on the cusp of the future.

What most people perceive as good taste is really a whole slew of dos and don'ts applied to one's initial first impression, which is generally an infantile fascination. When the equation of "what will other people think?" is added, and then the fashion factor is weighed, a snap judgment is made. This is then shrouded in a quick pseudo-deliberation, and then the final opinion. This is about as deep and impartial as judging art gets.

Pablo Picasso said it perfectly: "Good taste is the enemy of creativity."

If art is to be measured by popularity (and I don't begrudge this method), the most popular single graphic image of our time was the circular yellow happy face.

The point I'm so ineloquently making here is that the art we see around us is imposed on society by the hyper-squeamish. Allow me to give you an example: if I had a copy of Herman Melville's *Moby Dick* laying on my coffee table, I would be considered a rustic intellectual and a *bon vivant* of literature. But if I exhibited a large oil painting depicting specific passages out of that book on my wall, I would be thought of as a lurid lout, and my politically correct associates would, upon viewing this, shit their pants (figuratively speaking, that is).

Opinions have to expand in order to free art. We have all heard the old wisecrack, "Wine is just grape juice that's gone bad but hasn't yet turned to vinegar." Granted, simple fermented grapes have been cultivated for thousands of years and discreetly refined into hundreds of subtle flavors for fussy wine drinkers the world over. And if the grapes are left to oxidize, the juices will turn to vinegar. But there is also an abstract aspect to wine tastes. Vinegar can be processed and distilled into powerful and caustic solvents and further concentrated into volatile explosives. How does that fit into the narrow parameters of sophisticated wine tasting? Same grape.

I regret having to touch upon some sad notices. Earlier this year, the well-loved underground cartoonist Jim Osborne passed away. Osborne was known in the '70s as one of the most daring and unabashed outlaw illustrators in San Francisco. I don't see the young ranks of artists being filled today by his kind.

On March the 7th we lost an important elder statesman for the surreal arts, Mati Klarwein. Klarwein was the real thing and singlehandedly championed representational art throughout the darkest years for realist painting in the New York scene. He died after having struggled with prostrate cancer. Mati was a great source of inspiration to me during the late '60s and, later, became a main staple in *Juxtapoz.*

Unfortunately, my last bad tiding is also a passing of another outstanding artist. In mid-March the underground art luminary Mad Marc Rude succumbed to medical complications while living in Arizona. Rude was an early member of the LA punk rock art community and known to be as notorious with his fists as he was with a stippling pen or a tattoo needle. His demise is shrouded in mystery, but it is said that Nevada law enforcement might have played some part.

These gentlemen will be sorely missed.

–Robt Williams

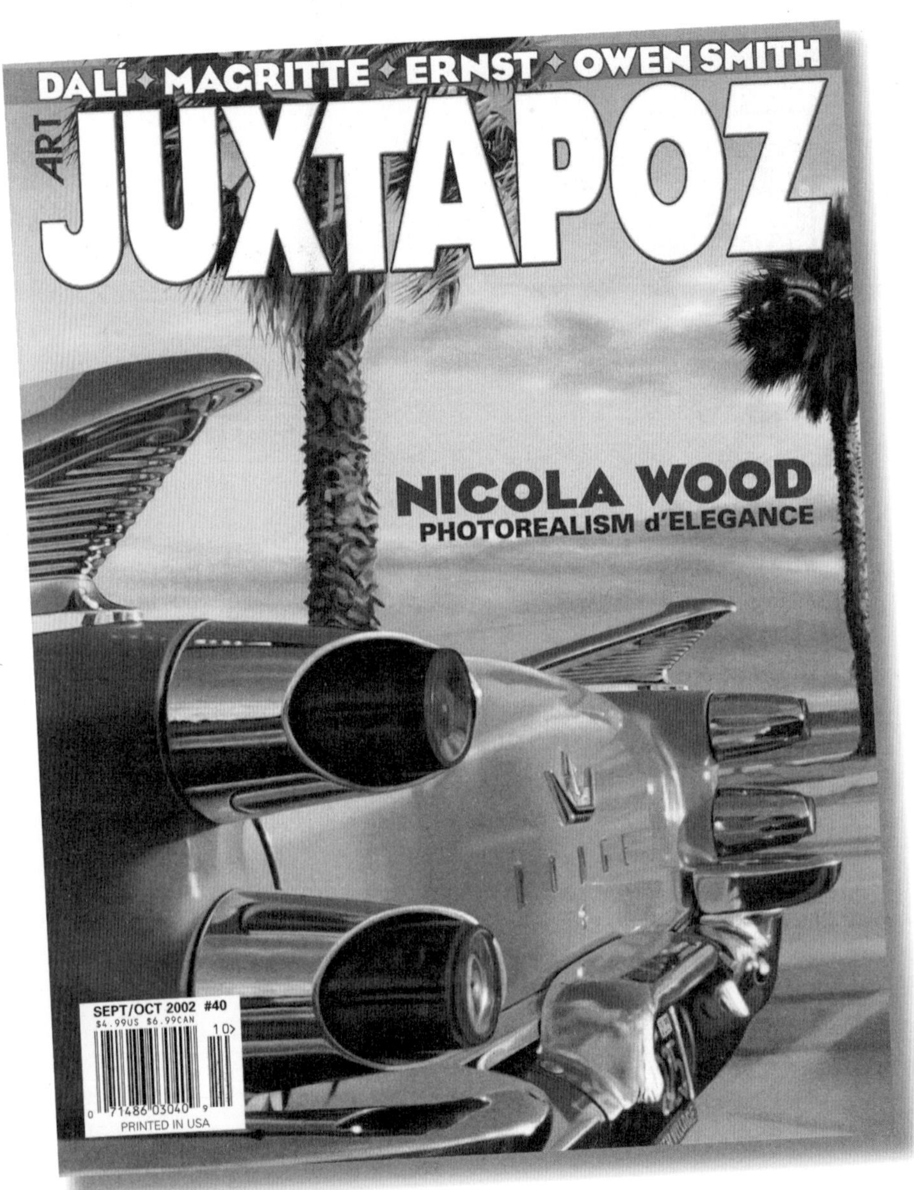

Cover art: Nicola Wood *Dodge Venice Beach*

Volume Ten Number Five Sept/Oct 2002 #40

Take Your Best Shot

THERE SEEMS TO BE ONE overriding characteristic among our readers. For some reason, the audience that reads *Juxtapoz* gains a great deal of satisfaction out of finding shortcomings with the work of the artists who appear in this magazine and feels obliged to write us about it.

From the inception of *Juxtapoz* magazine, we have politely suggested that, if you feel compelled to write "letters to the editor," you restrain yourself long enough to think and consider that lambasting some sensitive artist because their work does not live up to your ideals might reflect on you more than on the artist's work.

Don't get me wrong; we love getting correspondence. And we don't mind, and even enjoy, curt and cutting mail about what you like and don't like, and who you like and don't like. But as I have said time after time, "art is judged here, at the magazine, on a relative scale. There is good art, great art, and art that doesn't interest you. Bad art is the province of snobs."

Of all the derogatory correspondence, hate mail, character assassinations, adverse comments, maligning, denunciation, and pissin' and moanin' that has arrived in our mail box (or email), the largest single target has been me and my humble efforts. I get more criticism than any two other artists that have appeared in this publication, so I can sorta say this first hand. I feel that, being an underground and outlaw artist, receiving slanderous mail validates my work. The other artists have to speak for themselves.

But as far as we at *Juxtapoz* go, we would like to suggest this: if you are going to send a sour-mail, poison-pen letter castigating some poor bastard for his or her style of artwork, make it good! Analyze the work. Sit down at a desk and really compose a burning piece of literary abuse–a fiery opus with a lot of good expletives. Maybe get out a thesaurus or spell-checker and do it up right. Or better yet, visit a public restroom and gather some profane exclamations off the stall walls. Make this a strong and moving sonnet, worthwhile and worthy of us taking time to read it. Don't just go into the poor artist's modest works; let's dig up something personal on them. Who do they dare think they are? How do they do their hair? What do they wear? (I can't stand artists who wear brown shoes.)

Now, I can't promise we will print any of these abusive letters, but we just want to, once and for all, get a good idea of how venomous our readership can be.

I realize that none of us are beyond criticism. But I'm wondering why you communicators aren't writing these impassioned communiques to the overground and formalist art magazines. They are the dominant force that supports and propagates sterile and boring art. These are your real adversaries, I would think, not some innocuous artist in *Juxtapoz* who paints tits on a Rat Fink.

Juxtapoz, at its worst, has more visually rewarding and cerebrally engaging fare than you can find in a year's subscription of most of the other art rags. Remember, when you hate our magazine, hate it clear down to the barcode. And when you are at the newsstand purchasing *Juxtapoz,* look the magazine dealer straight in the eye, grit your teeth, and buy it with a vengeance.

–Robt Williams

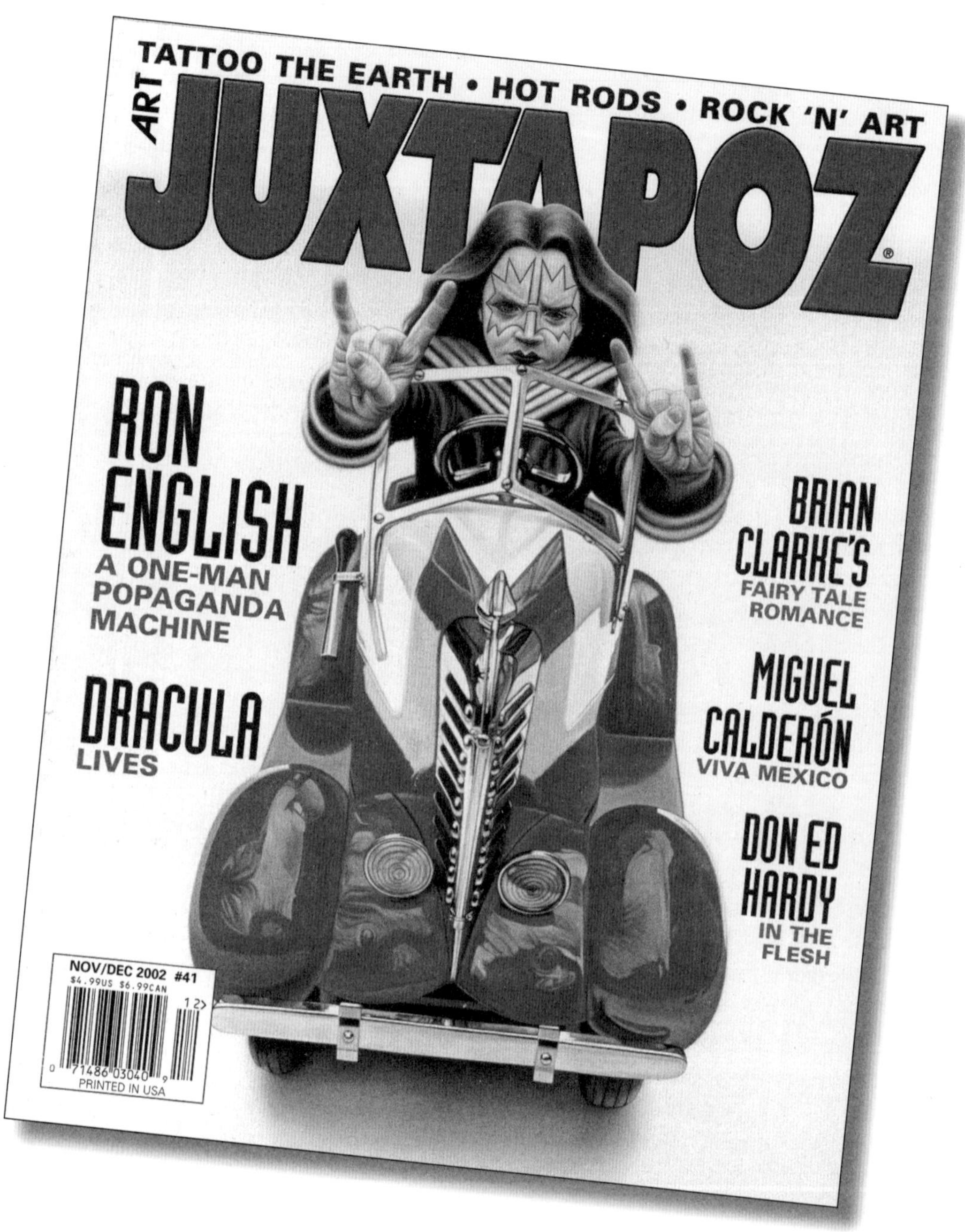

Cover art: Ron English *Kiss Kid In Kar*

Eight-Tenths Of A Decade And We Still Flourish

TWO EVENTS THIS FALL that predominate the interest of the staff here at *Juxtapoz* are significant to the direction and spirit of our magazine, and you should know about them.

Firstly, an art show at Cal State University Northridge (here in California) that runs through October 5th and picks up again at the end of the year at Cal State University Fullerton, remaining on display through January 2003. It is the much-touted Von Dutch show.

I hesitate from going into a lengthy dissertation about Von Dutch, but I would like to say this: Hopefully, you can come to the West Coast to see this show–it is a show not to be missed. I don't think even the organizers of this exhibition fully understand his significance. Kenny Howard (AKA Von Dutch) was the consummate backyard hot-rod artist, and he was gifted with an imagination that can only be compared with a "runaway train." In the early 1950s, he was my childhood hero and, later, a close personal acquaintance, for a time anyway.

Dutch had a very dark side to him. If you are a sensitive and caring liberal, you will have to rally your most tolerant objective emotions to understand Dutch as a man.

He was an iconoclast's iconoclast during a time when individualists were considered suspect. In political affairs, he had all the artistic trappings of a beatnik liberal but espoused a tough philosophy I can only describe as authoritarian absolutism (or far right). He advocated a governmental regime that would, in actuality, waste no time making him the first person rounded up and placed before a firing squad.

Nonetheless, even 10 years after his death, his legend keeps on escalating. Always carrying a firearm, Dutch personified the two-fisted art he created–you won't find any bunnies or tikis in his gnarled repertoire. He originated the now-famous abstract use of pinstriping and was the first to paint stylized fire (flames) on hot rods. He was a compulsive worker, brilliant inventor, master machinist, self-proclaimed great lover, and crackpot extraordinaire.

Our second event coming up this fall is a special art show commemorating eight years of *Juxtapoz* magazine. This exhibit will feature more than 75 different artists' works at Track 16 Gallery, part of Bergamot Station in Santa Monica, California. The show runs from October 26 till November 16, 2002.

This should be a landmark show at one of Los Angeles' prime gallery locations. I could say that this show would be a who's-who of America's top alternative artists, but we at *Juxtapoz* avoid who's-whos (and other forms of favoritism rankings), and artists who don't appear in this exhibit might well be selected for shows in the future. This presentation is a justification to give exposure to a lot of artists, and all the artwork will be made available for sale. We are certainly not interested in classifying specific artists as "*Juxtapoz* artists," *per se*, but a big group show like this will definitely stand out against most artworks exhibited in the many other galleries in the Bergamot Station complex.

Gee, I hope we don't influentially pollute the other galleries.

–Robt Williams

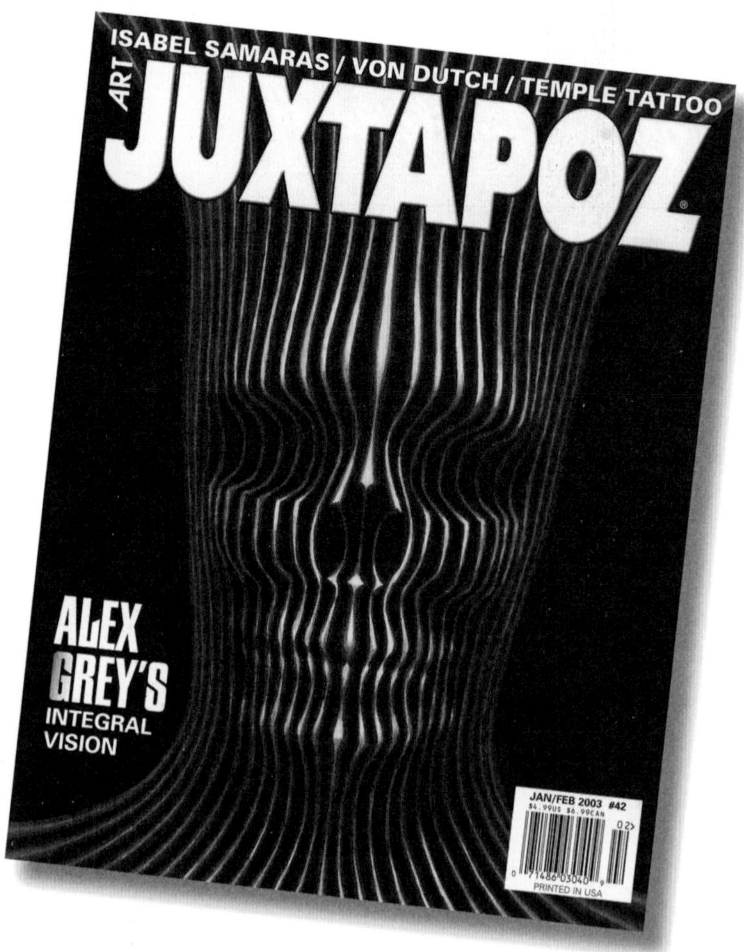

Cover art: Sean Sorensen *Blue Jean Burqa*

Volume Eleven Number One Jan/Feb 2003 #42

Oil Paint Ain't Axel Grease

AMONG THE VARIETY OF INFLUENCES and trends that *Juxtapoz* magazine has presented to its readers over the past years, one cultural idiom keeps cropping up. Some of the artists that frequent our pages have expressed resentment about it; I'm talking about our recurring use of hot-rod visuals and car culture.

Let me be quite frank with you and lay our cards on the table. Worldly, sophisticated *bon vivants* aren't going to be laying on their backs under cars, covered in grease, tightening up main bearings. Generally, purported intellectuals avoid the companionship of those who are mechanically inclined.

Twenty years ago, in a fit of excitement, I showed off my recently completed 1932 Ford roadster to an old friend who immediately put me in my place. After looking at the roadster, he said, "You know, you think you have really got a handle on being part of the hep automotive world. Well, let me tell you, I was out there at those early dry-lakes speed trials back in the '30s and '40s where the first hot rods were born, and I knew all those early speed-equipment innovators. Believe me, they were all dumb shits."

Well, to a certain extent, he might have been right. People with a high mechanical aptitude are usually left-brained or emotionless puzzle-solvers. Most artists and abstract thinkers are right brained: impractical by nature. I love hot rods, but I hate working on them. Many self-proclaimed geniuses berate the societies that cling to autos and motorcycles. And if you see this subject through their eyes, you can understand their indifference. They feel that methods of transportation have no more cultural significance than a toaster or a washing machine or any other appliance.

Fortunately for the international art intelligentsia, hot rodders are an endangered species. Law enforcement agencies have always exerted their influence to outlaw hot rods, and the late-'60s awakening of ecology seems to be the death knell for souped-up and modified cars and motorcycles. And now, with stringent environmental pollution laws, it will probably be just a short time before hot rodding is nothing more than a quaint legend like cowboys or pirates.

The idea of a hot rod was a wild and romantic notion. A kid 17 years old during the 1940s or 1950s, who has little chance of rising above a blue-collar life, buys an old automobile. Probably a Ford, since that was the lowest common denominator. He takes this car and strips off every part of nonessential metal, reducing the weight to almost half, and then alters the engine's horsepower with speed equipment. This car was dangerous to begin with. Now it's a virtual projectile. An old Ford that ran 60 miles per hour when it was new is now capable of speeds upwards of 120-140 mph. You can see the authorities' concern. The word "hot rod" is a metaphor for "thrill.".

Translate this into art. One of the bohemian guidelines for abstract art is "no responsibility." Art has to be unencumbered by regulations. Let's say a young artist accepts an important painting commission from a prominent hospital to do serene and pleasing art prints to hang in every room. These images have to be pastoral and restrained in subject and color. They have to integrate into an emotional environment with patients who suffer from anxieties and morose periods of depression. The art should be something like placid landscapes made up of gentle horizontal forms in pastel colors.

But the irrational right-brained artist figures it differently. "Shit, let's put some pep back into the libidos of these poor shut-ins." So, instead of rendering docile visions of tranquility, he splashes the picture plane with hot, red, fiery skies, illuminating scenes of nude, enslaved vixens braking their chains and whipping their captors with their own intestines, while invalids and other unfortunate, infirm souls are being healed by Christ while he's still on the cross–all of this while the Devil cowers in a muddy ditch, burying his face in his hands as a gesture of revulsion.

This analogy between art and hot rodding indicates a parallel with the same thrill based psychosis. The most inspiring art is almost always irresponsibly exuberant, no matter if the patients are affected adversely with headaches, diarrhea, vomiting, or bouts of severe depression after witnessing these masterpieces. Like with hot rod art, responsibility to good taste ends the minute you pick up *Juxtapoz* magazine.

–Robt Williams

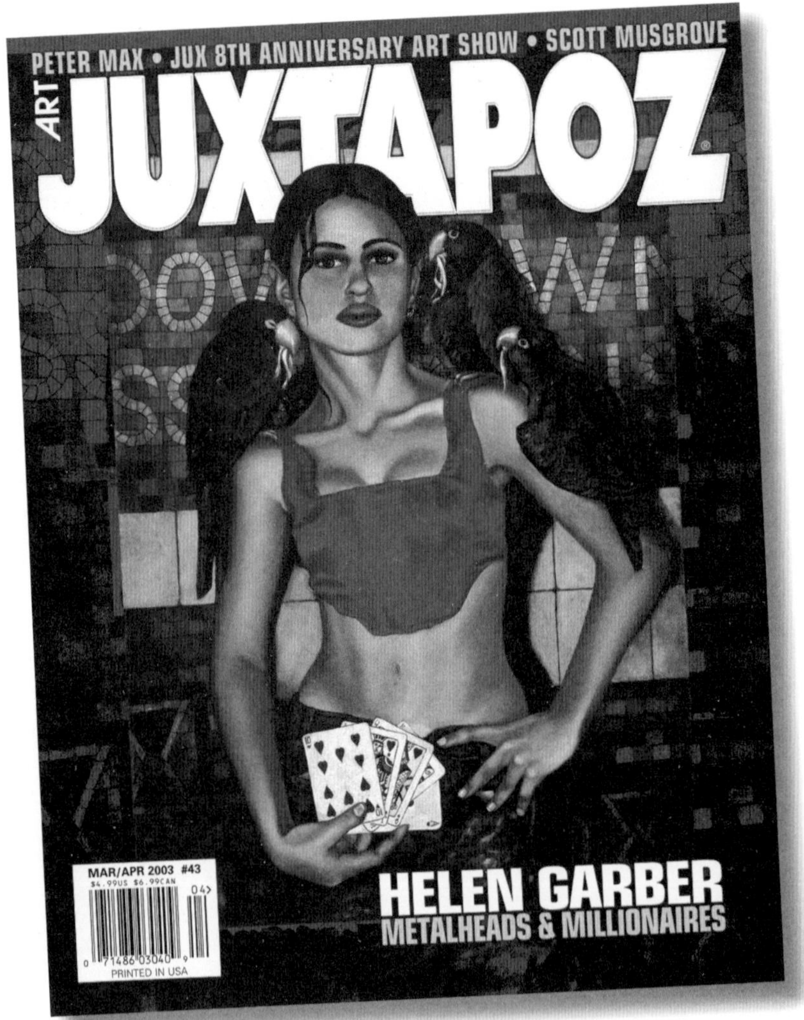

Cover art: Helen Garber *Self-Portrait*

Volume Eleven Number Two Mar/Apr 2003 #43

Postmortem Of The *Juxtapoz* Eighth Anniversary Party

OCTOBER 26 WAS OUR BIG PARTY at Track 16 Gallery at Bergamot Station in Santa Monica, California. Our Naugahyde anniversary (as the eminent LA Weekly arts writer, Doug Harvey, so imaginatively phrased it) was an enormous success; so much so that an extensive portion of this issue will focus on showcasing every piece that was in the show.

Let me preface the aims and intentions of our anniversary show to circumvent any lofty expectations about the motives of our pleasant little art soirée.

To begin with, this was a mercenary promotional party for *Juxtapoz* magazine, pure and simple; not a self-sacrificing impassioned act of cultural charity to better our misguided art community. It was basically a blatant attention-getting shindig to celebrate the existence and survival of ol' money-grubbing *Juxtapoz* magazine.

The art show was a secondary accoutrement to liven up the affair. At the time, we had no doubt that the art exhibit would immediately dominate and upstage our shitty little party–and that's exactly what happened. From its earliest inception, we realized that we had to put size restrictions on the artwork, or the show could mushroom into a "salon *du* berserk." This was like putting a condom on a hurricane.

Another facet that concerned me specifically was the fact that most of the artwork would most likely contrast so brutally with the other art generally exhibited at this enormous complex of galleries, and that therefore, our art would instantly be written off as "*Juxtapoz* art" and not be considered on the merits of each artist's individual expression. Fortunately, this didn't happen. *Juxtapoz* magazine exists as a service to the artists, not the other way around.

My other big fear was how similar all the art could potentially be. Remember, no one has ever seen 86 outlaw artists' works in one venue before–would this all be the same old dredged-up, familiar iconography? My concerns were quickly alleviated. The diversity of imagination and graphic skill was an obvious indication that there was a mutual life force extending far beyond *Juxtapoz* magazine and was certainly going to have a contaminating effect on what is thought of as the formal art establishment.

Despite rather anemic art sales, things could not have worked out better. The *Juxtapoz* panel discussion that followed two weeks later at Track 16, attracted a standing-room-only attendance with an enthusiastic audience.

Juxtapoz would like to offer its appreciation to Tom Patchett, Laurie Steelink, Cindy Ojeda, Scott Hopper, and the rest of the curatorial staff at Track 16 for the use of their gallery.

The question that keeps coming back to us is, "When is the next *Juxtapoz* party?" We'll keep you posted on that. Maybe for the "spandex anniversary."

–Robt Williams

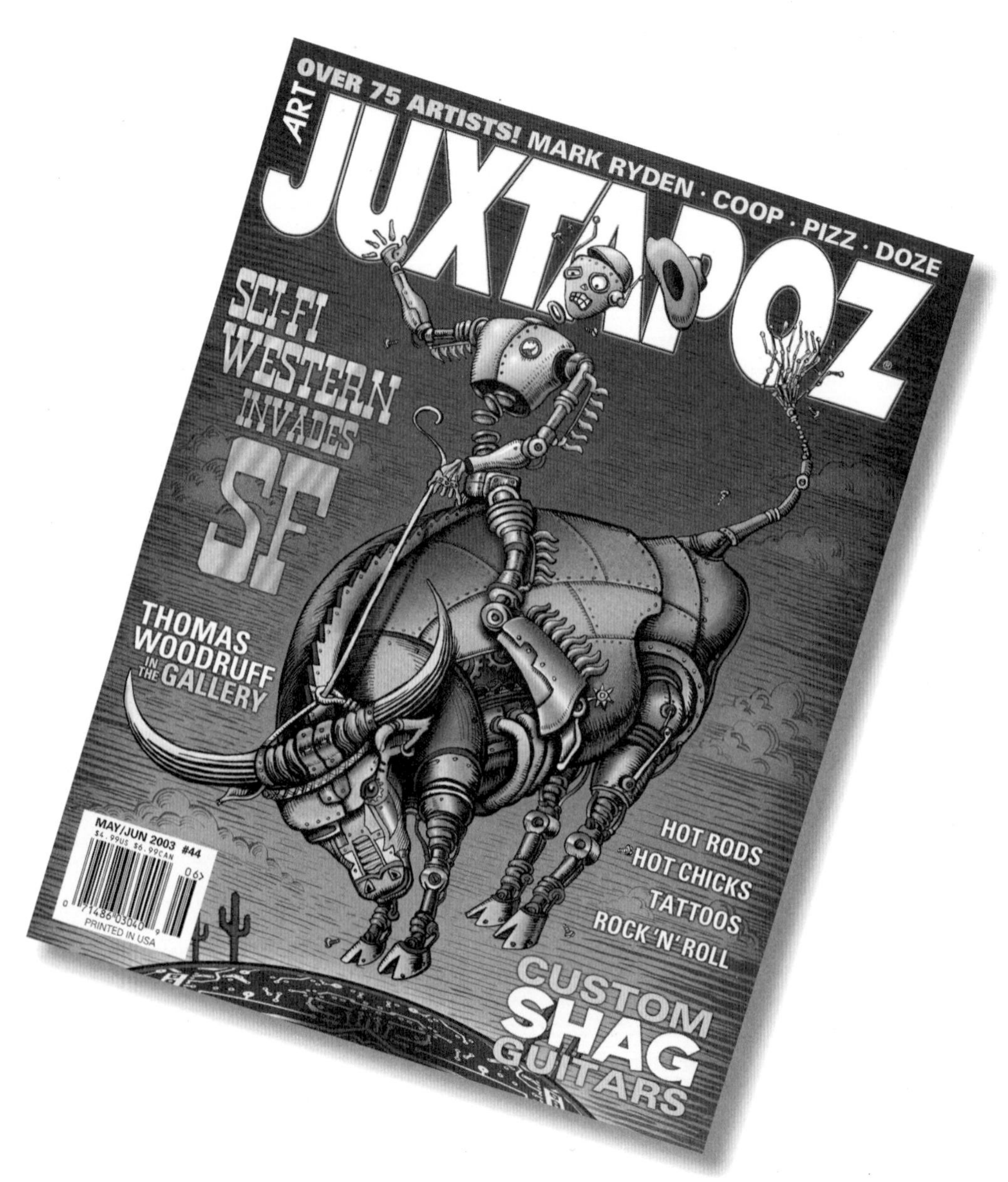

Cover art: EMEK *Rodeo*

How Loaded Do I have To Get To Be A Great Artist

YOU KNOW WHY THIS QUESTION sounds so peculiar? Because it flies in the face of professionalism. It's like asking a total stranger you see in the park some personal question about what coital position their parents assumed while they were being conceived.

Twenty years ago, this question would have seemed in keeping with other small talk bandied around by modern abstract painters and underground cartoonists. But now we are in a much more restrained period–and it's all about money. To encompass a much larger buying market, one has to make the decision to offend far less people. I've even weakened and succumbed to this spineless form of public patronization.

What I'm getting at is, what happened to all the maniacs who used to make up the groups of wild artists who were so prominent some time ago and who, during the '60s, used to be addressed as "kooks"?

Every once in a while, some individual will ask me, "Were you on acid when you painted that?" Well, maybe I was "high" on drugs, or booze, or caffeine, or nicotine, but it was probably the whole bohemian lifestyle that must be blamed. Being an iconoclast is like getting high on everybody else's fear of damaging their mediocrity.

Have you ever noticed how not only fine art painters but also house painters and auto painters tend to be alcoholics? I've often wondered if they might be drawn by the attraction to the distilled spirits and solvents they have to be around all the time.

Maybe it's the chronic use of the computer that's changed artists. Could staring at a user-friendly cathode-ray tube every day convert artists into translucent, pixel-eyed shut-ins who paint unfulfilled fantasies of imaginary barroom culture without actually having to smell the breath of real drunks?

Many of my old peer group of artists are dead now from burning their candles in the middle. Many a night we'd been drunken and doped up and screamed it like it was till early morning. Maybe the only art was the party. A number of my early art school friends would paint with a brush in one hand and a beer in the other. The pinstriper Von Dutch always had a beer can in his hand.

I enjoyed getting wasted, although I always took total responsibility for my actions. There was an intellectual posture in the use of some drugs. Psychedelic drugs actually altered your thinking processes without making you drunk. LSD allowed a person to perceive the subject of situation both laterally and abstractly. The elements of Zen seem to refocus logic with acid: "The apple isn't red; it's un-green." For the first time, an artist could see the same object from six or seven directions at once or even simply see through it to the other side. Things could be easily over-understood.

However, there have been some real inherent problems with drugs and art. To begin with, if you were to do art while on acid, you would tend to mesmerize yourself into believing everything you did was the most profound endeavor ever attempted by a mortal. That is, until you woke up the next morning and came across the piece of shit you so amazingly fascinated yourself with the night before the magic was gone.

For me personally, smoking marijuana and painting was a total waste of time. I would find myself painting the same thing over and over again. Nothing would ever get finished. Simple graphic functions became insurmountable.

Salvador Dalí was right when he said, "You can't paint drunk." I slowly came to understand that to be a good artist, you have to become a graphic athlete, always lucid and in shape.

Gosh, that kinda takes all the fun out of it, huh?

–Robt Williams

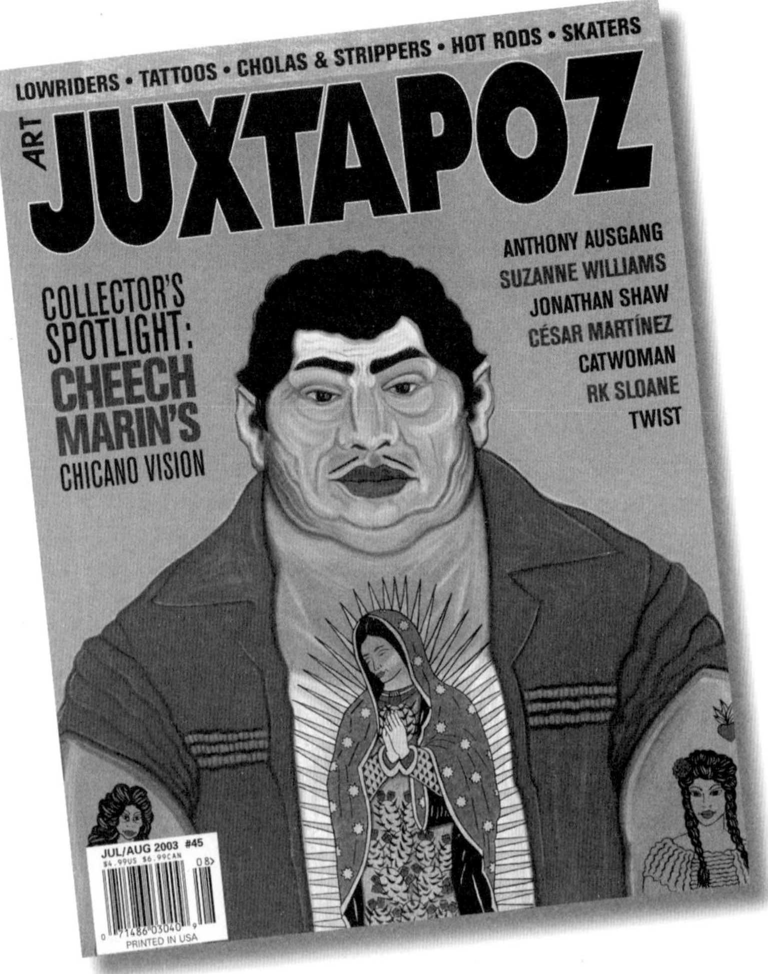

Cover art: César Martinez *Hombre que leGustan las Mujeres*

Volume Eleven Number Four Jul/Aug 2003 #45

Fighting The Ghosts Of Dead Art Critics

IT HAS BEEN A FOREGONE CONCLUSION that the premier artist of the first half of the 20th century was Pablo Picasso, and (not surprisingly) that the principal artist of the last half of the 20th century was Andy Warhol. This looks like the way history is going to be written.

But a premonition comes to haunt me about the now upcoming, most preeminent grand master at the beginning of the 21st century. Without a doubt, the most publicly heralded artist, painter, and graphic creator of our immediate period in history is the landscape print flogger Thomas Kinkade. I don't really know any other way to describe this phenomenon. Mr Kinkade's bucolic prints of warm, teddy bear-esque cottage scenes are the number-one focal point of American art appreciation. He is the undisputed king of art, despite the formal art world that usually insists on doing the crowning.

How do you criticize this man's work? Where do you start? His homey little gingerbread domiciles lack functional architectural principles. Thom never seems to render the human form with any knowledge of physical structure, and he can't bring any accuracy to mechanics, machinery, autos, etc. He primarily depends on a soft, scumbled glow of light to sweeten the atmosphere of his cozy little saccharine depictions. Still, I am no one to stand in judgement of him. He is, without question, the egalitarian maestro–the artist of the people–and he does make a lot of people happy.

The thing I really most appreciate about him and his work is that it pisses off the very people who made my life miserable when I was a young artist. I am referring to the earlier art authorities who have set the course of painting for the last 60 years. It was because of their actions that *Juxtapoz* magazine evolved and came into existence.

I don't want to demean modern and abstract art. These are legitimate pluses in art history. But it seems that, years ago, when non-objective art was struggling to establish itself, realistic art was the sacrificial lamb that had to die to enthrone modernism. And I think I can identify the culprits, so hear me out.

Since the 1880s, the intellectual content had been getting increasingly more important in the arts. And when modern art was winning its wings with the public after the First World War, it was essential to deemphasize photographic exactness for emotional and geometric expression. Realism seemed to stay in the forefront in the form of surrealism until after the Second World War. The same was true of the great muralist movement (social realism) that was so popular in the 1930s.

The postwar era brought about the age of "pure art"–art of abstract theory. This, in many people's minds, made the physical *objet d'art passe*, and, in the theoretic concept of the action of creating the art, became the art in itself. This modernist thought process was the direct handiwork of New York art critics and writers Clement Greenburg, Harold Rosenburg, and New York's then-current group of *faux* intelligentsia. They postulated a philosophy for art to be unencumbered, allowing for its own intellectual pursuits. They said it must be free of restricting art tradition that relies on a visual and verbal language which exercises the vanity of dexterity and poetic draftsmanship.

It wasn't said in this many words, but the implication was that pictures that depend on recognizable graphic stimuli appeal to simple people with limited conceptual skills–in other words, amusement for rank-and-file morons.

Maybe all the fault shouldn't fall on the shoulders of the man of letters who was the prime promoter of Jackson Pollock and the abstract expressionism movement, Clement Greenburg. Nonetheless, he and his strong influence were instrumental in the persecution of representational art in order to gain the approval of abstract expressionism in the public's eye.

Abstract expressionism and realistic art at that time could not live side by side; they simply contradicted each other. Now, in a more open-minded environment, they could probably coexist comfortably together. But during the 1950s and 1960s, for an art movement to be taken seriously and have power, it had to dominate and command the playing field–and abstract expressionism did just that.

Realistic art did, however, survive that long period as a quaint sub-art. Through the years, *American Artist* magazine always gave realism a safe home, printing good articles about illustration work, flower painting, hobby painting, and whatnot, but never dared to raise its voice above that of *ArtForum.*

Juxtapoz has never practiced that humble decorum. Our aggressive range of taste is something like the flavor obtained from the southern end of an anal thermometer. And to show that we, as artists, don't have any hard feelings about being suppressed, ostracized, and treated like shit for 60 years, I'm going to implore the other board members of this magazine to take on the burden of trying to save, and breathe new life back into, dead ol' milky-eyed abstract expressionism–that is, of course, only if everybody else refuses to touch it. And we should also show the same charity of heart for Thomas Kinkade's art when his popularity starts to fade.

–Robt Williams

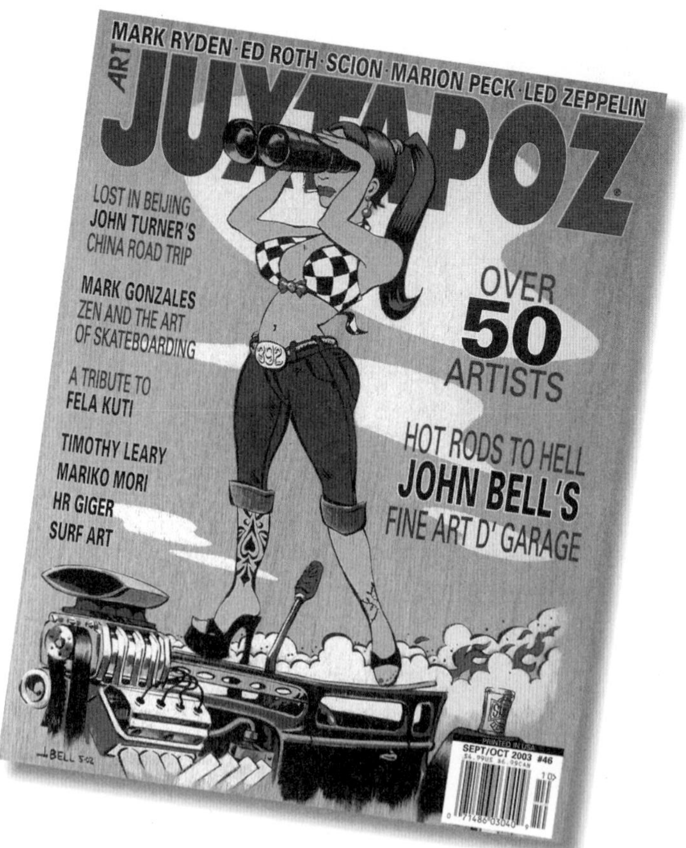

Cover art: John Bell *392*

Volume Eleven Number Five Sept/Oct 2003 #46

Rational Doctrine That Justifies Pie In The Sky

INNUMEROUS AMOUNTS OF image-producing artists that *Juxtapoz* magazine has become aware of during the last eight years make it obvious that a lot of people think in picture parables. The interesting thing is that just about all of the visual language can be categorized into familiar classifications, and, strangely enough, few seem to go exploring or think outside the loop. Well, a few artists do, but these are the ones that seem to slip through the cracks.

In my estimation (this is in my humble opinion only), there seem to be about eight or nine categories of fantastical art that appear throughout history and still manifest themselves today. What I mean is that when a piece of art is created and the artist wishes to deviate from exact physical realism of subject matter in his/her work, any fancifulness of imagination seems to have to fall within the parameters of some rationalized doctrine.

Here are some of the premises I find that altered representational art comfortably fits into:

Probably the oldest and most respected would be religious visions and miracles from sacred manuscripts, like winged people in the sky, seas parting, etc.

After that, also from antiquity, are occult prophecies and metaphysics–supernatural stuff like raining snakes, tricking zombies into eating salt, ghosts, and what have you.

And then, later in the 19th century, that interesting phenomenon of fairy-tale belief and fairy art. This is an offshoot of medieval and Norse legend imagery.

Modern art's most well-known movement, surrealism, is the next category for the justification of abnormal art. This actually sprang from dream art and goes way back in time. Dream art, the mystical domain of the subconscious, gives the artist a legitimate excuse to paint anything that pleases their flights of fancy.

The contemporary art mode of our day that really allows for pushing the fantasy envelope is science fiction art. But you are slightly limited by having to bring the reasoning back down to earth so we (the onlookers) can use the art to anticipate the future, the past, and other space-time never-never lands. Sci-fi art does allow for an inexhaustible range of possibilities of alien monsters and technocratic wonder machinery to be dreamed up.

After this, the classification standing out most in my mind for gratuitous realism is referred to as "outsider art." This is really too general a term, in that it covers the large, interruptive playing field of primitive abstract and naive savant art. This is probably the most charming of all the "isms." A few of my artist friends have attempted to fit into this formal doctrine, but it soon becomes obvious if they can't measure up to fulfill the "gifted simpleton" prerequisite that makes naiveté art so enchanting–everybody can't be mentally impacted.

Another form of art (which is akin to both outsider art and surrealism) making concessions for a "runaway train" art hypothesis is insanity art. Occasionally, modern artists have tried to operate under these credentials, resulting in a silly and unconvincing awkwardness. Two genuinely successful "crazy artists" that come to mind are, of course, Vincent van Gogh and 19th century fairy painter and murderer Richard Dadd.

Tattoo artists function under a historical premise of "emblemata," or what is traditionally known as heraldry–coats of arms, etc. As downtrodden as this art form once was, it is now apparent that tattoos can give an emblematic authority to any image through its distinction of being on the most precious of all canvases, skin.

Juxtapoz has inherited a large group of illustrators who comprise yet another classification: seeing themselves as heirs apparent to the pop art movement. Believe me, the jury is still out on this, and it might stay out until the museum directors and art critics are replaced by more sympathetic dilettantes. The pop art realm is now one of the most orthodox branches of the academically accepted art world. Trying to casually slip unnoticed into the restrictive pop art world with innocuous cartoon characters, Polynesian luau idols, and iconic tableaus of Betty Page is like trying to get into the New York Philharmonic Orchestra with a Marine Band harmonica. It's not a question of good or bad–the two universes just don't interface.

The reason I've formed this simplistic list of premises for imagist art is to make it apparent that no one has to be locked into secure theoretic cocoons in order to safely present themselves and their work to some kind of official or commanding overseer with hopes for valid acceptance. If you are an artist and find yourself in that position, then you are subjecting yourself to the wrong judges.

Working without a recognized rationale is scary territory. What do you say when someone asks you what kind of artist you are? What is your official title? I'm curious to hear how you describe yourself. Remember, whatever you tell the public is the way you choose to portray yourself.

Listen, why did the chicken cross the road? The question is totally inapplicable and infelicitous. The fact is that municipal highway engineers inadvertently laid a thoroughfare through the predestined path being instinctively transited by poultry. The word "road" is relative. In this case, the chicken is not a noun. It is an abstract device and exists not in physics, grammar, math, or philosophy, but in art. Explain this to your public.

–Robt Williams

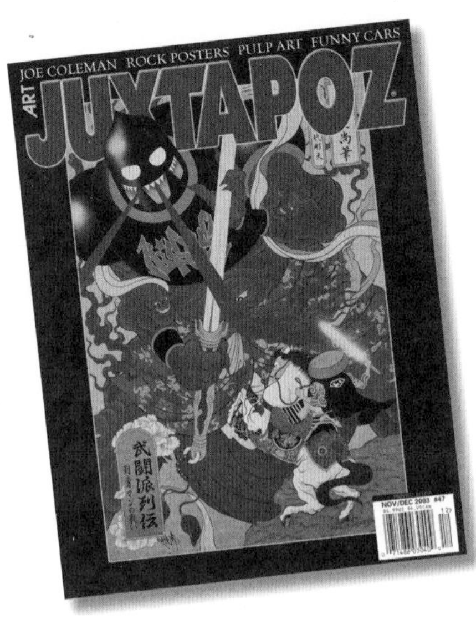

Cover art: Hisashi Tenmyouya *Tattoo Man's Battle*

Volume Eleven Number Six Nov/Dec 2003 #47

The Mouse With The Iron Fist

I DON'T HAVE A GOOD MEMORY, but I do remember a news item I heard in 1966 with crystal clarity. I was driving to work at Roth Studios in Maywood, CA, and just before I exited the Long Beach Freeway, the news commentator on the radio announced the death of Walt Disney. He then went on to make a very curious statement that Disney's date of passing had actually been three days earlier. To quote the spokesman for the Disney Corporation, "The death date was kept confidential to give time to adjust the stock market." To adjust the stock market!!!

At the time, I was only 23 years old, but I was highly distressed that the date of death for such an important man was hushed up to manipulate Wall Street. That was 37 years ago. Maybe "adjusting the stock market" these days is called "insider trading."

As a child, I worshiped Walt Disney. The fourth name I memorized as an infant, after Mommy, Daddy, and Bobby (myself), was Walt Disney. I satiated myself with all Disney products: comic books, toys, gift premiums, etc. I saw Disney's first TV show. I visited Disneyland the first year it opened.

But as time went by and I matured, I discovered other animation studios of the period: The Fleischer Brothers, Walter Lantz, Warner Brothers, Tex Avery, and Ub Iwerks (Disney's old partner, who originally designed Mickey Mouse).

Time went by, and during the late 1960s, I was deeply involved in underground comix–my Disney fascination set aside. I remember I was in a psychedelic shop, and I spotted an amazing black-light poster. It was a large print in day-glo colors with almost all of Walt Disney's characters engaged in the most extreme sexual perversions. Mickey, Minnie, Goofy, Pluto, Donald, all of them in the heat of licentious impropriety. Some of the dwarves were molesting Snow White; other dwarves were involved in anal coitus. Despite the lascivious nature of the images, the composition of the artwork was absolutely brilliant. The actual rendering of the cartoon characters was right on the money, as if they were drawn by Floyd Gottfredson or Carl Barks, Disney's top comic-book artists. Shortly after, the word from other underground artists was that the Disney Corp was horrendously jerked out of shape by the pornographic poster and had offered an enticing reward for the culprit.

Now this is amazing to me. It wasn't long before everybody in the comix underground knew who the artist was. He was the famous EC Mad comics artist, Wallace Wood. No one would turn him in. I am sure that even a number of artists on the Disney payroll knew his identity. This confirmed some kind of hero status on Wally Wood.

Walt Disney did have a valiant and noble side to him. In 1940, with the film Fantasia, Disney tried his first foray into highbrow entertainment. Using the conductor, Leopold Stokowski, and doomed assistance of Salvador Dalí, Disney put together one of his most challenging movies. Unfortunately, it was 15 years ahead of its time and was something of a flop. In the end, the film did make an enormous profit, but it took 30 years. Never again did Walt Disney venture into the artistic fog of abstract culture.

During World War II, in occupied Europe, a cartoonist named Calvo drew a series of cartoons that made up an anti-fascist book which was nothing short of some of the finest cartoons ever done. These were highly inflammatory caricatures of the axis countries presented as brutal animals. The Germans were portrayed as wolves, the Italian fascists as lackey hyenas, and the Japanese as thieving monkeys. These books were strictly the propaganda of the French and allied resistance and would have cost Calvo his life if he had been apprehended.

Somehow, the legal advisors for Disney Studios considered this a copyright infringement because of its use of little animal characters. My later postwar copy of Calvo's book has all of the animals' bulbous noses removed to comply with Disney's stringent trademark regulations.

I know for a fact that during this period of time, at least two units of Luftwaffe fighter planes were emblazoned with Disney cartoon characters. I've seen photos revealing two different variations of Mickey Mouse as squadron mascots on the tail rudders of Messerschmitt ME 109s. I doubt that Disney's proficient legal staff contacted Hermann Göring with a cease-and-desist notice.

Walt Disney has always taken the safe road of popularism. Disney, as a corporation, fully understood the dangers of profiting by association, avoiding lurid material that might infuriate church and civic groups, groups who felt cartoons are the sovereign domain of innocent children and should be monitored accordingly.

When Ub Iwerks was an active partner with Disney during the late 1920s, he had the authority to give Mickey Mouse a much more adult disposition. In one early short, Mickey is flying with Minnie in a two-seater airplane and he, without provocation, reaches around and forces a full-mouth kiss from Minnie. She resists his aggression, but the embrace still occurs. Iwerks dissolved the partnership and left Disney. Years later, he returned to work for Walt, but he no longer had the influence he had once had. Mickey Mouse would get no more stolen smacky-mouth.

The degree of joy and entertainment produced by Walt Disney and his empire during the last 75 years makes any criticism a moot point. But the reason I presented this petty expose is to set the stage for a couple of potentialities that could have manifested themselves if circumstances had been different at the right time.

If, in the early 1940s, the general public had understood and appreciated the movie Fantasia as adult fare, Disney would most certainly have followed a course much more conducive to fine art and explored a sophisticated use of cartoon characters.

Secondly, if Ub Iwerks' influence had been heeded, and a much more straightforward and mature person had been given the characters, the American public might have leapfrogged the catatonic, I Love Lucy no-brainer entertainment that was so pervasive in the 1950s. Cartooning could now be advanced by 20 years, and the arts progressed along with it.

Walt Disney was in a position to both pull people into art and form an invigorated fine art that would be palatable to the average Joe. If this had happened, there never would have been a need for *Juxtapoz* magazine. The more representational art and cartooning are allowed to progress, the more adventurous it will metamorphosize itself, and the more stimulating it will become to the rank and file.

Looking back a hundred years, our great-grandparents could not have comprehended Rat Fink, much less Shag's futuristic cartoons. We have moved from the severe age of "no nonsense" to the abstract age of "all nonsense."

–Robt Williams

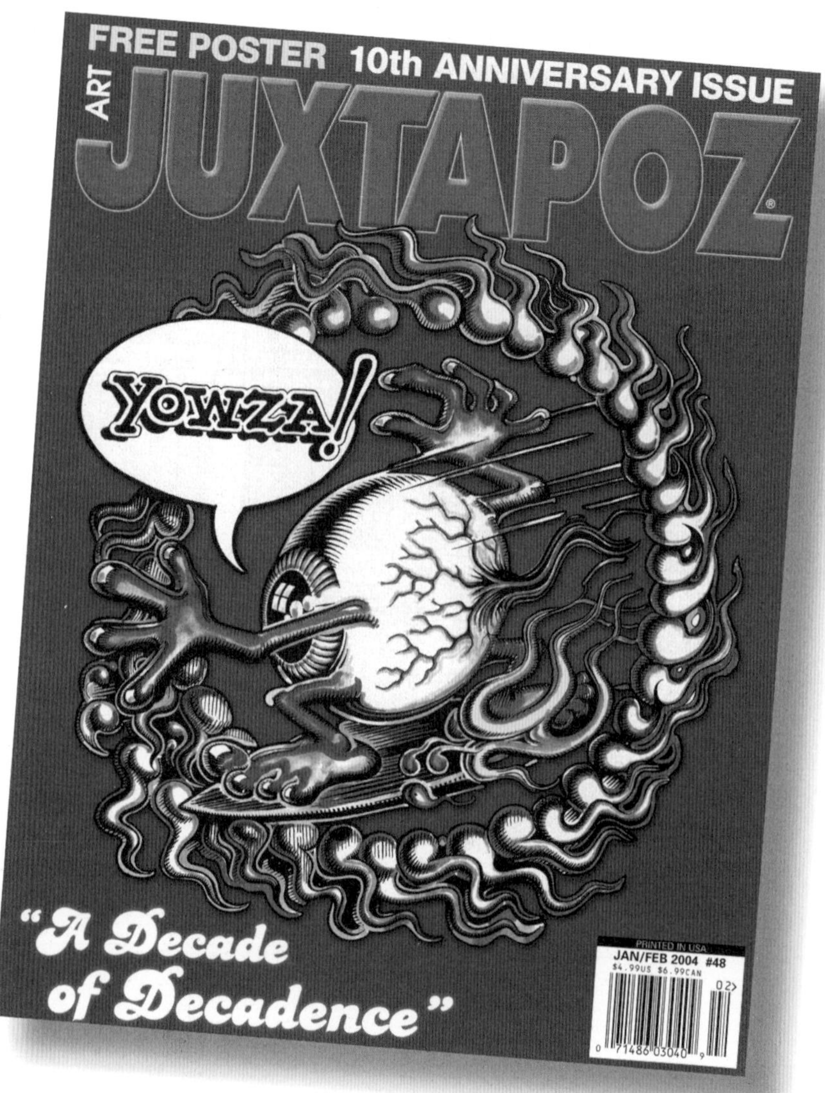

Cover art: Rick Griffin *Yowza!*

Ten Years Later, A Reassessment

I WAS SITTING BY THE WINDOW of an In-N-Out Burger in Van Nuys, about to eat my cheeseburger, when I had a compulsion to go use the restroom. There were no customers in the restaurant at the time, so I figured I could slip into the restroom and get back before my burger got cold.

When I returned, I found a disheveled homeless reprobate sitting in my seat, eating my cheeseburger. I flipped! I ran up to him and screamed at him, "What in the hell are you doing? That's my cheeseburger, you thieving bastard!" The bum looked up at me and said, "I didn't see your name on it."

I was incensed. I looked down and spotted his dirty, frayed knapsack full of his only worldly possessions. In the wink of an eye, I grabbed his bag and was out the door. I was standing out behind my car, going through the bag, and to my surprise, I found inside eight or 10 tubes of paint, brushes, art supplies, and two beat-up copies of *Juxtapoz.*

In a flash, this bum was in my face, yelling at me, "That's my bag, and I don't see your name on it!" I jerk out one of the *Juxtapozes*, turn to the staff masthead, and say, "Yeah, here it is at the top of the page!"

Now, would that story be appropriate for *ArtForum, Art News, Art Business News*, or even *American Artist* magazine? I don't think so. Only *Juxtapoz.*

With this issue, we are celebrating our first decade of magazine circulation. Before *Juxtapoz*, there was a vacuum in art publications. Almost all art periodicals pushed the attitude of faux objectivity–a sort of no-nonsense baloney. *Juxtapoz* would concentrate on subjectivity, the more authentic form of human expression, a pro-nonsense malarkey. *Juxtapoz'* incarnation, in its inception in the early 1990s, was not easy coming. It was obvious that getting art reviews for lowbrow, outlaw, and underground painting and art within the then existing orthodox art magazines was a losing proposition. Probably the most tolerant of the top three art journals was *Art in America*, but even they were far too formalist and bogged down in pedantic art-speak. Their interest in actual retinal gratification was their least concern.

The 1980s and 1990s saw the irrefutable age of minimal and conceptual theory. What was considered great art of that time, and pandered to by all the art writers and critics, was something like maybe three large wooden blocks stacked as only the artist can stack them, or maybe an arrangement of white Christmas tree lights on a black wall, or perhaps a manifesto-blessed pile of sand. They were the kind of defiant art installations that revelled in spiting egalitarian sensibilities and allowed a lot of fodder for intellectual art theorists. These profound ambiguities would give art writers and art critics nocturnal emissions. Your mere challenging of these art pieces marked you a fool.

This was the wasteland in which underground and representational artists were trying to get a foothold. The only hope for write-ups were in men's magazines, pro-drug publications, tattoo magazines, and music trade magazines. It was clear that there were more than enough artists, as well as a keen interest among the general public for a special magazine that would offer exposure to the perceived flotsam that the formal art world was scared to touch.

Since I had been in the magazine business as a young man, it seemed possible to find an adventurous publisher who might dare to undertake an unorthodox art periodical. I wanted to fashion it in the style of the rogue French art journals published by the dadaists and surrealists during the 1920s and 1930s (*La Revolution Surrealiste, Minotaur*, etc). But I still wanted the outlaw-cartoon flavor of underground comix of the 1960s. I went to a number of tattoo and girly magazine publishers who declined, or even refused, to help me out. But eventually, with the help of Greg Escalante, we approached the head of Thrasher skateboard magazine. Years earlier, after reader requests, I had artwork shown in *Thrasher*, so they knew they could get a positive response.

Nonetheless, an entire publication of fringe group art, some of it pornographic, most of it antisocial, all of it off the wall, would be financially chancy for even the gutsiest magazine publisher.

With the head of *Thrasher/High Speed Productions*, Fausto Vitello, we found the publishing and distributing strength to go ahead with the magazine. Craig Stecyk was the ghost henchman in the background, along with Greg Escalante and Suzanne Williams, forming the backbone of this magazine's skeleton. Ed Riggins bore the weight of newsstand circulation and rounded out the *Juxtapoz* machine.

The magazine caught on almost immediately. In the very beginning, it was our intention to search out artists who functioned best under the dark cloud of criminal ethos, not necessarily in respect to heinous felonies, but asocial in regards to mental psychosis–in other words, finding artwork by true nonconformists and iconoclasts.

My first act during the formation of *Juxtapoz* was getting together with the psychedelic poster artists and *Zap* comic book artists to ask them for their support. One day at the Farmers Market in Los Angeles, I made my appeal to Spain Rodriguez, S. Clay Wilson, Victor Moscoso, Gilbert Shelton, and Robert Crumb. And then I made my plea to Ed Roth. After gaining their support, I then went to Timothy Leary, as well as Ron Turner and George DiCaprio, both underground distributors and alternative press luminaries.

Besides paintings and drawings, the magazine was designed to advocate the great "disregarded arts," such as hot rod art, surfer art, biker art, tattoos, skateboard graphics, graffiti, pin-up art, disenfranchised illustrators and their work, movie posters, carnival banners, rock 'n' roll art, and any other arts that the blue noses would not honor.

This remained the direction and thrust of *Juxtapoz* during the first three or four years. But what started out as a refuge for artists who dared to champion non-academic art and mongrel cartooning would later come to face changes. As *Juxtapoz* magazine's circulation grew, the old West Coast underground that was so popular during the 1960s was withering away. To put it euphemistically, the Love-In was over. The Age of Aquarius gave way to the era of "me first, gimme, gimme."

By the late 1990s, the average *Juxtapoz* reader was under 25 and had never heard of underground comix. The concept of the magazine being based on an artistic struggle that had started back in the 1950s was nothing more than a vague, esoteric curiosity that had now become completely irrelevant. One thing was sure: *Juxtapoz* now had new blood in its veins.

With the meteoric growth of *Juxtapoz* came its first growing pains. Many small businesses started to advertise in *Juxtapoz*, and a lot of them had special interests. Unfortunately, these interests attempted to influence the magazine's editorial direction. This was the problem the large auto magazines faced: they all became parts and accessories catalogs.

It wasn't until the turn of the new millennium that we were confronted with the question of what were silly passing fads and what were legitimate social trends–for example, Rat Finks, tikis, skulls, girls in martini glasses, big-eyed children, female devils, retro jazz-bo beatniks, etc. How could something as vital and influential as *Juxtapoz* magazine stop dead in its tracks to embrace these simple iconic fascinations that kept reappearing?

After a while, the answer to the attraction of the lighthearted cliches became apparent. These simple cartoon forms bound our readers (and other young people) together. There were no deep, dark, secret Polynesian meanings in the tikis; they were simply the binding mortar for friends and strangers. Water had found its own level.

By 2002, an unsettling phenomenon was beginning to make itself known, and *Juxtapoz* has done everything in its power to avoid it. The American general public, and its youth in particular, have started to become benign and complacent. I am not the only one to notice this. A number of people have mentioned it. The majority of the population will unquestioningly do as they're told. Whether this is ethically right or wrong is not our question. The problem in the arts is where we are going to get our iconoclasts and free thinkers. Where are all the young progressive individualists? They can't be found at the sports bars, and they're not at Starbucks.

Our star editor, Jamie O'Shea, along with Annie Tucker, our ace managing editor, is steadfastly helping us seek out singular-minded artists. All of us here at *Juxtapoz* are pledged to promote unsanctioned artists and their brash creations.

One-tenth of a century later, a hundredth of a millennium later, a nanosecond of eternity later, *Juxtapoz* magazine still meets its deadlines. And will strive to do so for the next 10 years. Stay tuned.

–Robt Williams

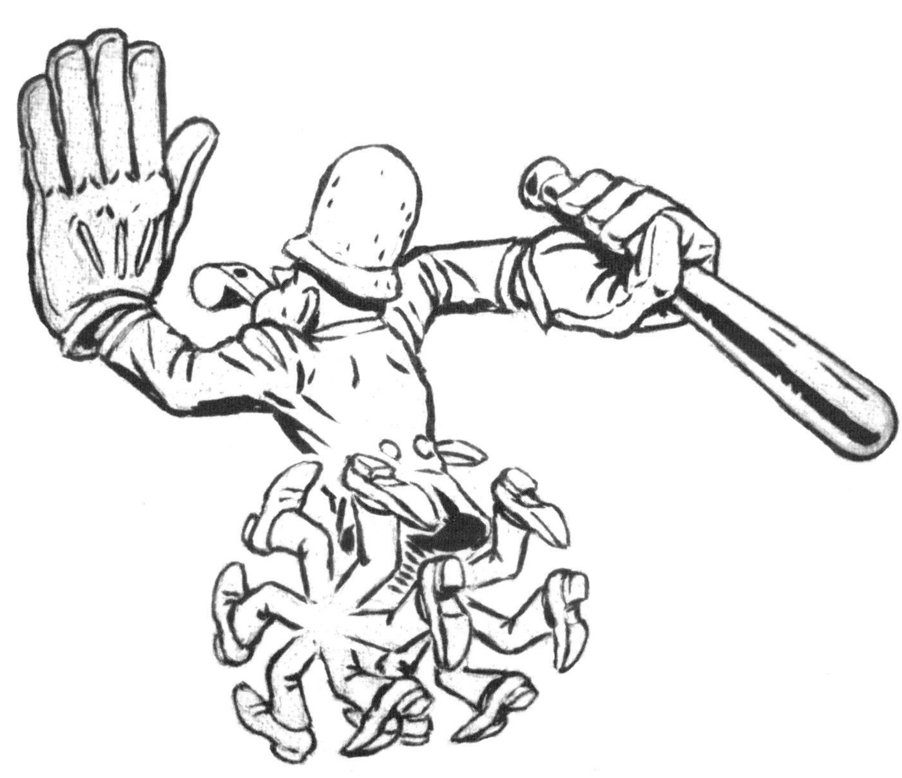

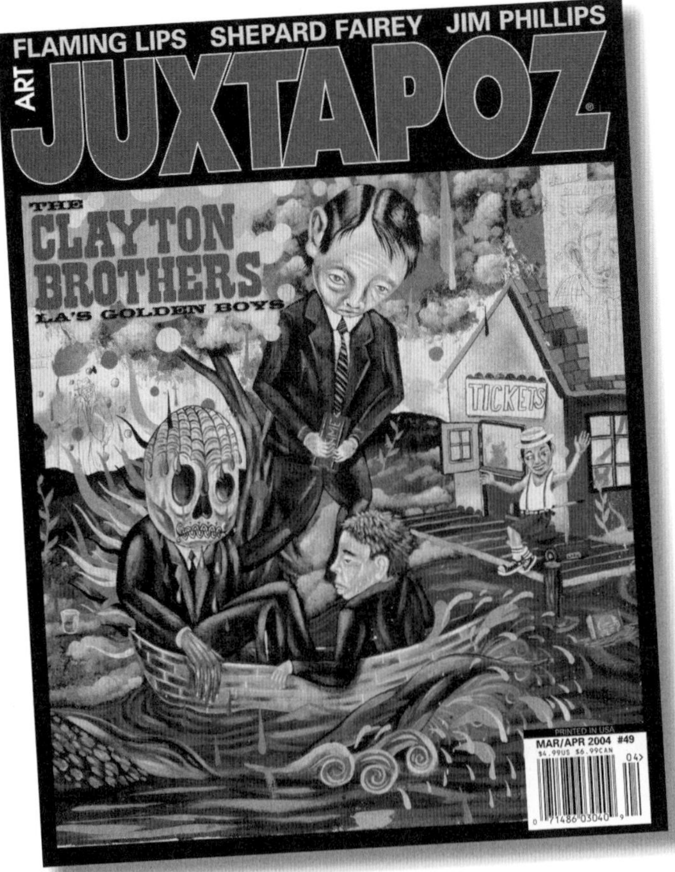

Cover art: The Clayton Brothers *Six Foot Eleven Series*

Volume Thirteen Number Two Mar/Apr 2004 #49

Living With Rejection

AT THE BEGINNING OF THIS YEAR, I received the last reviews on my new book, Hysteria in Remission, and I acquired the critical acknowledgment I have come to expect with the material I present to my precious supporters. One review in particular summed it all up. The National Library Association Journal stated that my book was, "interesting and extremely well done, but if public libraries wanted to avoid any first amendment court cases they would show prudence in deleting my book from library shelves."

It seems to me that rejection and repudiation have followed me throughout my entire career. I have become so accustomed to official censure that I unconsciously anticipate it when preparing any artwork I do. Consequently, I often forget that for other artists, especially young beginners, rejection is a form of condemnation.

I would estimate (in my 40 odd years as an artist) that I have had at least 100 ideas and sketches rejected by ad agencies, album cover art directors, and magazine editors who have given me thumbs down or asked me to revise work I have submitted. My luck with fine arts galleries hasn't fared much better. I would guess that I've been politely turned away from more than 60 galleries. This isn't including group shows. Of course, most of these galleries are long out of business and have been forgotten. When I've discussed this with other older artists they've shared similar experiences. But, my situation appears to be more acute. It was obvious I was dancing to the beat of a different drum, and not in step with the hoi polloi sensibilities that define good marketing. Earlier, as a novice, rejection emotionally felt like being cut with a sharp razor that stung for days. Today, it's like being whacked with a dull butter knife on the heel of my shoe. Now, if I don't get disapproval my will to resist conformity seems as though it is atrophying.

In the course of day to day life; acceptance and rejection are the unquestionable parameters which makes society function. Rights and wrongs have to be tangible. Human conditions like feast, famine, civil behavior, war, peace, business, money, health, marriage, safety, and the advantages surrounding our lives are based on dos and don'ts. The alternative to this is chaos.

But with art, approval only means you've found sympathetic accomplices. While rejection, on the other hand, means you've run across your detractors.

I apologize to our *Juxtapoz* readers for more of my self-possessed personal reflections and my seemingly conceited self-depreciations, but I think using myself as the observer is pertinent to what I am trying to express to you. So allow me to go on an anecdotal ghost hunt to add substance to what I'm getting at.

Over a hundred years ago, when it was very fashionable to believe in ghosts and fairies, a European professor first used the term "ectoplasm" to describe the cotton candy like nebulous material people thought ghosts were made of. This term also identified the soupy froth that spiritualist mediums would get shills to puke up during seances as proof they were possessed.

Can you imagine that a professional Victorian doctor has defined the exact ethereal slop that ghosts are made of? I don't know about you, but my overactive imagination totally embraces this notion. I don't mean the spooky belief systems and et cetera. I mean the mental projection of imaginary goop that could do anything, which thousands of people believed in a century ago.

Okay, are you with me? Let's take this humbug one step further. Let's drag this into the context of art. Now, use your imagination, and try to envision your own interpretation of an artistic mystery substance that you could mentally form into anything you might dream up. An example would be to discipline your thought processes enough to envision a total environmental situation where every form and shape, including limits like ground and sky, would be made up of chrome plated entities. Or better yet, say you want to create a private cerebral universe of every object translated into a substance like clumped-together sunlight having the consistency of red day-glo mashed potatoes.

Now that you have contemplated (however seriously) a concept of your own personal abstract unified ghost neither land, how do you think "rejection" would affect it? Criticism of this private art Valhalla is like saying "on Tuesday I hate everybody who wears green socks."

Art history doesn't acknowledge what's not successful, so we are left with all the serious real (not real) values of the past. For the last 200 years, some of the greatest artists of western civilization have vied for the honor of winning the prestigious *Prix de Rome*–a trip to study in Rome, the work of the masters. And, ever since I was a young artist I have secretly dreamed of garnering this great honor for myself. What are the chances of fulfilling my aspirations if I were to tell the *Prix de Rome* board of judges all about my artoplasmic world that my rejected self lives in?

This is why we have *Juxtapoz* magazine.

–Robt Williams

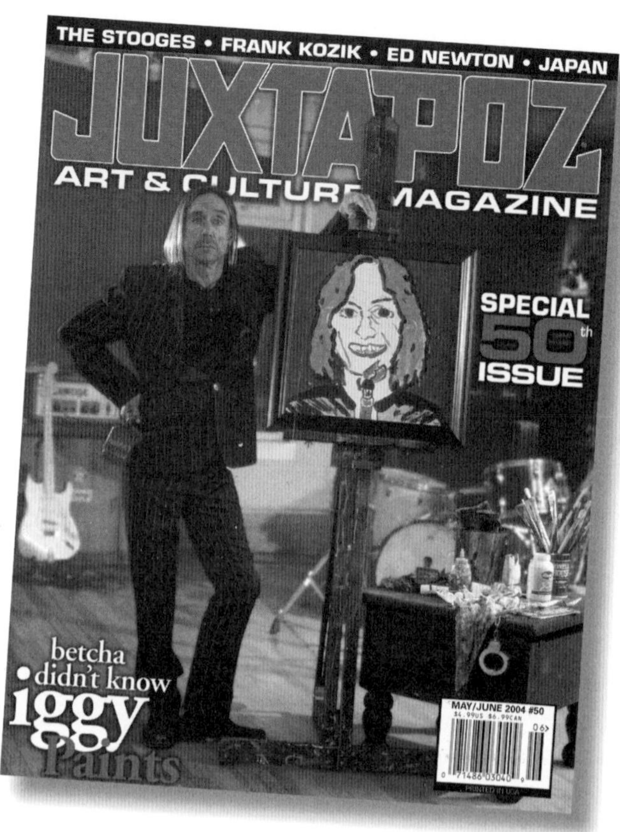

Cover art: Ewolf *Portrait of Iggy Pop*

Volume Eleven Number Three May/June 2004 #50

Bits And Pieces, And Observations From An Irate Reader

NOT EXACTLY IN OUR BALLPARK, but certainly worth of our attention, is the enormous James Rosenquist exhibit currently at the New York City Guggenheim Museum. This sort of fare would generally be beyond our rough-hewn milieu, except for a couple of points of interest.

Although blanketly categorized as a "pop art show," the Rosenquist show is the first in recent modern memory to reach national notoriety in a top 10 museum, with hand-blended oil paintings dealing expressly with representational art. And with this, a number of people (myself included) seriously believe that contemporary art might have just passed the corner and made the turn.

This astounding exhibition was the brainchild of America's preeminent museum curator of 20th century art, Walter Hopps, and the show has broken all attendance records at the Guggenheim. This is the same museum that, just a few years ago, broke all previous records with its successful motorcycles as art show.

Rosenquist has tried to extend the definition of his work beyond the simplistic bounds of the title "pop art" but, it seems, with little success. Walter Hopps has given it the much more spacious classification of "imagist"art. A term he has generously used for a number of *Juxtapoz* artists, including myself.

Hopps is, according to an article in the January issue of *Smithsonian* magazine, credited with organizing the first pop show in 1962. I do know Walter was the person who put together the first underground comix show in the early '70s. And in the late '50s, he tried to pull Von Dutch into the orthodox art world. I don't think there has been another prominent modern art curator who has ever had the gall to stick his neck out like that.

My next matter of business is a response to an interesting letter (via email) from a concerned reader. I generally avoid defending *Juxtapoz* against disgruntled readers, but this constructive criticism in the March/April issue, from a Mr. Chadwick Buxton, seemed sincere enough that I felt compelled to reply.

To begin with, Mr. Buxton explains how he feels our publication has taken a nose dive in substance. Now I don't want to sound condescending to Mr. Buxton, and we do appreciate his concern in keeping us informed on our endeavors as seen through our readers' eyes, but the majority of our other readers' responses have commended us and assured us of their exact opposite position.

The second matter he brings up is our chronic overexposure of "that Mark Ryden dude." I think I see what you are getting at, so let me explain *Juxtapoz* magazine's position.

One thing I tried to avoid in the creation of this magazine was the exclusive "in crowd" hysteria that is usually generated in rock magazines and teen and movie star fan magazines. We are the only magazine that consistently tries to post artists' photos with each article. This is intended to help familiarize the public with the artist as a real person. We also have a photo section called "Beatdown," showing the artist and their work in everyday social life. Unfortunately, this photo review can sometimes be construed by modest and sensitive people as an arrogant promenade by egotistical, self-possessed lime-lighters. Chadwick, I'm sorry, but we are just going to have to live with that misinterpretation. The matter of *Juxtapoz* magazine promoting our own star artists is not as cut and dried as it seems. We deal in the art–the personality and promotion of the artist is their affair. Mark Ryden reappears in *Juxtapoz* magazine because Mr. Ryden is a capable artist that has brought to the table a style people enjoy.

The next matter is Chadwick's disdain for 1960s psychedelic art culture. I could go on for volumes about this but just let me paraphrase by saying that if there hadn't been a '60s underground youth movement, *Juxtapoz* magazine probably wouldn't exist today, and Mr. Buxton's ass would have long ago been drafted to fight in a fourth decade of the never-ending Vietnam War.

Another matter Chadwick brings up is the re-occurrence of big-eyed girls, bad biker art, skulls, and what-not from the same group of artists. Chadwick, we are an outlaw, underground, lowbrow art periodical. You might find facets of our art constituency dim-witted, but we are the only magazine that endeavors to utilize the whole mental playing field to find whatever the hell we feel has graphic energy. We want the artistic longitude and latitude to go from the sacrosanct ceilings of the Sistine Chapel to the step by step illustrations depicting the proper insertion of the polyurethane butt-plug.

Mr. Buxton's last remark is, I feel, his most important. He implies that we are so wrapped up in ourselves that we miss other creative artists who we haven't had the patience to find. On that point he is partly correct. We are certain that there are a lot of yet unseen interesting artists in the world population. Chadwick, we are looking for them. But let me warn you, we are not interested in every high school art major that deludes themselves into thinking they are ready to dazzle us. And, you have to remember, our magazine is not beyond reproach. In fact, we take pride in our gnarly and profane subject matter.

Chadwick, maybe this lurid publication just isn't for you. Perhaps you may have pissed away five dollars on a shitty magazine.

–Robt Williams

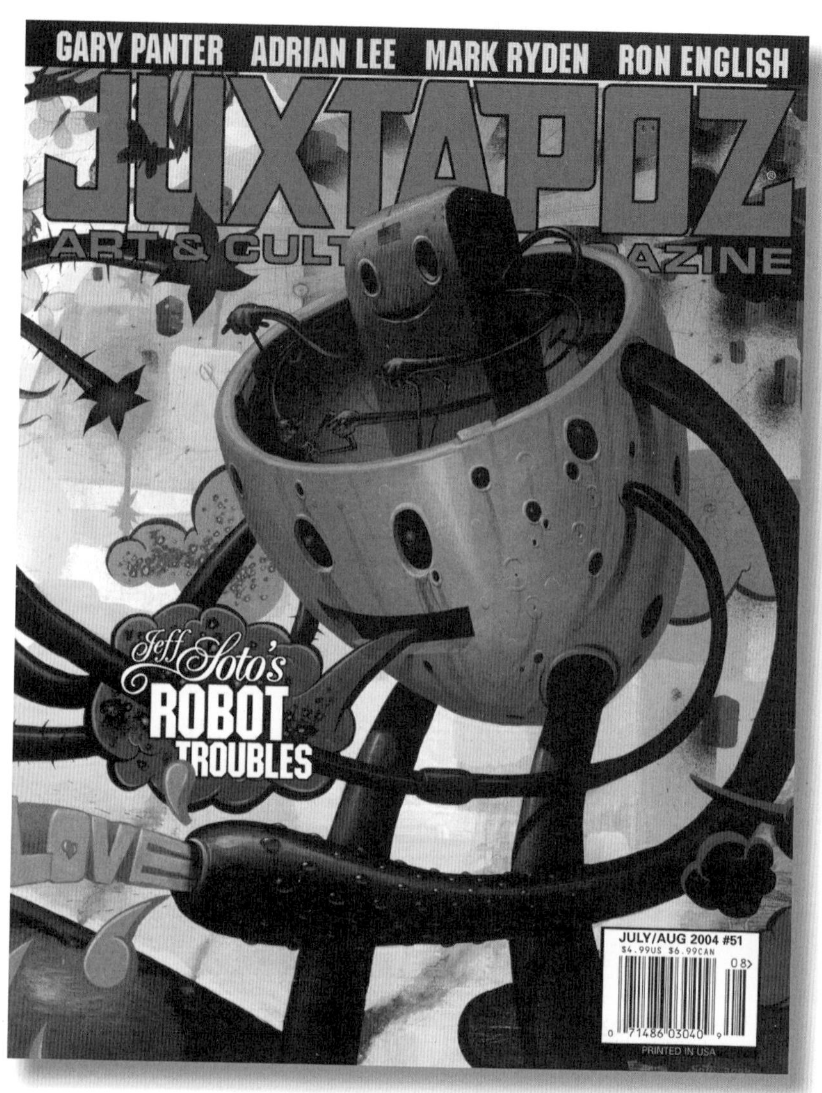

Cover art: Jeff Soto (detail) *Gumivore Love*

The Results Of The 10th Anniversary Art Show

APRIL FIRST THROUGH THIRTIETH were the dates of our second *Juxtapoz* art show. This one, commemorating *Juxtapoz'* 10th year of successful publishing, contrasted considerably to our eighth anniversary show two years ago.

Our past show was also a stellar phenomenon but was held at a much more formal and auspicious gallery, Track 16, in the prestigious middle of the Los Angeles art hub, Bergamot Station. With that show, the *Juxtapoz* brand of progressive retrograde art (lowbrow to some) obtrusively conflicted with the more mainstream conceptual and minimalist content that is so seemingly compulsory in academic gallery settings. We did well, and it was a honor to have had an opportunity to flamboyantly present our varied styles to a constipated art world.

However, this 10th anniversary exhibit was held in San Francisco in a much more rustic atmosphere. During the 1950s and '60s, the Bay Area sprang up as one of the West Coast's early underground hotbeds and has always been hospitable to bohemian artists and their eccentricities. We were totally at home there (after all, San Fran is the location of Juxtapoz magazine), and 111 Minna Gallery couldn't have been more conducive to an uproarious art show and party. The Minna St Gallery has hosted a number of underground and alternative functions over the years, and I have always enjoyed their youthful environment. Our editor, Jamie O'Shea, managing editor, Annie Tucker, and marketing director, Lindsey Byrnes, along with the help of our boy wonder advertising chief, William Haugh, were the organizing functionaries of this uninhibited cultural soiree. Many thanx to them. Libations were flowing as though it were the artists' last day on earth, and for many, hangovers were their door prizes.

The long list of artists and their work was impressive. It read like the tiki, Rat Fink, and dysfunctional illustrators' association who's who. I say this with great respect for my fellow artists. But remember, none of us were gracing the walls of the omnipotent San Francisco Museum of Modern Art down the street, just 300 yards away.

I am sure that there are going to be more of these spirited bacchanals in the future where we'll continue to "express" ourselves.

–Robt Williams

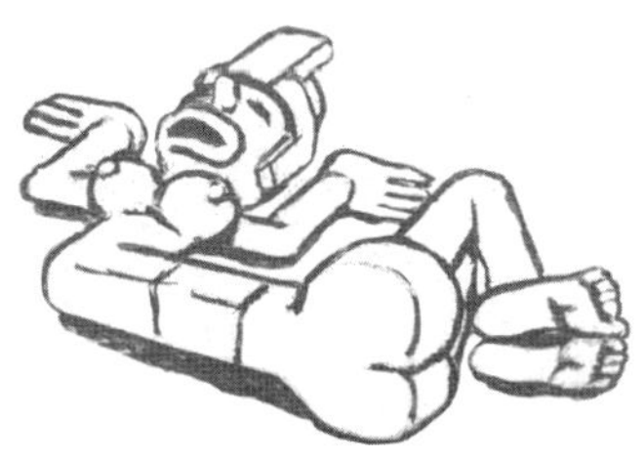

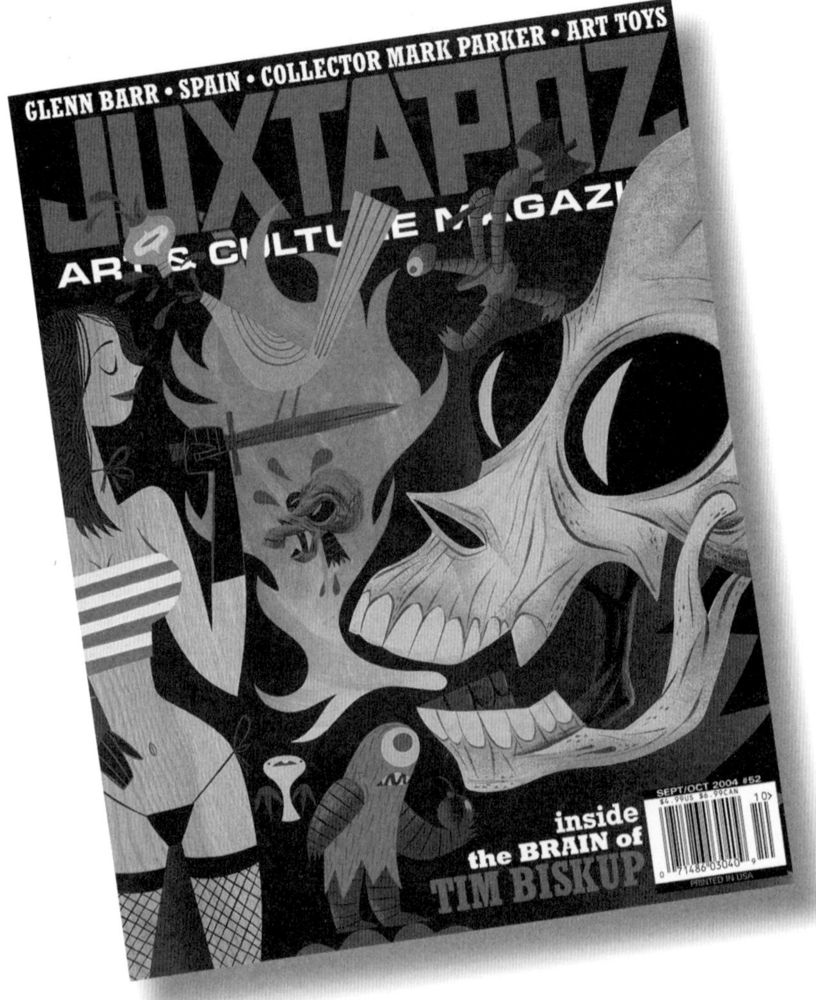

Cover art: Tim Biskup *The Broken Beak*

***Verbum Sapienti Artisa* (An Artist's Warning)**

FROM TIME TO TIME I will encounter young artists who have reasonably well-developed drawing skills and possess a fluid imagination who keep asking the same question, "Why should I deal with galleries and piss away large amounts of my profits when these shysters do little or nothing for me?" I addressed this question seven or eight years ago, and I guess it's time to restate it–maybe this time with some suggestions for those of you who might be a novice. I regret if I sound like Mr. Know-It-All, but this is a bumpy road I've traveled, finding adversity every inch of the way for over 30 years.

If you are an artist who has any intention of being a painter, sculptor or photographer and functioning in an art world (high or low) you need to have intelligent representation. If you think you can promote and sell paintings out of your apartment or your garage indefinitely you might want to prepare yourself for a dismal future no matter how good you are.

There are four basic factions that make up the great cultural art machine: The art school where you learn (or where you are indoctrinated), the gallery where you try to survive, the museum where you try to be officially recognized, and the foundations, benefactors and underwriters who might endorse your recognition with financing. There is a fifth faction, the critic, but their support comes with recognition.

The four above mentioned art institutions have one important element in common. They all maintain or help maintain real estate. A special space where art can be sanctified holy ground where any object placed in its inner perimeters becomes sacrosanct. Unfortunately, art is about putting your artistic achievements in a predetermined powerful location where the multitudes, as well as the specialists can adore it. I didn't make up these rules, I just have to subjugate myself to them like other artists.

Nonetheless, let me give you ten tips that might help you through the smoke and mirrors.

Number one: to begin with, finding a gallery is essential. If you are a capable draftsman with a precocious imagination and you haven't embraced the modernist credos of conceptualism, minimalism or abstract expressionism, you are going to face dissension. I don't know why it is, but any art that speaks clearly and exhibits any hand skills is always deemed "Facile" and is seen as the endeavors of a dimwitted illustrator. Consequently, finding a good gallery can be agonizing. Fortunately, there are new alternative and low brow galleries to find like-minded artists to show with.

It has always been my inclination to try and ensconce myself into more traditional modernist galleries to invoke energy into a stale and stagnant art world. However, believe me, this is where you are really asking for rejection.

Number two: Make early agreements with galleries so problems don't occur later. To begin with make it clear that you want to get paid at the time a buyer makes their payment. Galleries hate this kind of deal but if you wait thirty or sixty days for payment, you might be shit-out'a-luck. Lots of galleries prefer to pay their outstanding debts before they pay their artists. Remember, artists are a dime a dozen.

Number three: Do not price your artwork at the same altitude as your ego. Always sell your work as low as you possibly can. This not only encourages sales but you also develop a record of successful sales. When the art is priced reasonably, it promotes a secondary market–this is the true test of a successful artist. Remember, a lot of those big sales you hear about from hot, up and coming artists are works that don't seem to sell beyond the first buyer. Truly valuable artwork sells itself from buyer to buyer with little or no promotion. Solid sales means the price will naturally increase.

Number four: If you have an agreement with a gallery for an impending art show and the gallery owner has a buyer for one of the paintings, but the buyer wants to buy the picture in advance and bring the painting back to the show when the exhibit takes place, watch out. This almost never works out. Galleries are generally hand to mouth operations, and if you lost just one "carrot on a stick" the whole dynamic of business incentive might collapse. If the buyer wants the painting they can wait.

Number five: Don't get drunk at your own art show opening. This sounds funny, but it's a problem. The first three or four hours at the beginning of an art show (the opening) is the most crucial period for sales and promotion of the artist and their work. To get shit-faced and miss this opportunity would be reprehensible. The trick is to get everybody else shit-faced so you can negotiate your supporters into a malleable state of appreciation. Later you can get as soused as you want. You can pursue your indulgences as a lush or drug addict when you're not wasting the precious gallery promotion of your work. Remember, art openings are like anal sex, all the real action is in the beginning.

Number six: Don't stab your gallery in the back. Under no circumstances make any clandestine side deal with a buyer who has seen a specific piece of work while your art show is in effect. The standard rule of thumb is to wait six months after an art show has ended before you put any unsold artwork on the market again. You can not expect a gallery to spend their money on rent, advertising, promotion and insurance in order to give your work exposure, only to have you slip around making a secret sale to some clown you've cultivated so you can keep all the profits.

Number seven: Don't copy other artists. This sounds real basic, but it seems like more than seventy percent of artists can't resist lifting or appropriating images and themes from other sources. This habit is usually euphemistically excused as using "pop culture." Most graphic work that's been in print is either registered or copyrighted, and photographs more so. When showing at a gallery, the gallery becomes partially libel, and in some cases will have the artist sign a statement of responsibility.

Number eight: Galleries don't exist to create pompous asses. Next to the artist's drinking problems the attitude of the gallery's central figure (the artist) is the second biggest sales deterrent. Many, many artists, even famous artists with years of experience having art shows in blue chip circles sometimes slip into euphoric bouts of vein ecstasy in front of adoring fans. Keep in mind, after the crowd is through basking in your glory, they are off to the next gallery opening to anoint the feet of the next living legend.

Number nine: Don't throw the first rock. Do not demean other artists, especially the artists in your own gallery. Art is not equitable so forget justice. Have no doubt that the gallery is going to use your buyers to sell the work of their other artists. Granted, it's the shits, but live with it. Your only consolation is to bring in more customers and hopefully expose what losers your work has been supporting.

Number ten: Be aware of the social repercussions of your own work. I am not trying to inhibit you and your work, in fact the more extreme and far out your efforts are the more I applaud them. But you have to be responsible for what audience you are seeking. The more sedate, sentimental and trite your work is, the better chance you have for encompassing a larger following. The more off the wall and oblique the subject matter the more you start reducing your audience down to people with more investigative attention spans. You add to that off-color subject matter (sex, genitals, tits, rear ends, bodily fluids, open wounds, suggested violence, and etc) and your following declines even more. My philosophy has always been, go for the small arcane audience who find themselves compelled to search out intelligent and interesting subject matter, and let everybody else entertain themselves the best they can. But finding a gallery that shares this social indifference is harder than finding an audience.

I may sound cynical and bitter, but I'm not. I just pacify my frustration with Juxtapoz magazine.

–Robt Williams

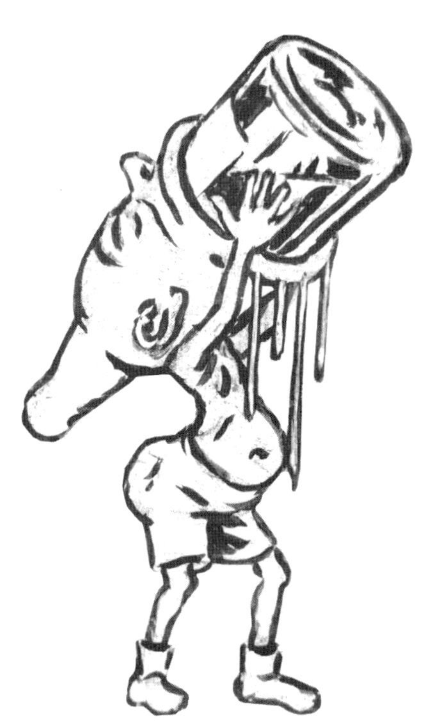

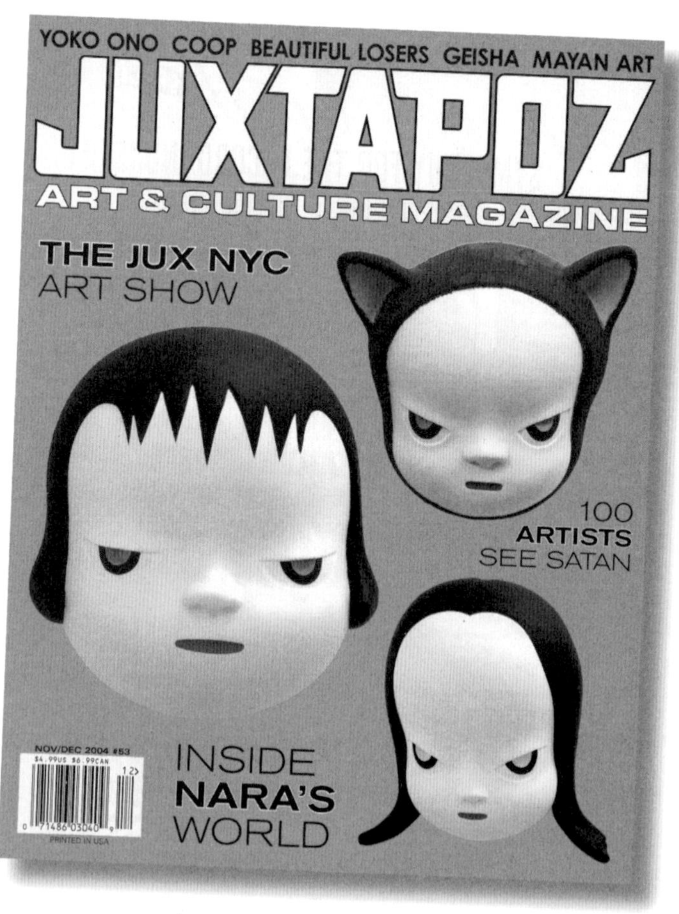

Cover art: Yoshitomo Nara (clockwise from left) *Puffy Girl, Upset Kitty, Amuro Girl*

Volume Eleven Number Six Nov/Dec 2004 #53

Crossing The Isthmus Of Art

RECENTLY, THE SALES FIGURES CAME TO ME for *Juxtapoz* magazine and we had quietly slipped into second place among art magazine sales. We are now out-selling our venerable newsstand contemporary, Art in America.

The enigma is: How can a decade old art publication like *Juxtapoz* have such a successful circulation record, and not in some way infiltrate the higher echelons of fine art? Well, yes, there have been cartoon and representational art influences cropping-up in major museum art shows in the last six or eight years. But, this is insignificant compared with the enormous amount of young artists that function within *Juxtapoz'* sphere of influence.

It would not be inconceivable to see the day come when disenfranchised artists well out number conceptual and formalist artists who now make up the more orthodox art institutions. In fact, only a small strand of separation (an isthmus of difference) keeps us from colliding today.

Hypothetically speaking, if *Juxtapoz'* circulation was to double in the next couple of years, I could easily imagine, by sheer mass of artists, the so-called lowbrow art idiom forming an irresistible wave and flooding over this thin isthmus currently dividing the two worlds. "I love art, but I love money."

There seems to be a small problem with my hypothesis. *Juxtapoz*, in the last three or four years, has experienced a large inadvertent metamorphosis, one the recognized art world is not ready to adjust to. A number of our more ambitious alternative artists have mistaken Popularism for Pop Art, although it does seem as though the two have little to do with each other. Pop Art is the bastard nephew of Dada. Dada's primary axiom is: "This is art, fuck you."

Pop Art, in a less embittered stance, takes common place items, images and ideas then coarsely, impersonally, and matter-of-factly makes you look at them. There is no warmth of sentimentality to it. In fact, any over exuberance of care, craftsmanship or personal pride spoils Pop Art. The idea here is the cold, objective strength of indifference.

Painting prosaic portraits of your swap-meet toy collection, tiki altar, or illustrations of nostalgic cartooning can never be "Pop Art." I am not the mean man that made these regulations–these are the bylaws of the cold-fish that pull the strings in the world wide art consortium.

Creating cute little cartoons that everybody loves and happy precious little characters that lend themselves to merchandising is "Popularism." The world's greatest "Pop Artist" is Andy Warhol. The world's greatest "Popularist" is Paul Frank.

Now you can see that this thin isthmus between these two cultures is, in reality, a continent apart. When the posters, toys and ephemera get more important than the principle artwork, the philosophy enters a new realm. Whoever can sell the most merchandise becomes the most distinguished artist. This egalitarian philosophy defends popular demands–this is true art democracy.

On the other hand, the more romantic, artistic and bohemian credo endorses the ethic of total freedom, and that means freedom from financial and economic restraints–the art is the art.

Juxtapoz is confronted with this dichotomy. I love art, but I love money. What about integrity? Bad breath is like the lack of integrity, everyone else suffers from it except ourselves. Eventually Popularism will take over. Why? Because it's the most popular.

–Robt Williams

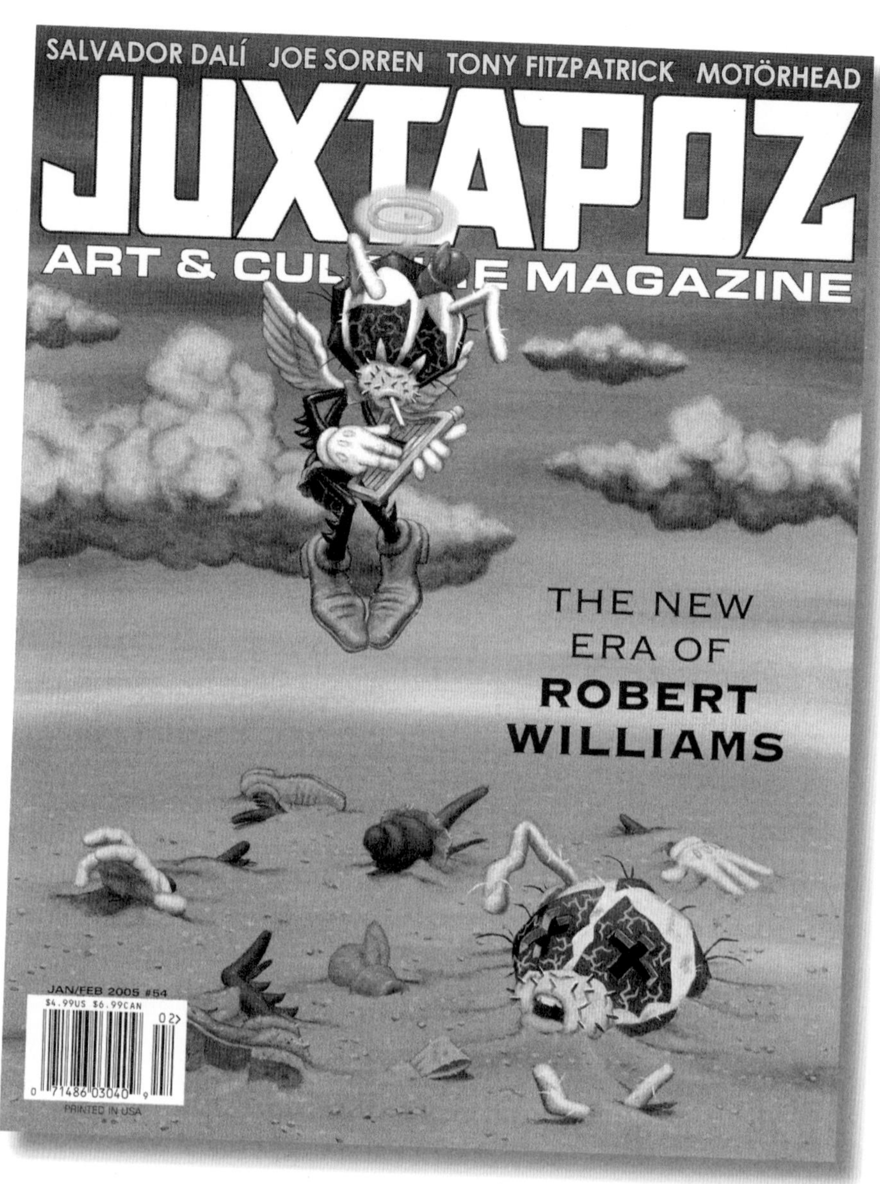

Cover art: Robert Williams *Mortal Contemplation*

Evaluating Juxtapoz' First New York Incursion

ON SATURDAY, OCTOBER SECOND, the doors opened at Fuse Gallery for *Juxtapoz* magazine's first exposure in the Big Apple. As far back as 18 years ago, New York City had experienced underground and lowbrow growlings in small venues like the Psychedelic Solution, CBGB's, Danceteria, and World Club. These simi-galleries (or in many cases, music clubs) owed their small successes to the earlier galleries that fostered graffiti art and punk rock art during the 1970s. Predecessors like: The Mudd Club, Fun Gallery, and P.S.1, to mention a few. So, New York is by no means ignorant of the alternative art scene.

However, the New York City fine arts establishment still sets the standard for the rest of the country with respect to constipated adroit aloofness. But, believe me, on Saturday night, the Second of October, the Fuse Gallery was no place for snobs. Some of the best imaginative artwork was on display in New York, in a scaled-down exhibition that gratified an enormous gathering of receptive art lovers.

This was the third *Juxtapoz* sanctioned art show within two years. The first being in Los Angeles, and the second was held in San Francisco. The Fuse Gallery had the perfect bohemian ambience for our NYC show, and was reminiscent of the old Psychedelic Solution shows held a decade and a half earlier. None of these three shows would have been possible without the astute direction of our editor, Jamie O'Shea, who has had his hand on the strobing pulse of our faithful readers. And, of course, a special thanks goes out to our marketing director, Lindsey Byrnes, along with Erik Foss, Mike McGrane, and David Schwartz at the Fuse Gallery.

Another matter I would like to bring up (since I've just pondered the past) is the recent passing of the noted *Juxtapoz* biker artist, Dave Mann. He was the featured artist in the spring 1997 issue, with his work gracing our cover.

Dave succumbed to a long bout with emphysema, and died September 11th, ending my long time friendship with him. Dave's story was a long and colorful one. Back in 1966, he first got his start as a published artist with Ed "Big Daddy" Roth. His title as the premier biker artist did not come easy. As his work was beginning to gain notoriety in the biker world, other artists challenged his prowess. But, with his personal experience as an outlaw himself, he painted an undeniable truth that ensconced permanently in that rough-hewn world. Dave didn't shy away from chrome or blood. For years he was the principal artist for *Easyrider* magazine, as well as being the graphic spokesman for an entire culture. Surprisingly to many, he tried to rise above that world. For years he dallied in the realm of fine arts surrealism, and he was extremely good at it. But in the end, his work belonged in the hearts of the outlaw biker world.

Dave's ashes are being built into a special chopper gas tank so he'll always be on the move. He is survived by his wife Jacquie Mann, who remains back in their home in Kansas City, Missouri. December 12th there will be a tribute to Dave Mann in Ventura, California, at Chopperfest, an event being held at the Ventura Fairgrounds. Good bye Dave, it was an honor to know you.

–Robt Williams

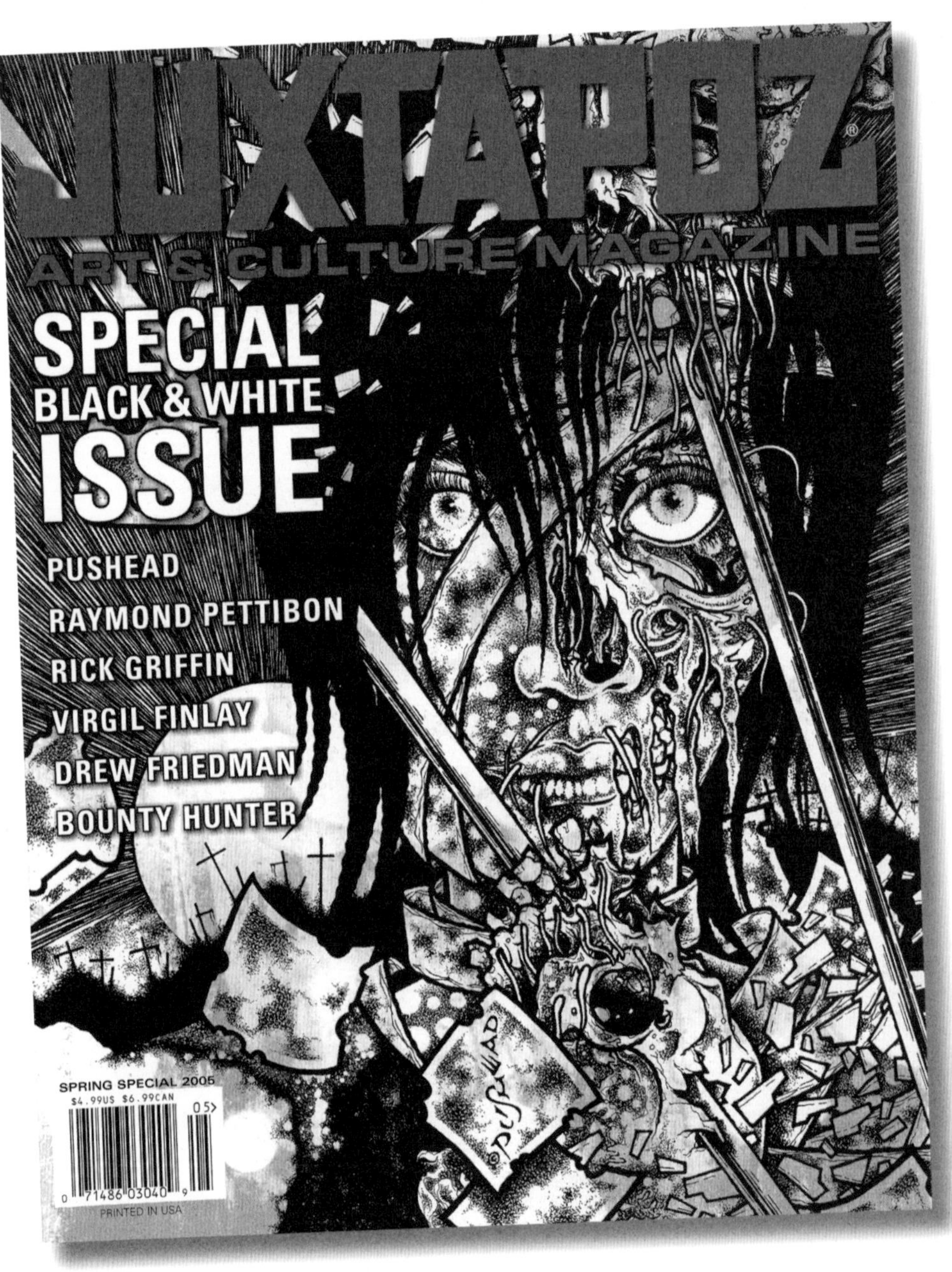

Cover art: David Trulli *City Girl*

Brainstorms Contained Within Black Boundaries

THE FOREFATHER OF UNDERGROUND COMIX, Robert Crumb, once referred to black and white drawings and cartoons as "just lines on paper." A profoundly stated remark, but poignant with compelling irony. The truth is, it's the intended thought being conveyed within the boundaries of a drawn area that is the subject, not the harmony of the drawn line itself.

Black and white renderings speak clearer, louder and more concisely than a full color painting. Beyond the thought and purpose of a drawing, you can later come back and consider the lyrical beauty (or the lack thereof) of the actual drawn line that is telling the story.

Yes, I admit, in some cases the very character of the line, the thickness, the form, the scratchiness, the precise execution of the shape means much more than the idea that the drawing is trying to convey. In other words, in this case the graphic language, or means of delineating thought, becomes the thought. This expressive use of style makes the line, and not the message, the art-thought or message really doesn't matter. Nonetheless, most young artists underestimate the importance of learning how to draw. It has been an unfortunate attitude in the arts (for the past 50 years) that drawing is a quaint sideline and real geniuses pride themselves on concepts while knaves doodle their lives away.

On the other side of the coin, it should be stressed that the principles of art should never be degenerated down to egotistical drawing contests. Beautiful draftsmanship is a virtue, not a regulation. And who is to say what is beautiful. Just because a drawing is created which represents something accurately it still has no bearing on abstract appeal. And abstract appeal is where the imagination resides.

This human predilection to draw goes back at least 35 thousand years. This need must be intrinsic in everyone's DNA. Whether it is pen and ink, brush with ink or black paint, charcoal, marker pen, or intaglio chicken scratches on a steel plate, the thoughts communicated by drawings today are as modern and fresh and relevant to us as they were thousands of years ago when the first caveman grabbed a burnt charred limb and tried to render a bare breasted stick-figure on a flat rock.

With this example in mind, allow me to offer you this special black and white edition of *Juxtapoz* magazine.

–Robt. Williams

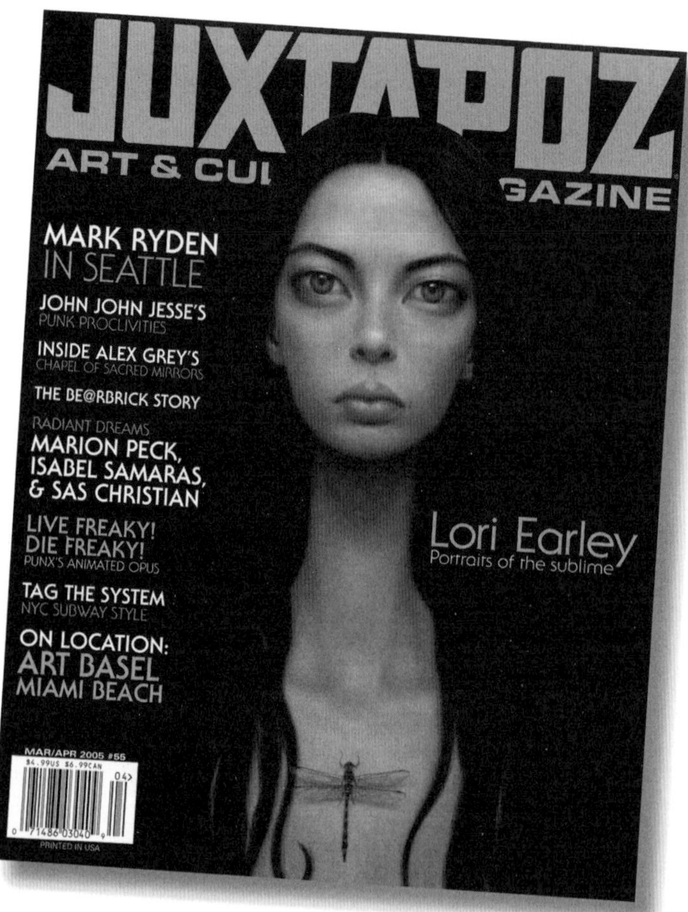

Cover art: Lori Earley *The Hunter*

Volume Twelve Number Two Mar/April 2005 #55

The Age of Complacency

JUXTAPOZ MAGAZINE, along with almost all other arts periodicals, avoids the emotionalism and partisan reactions to political events that dog our lives. And, I certainly wouldn't want to break ranks by slobbering out my eccentric views, but I would like to offer some observations about politics and the artists who try to invoke their influence.

We have currently reelected our president, George W. Bush, and our course in government is now irreversible-for the next four years anyway. Consequently, allow me to air my limited insight on artists and politics. As far as history goes, they seem to be inseparable, and war has apparently had a tremendous effect on art movements. The French Revolution and the Napoleonic Wars ushered in Romanticism and the birth of Bohemians. This brought about the notion that almost all artists are liberals, leftists, or anarchists–and to a certain extent this is true. Artists as a whole like to think of themselves as freethinkers, but you can't be an open-minded iconoclast if you continually have to answer to authority and serve a system that wishes to control the status quo.

I've rambled on about this in previous issues of *Juxtapoz*, but indulge me one more time. In the late 1840s and early 1850s, a series of riots broke out in most of Europe's capitols. From this social unrest sprang Marx and Engels, and the Communist Manifesto. For idealistic and utopian minded freethinking artists and writers, this was the cure-all for all political evils.

The Franco-Prussian War, in 1870, reignited these revolutionary beliefs and sparked the commune tragedy in Paris. From then on, liberal and artistic sympathies embraced the Communist dream. From this confused tempest of clashing ideals came the seeds of modern art which eventually took root. World War One was the final catalyst for the creation of the "lost generation" or, as some came to call it, the Beat Generation. Hence, with the 1950s launching of the Russian satellite, Sputnik, the next Bohemian title came to be "beatnik."

But, by no means, were all artists leftists. One of the most interesting and influential trends to come out of early twentieth-century art was futurism. Although starting in Paris, it was spawned by an Italian artist named Marinette. The futurist intention was brutal; man was inferior to machines, and superior art could only be measured against the perfection of machinery. This was the immaculate clockwork ideology of Fascism. These poetic horrors were the inspiration for Mussolini, and in turn Hitler.

But generally, the rest of the modern art brotherhood still fraternized with Marxist, Leninist, or Trotskyist hyperbole. There were exceptions: Salvador Dalí was thrown out of the surrealist movement because of his praise for the Spanish Fascist dictator, Generalissimo Franco, and some say his tolerance of Hitler. On the other hand, Picasso was a contradiction in terms; a wealthy Communist who enjoyed both worlds.

During the cold war of the 1950s, beatniks flourished in both the theoretical leftist world, and the existential neither-world of no responsibility, totally freeing themselves from the anxieties of the impending fear of nuclear war.

It's been said by many (myself included), that the hippie phenomenon of the late 1960s was a key factor in our disengagement from the Vietnam War.

One of the more unusual factions of Bohemian life is the biker culture, by nature extremely right wing, but yet proud to live the libertine life-style with drugs, sex, and disregard for authority. An example of this is the conduct of the artist, Von Dutch. He lived the existentialist life of drunkenness, drugs and lechery, but at the same time espoused a tyrannical social policy of population control. I had heard him, on a number of occasions, state that "anyone who is incapable of creating something for society should be executed." This was always curious to me because he would have been the first one his authoritarian regime would have hunted down and exterminated.

However, it is the current generation of artists that have broken the historical pattern of social activism. The youth turn-out for voting in the last election was like lambs resisting the discomforts of being extracted from their television sets and facing the shock of missing an episode of their favorite sitcom. When you look into the eyes of artists today you see hep apathy–where is the great storm? Where is the boiling fury?

This insouciance won't last long. The religious right will clean up our act. No more pornography–that translates down to Betty Page imagery. No more idolatry–that means fiddling with Polynesian figurines. No more graphic exploitation of children–that implies any usage of syrupy Margaret Keane depictions of doe-eyed waifs.

–Robt. Williams

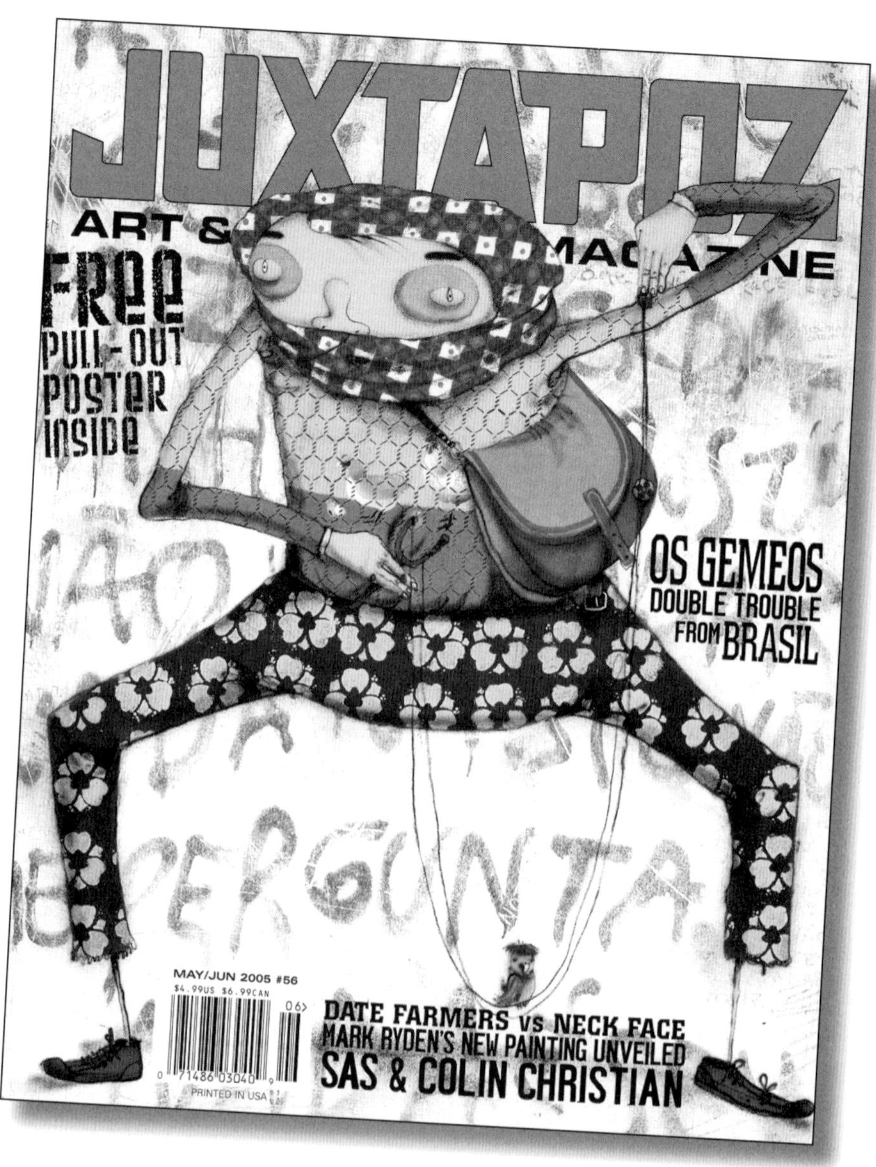

Cover art: Os Gemeos *Untitled*

May/Jun 2005 #56

The Devil Is In The Details

LAST MONTH, I HAD A CHANCE to see the works of high school art students selected from around the United States, in a special exhibit at Otis College of Art + Design. I've waded through many such amateur presentations over the years, and have always found them a little disappointing. But, to my amazement, as I walked through the show I began to realize that the vast majority of these young peoples' work was well done representational artwork, and some of it rather professional.

It was reassuring to know that the artists of the future might again embrace the virtues of craftsmanship, but to me the real question is: Is there an intelligent and patient audience for this kind of work sprouting up at the same time? It is important for the *Juxtapoz* reader to understand that well executed and tightly rendered artwork, by skilled and competent artists, has been considered intellectually insignificant by the international fine arts community for more than fifty years.

What I'm saying is, that for over half a century, art connoisseurs have allowed themselves to become too self-engrossed with their relative presence in front of art to actually see the art itself; something along the conceptualist philosophy of "I declare this pile of sand to be brilliant, therefore I am brilliant in my predication." Artists know what I'm talking about.

The worst thing an artist can do, when working within the conventional art world, is to load up a piece of artwork with too much forethought and detail. Preoccupied art admirers can't digest creative expression that requires their exhaustive investigation. The average art enthusiast expects art to offer itself to them as a joyful epiphany, and then release them to move along to the next wonderment. For the normal art fancier, taking too much time, stopping and trying to understand a lushly detailed piece of art is stifling, and it challenges one's ability to condone the work with an aloof perspective. Modern art has evolved into simplicity for a reason–the average art aficionado has the attention span of a paramecium. Authorities say that the usual museum visitor spends, on average, less than 11 seconds looking at any one given piece of art.

One artist told me that art museums should issue the art devotees skateboards, to helpfully glide them through the exhibits without bogging down on anything poignant. In this respect, the devil is in the details. Unfortunately, a high percentage of well established art experts are simply not visually oriented. And what's worst is that almost all of these intellectual dilettantes will never be able to be converted over to the visually investigative world of imagist art.

I find that some of the best art collectors come from outside the formal art establishment. Places like the comic book world, the realm of science fiction, and the collector world of esoteric art such as posters, gum cards, music ephemera and unorthodox illustration. Unfortunately, new art invariably requires a new sphere of admirers and collectors. This mode makes allowances for the use of detail-devils. So, conversely, would leave the formal art society contemplating the antithesis, "angels in the lack of detail."

On the 30th of December, this past year, the art world and *Juxtapoz* magazine lost a good friend. The big band leader, Artie Shaw died after a long illness. He was 94. As a young man, he had aspirations of becoming an artist, but instead found tremendous success in the music world as one of the premier jazz musicians of the mid-20 century.

As an art supporter, he was good friends with surrealists Salvador Dali and Yves Tanguy, the German expressionist George Gross, and contemporary art stars like sculptor Larry Bell, and pop artists Ed Ruscha and Kenny Scharf. Artie understood artists like Robert Crumb and Joe Coleman, and was an avid reader of *Juxtapoz* magazine. And, he made no bones about his appreciation of artists who could actually facilitate with craftsmanship. Artie, we're going to miss you–give 'em hell in Hades.

–Robt. Williams

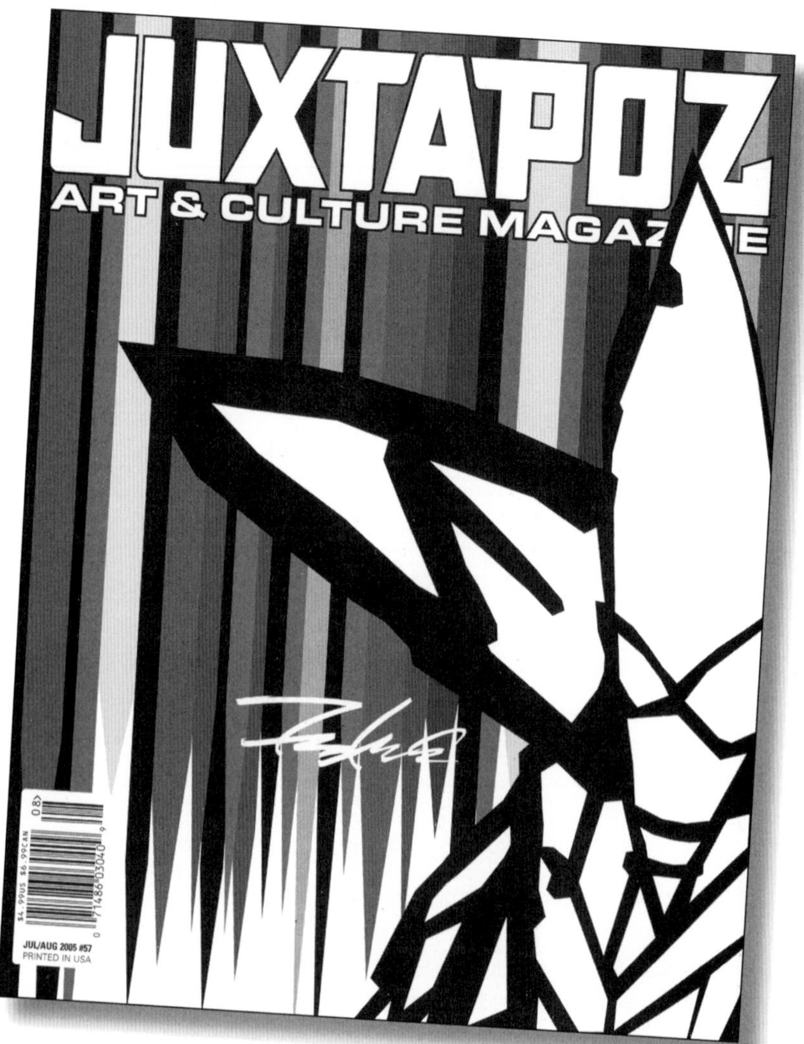

Cover art: Artwork by Futuro, Graphic design by Eric Elms

Jul/Aug 2005 #57

A Requiem For A Prince And Our Unrealized Selves

AS AN OLDER ARTIST, I see a lot of old friends and comrades leaving this vale of tears–and this makes one wonder what significance our dearly departed friends have on the new artists that have just entered the art world. On March 20th, a Sunday morning, a close friend and confidant, Walter Hopps passed away.

I had dropped Walter's name many times in *Juxtapoz* magazine, but to many readers it seemed as though I was just touting some old esoteric acquaintance–and anyway, how could anybody over the age of seventy have any bearing on the energy and volatility of a raging art chronicle like *Juxtapoz*?

Let me put this in a more understandable context. Of the four or five venerated art magazines currently on the newsstand, *Juxtapoz* is considered by the formal art institutions as a precocious fad-rag for illinspired young dabblers. Despite its enormous growth and sales record, this magazine is nonetheless regarded by art authorities as a passing trifle. But Walter knew exactly what this magazine was. He, more than any other art visionary, understood the potential storm that had been brewing for over 50 years. He had the ability to foresee how the popular arts could very easily evolve into the fine arts of the future.

I wouldn't want to suggest that I am an expert on Walter's position or accomplishments in the world of art, but it must be understood that his effect on modern art was substantial. During the last couple of years, he was officially awarded the international credentials as one of (if not solely) the premier museum curators of our time. Not too bad for a maverick art historian who was booted out of his job as museum director of the prestigious old "Pasadena Museum" in (Southern California), for drug abuse. Walter was "the man" and the preeminent art facilitator, right up until he took his last breath that Sunday morning. He, along with Ed Kienholz, started the Los Angeles based Ferus Gallery in 1957. This was the gallery that changed art on the West Coast forever. Walter told me that he gave Andy Warhol his first show.

Walter Hopps was at the very top of the art food chain. He was the curator of modern art for the Smithsonian Institution, and later the senior curator for the famous Menil Collection in Houston, Texas. In 2004 he topped off his career with the record breaking James Rosenquist show at the Guggenheim Museum in New York City. But Walter was frail, his health was never very good.

Walter had a princely characteristic that tied him to the alternative art scene. He was a born bohemian, and he loved the romantic life of self-indulgences. He instinctively knew that the underground and outlaw world of art had a pulse that would beat through all adversity.

In 1955, Walter attempted to pull hot rod and motorcycle artist, Von Dutch into the fine arts world, but had no success. In 1971, he had the nerve to present a *Zap* comix art show at the Corcoran Gallery in Washington DC. When I first showed Walter a *Juxtapoz* magazine in 1994, he immediately sensed what this would mean to young artists.

Walter's last curatorial duties were a heartfelt show for George Hermes at the Santa Monica Museum of Art. Prior to that, he co-curated a show with Tony Shafrazi which I was lucky enough to participate in, in New York last January. Walter was planning an "imagist" show in 2008 at the Guggenheim. This would have certainly included a number of *Juxtapoz* alumni. What an opportunity this could have been!

Please understand, there is no other "Walter." There isn't even anyone close. So, if you are a young artist, and you haven't heard of Walter Hopps, believe me, you are better off–you won't have to bear the sorrows of this incredible loss.

Our best wishes go out to his widow, artist, Caroline Huber. With his last curated show still installed, a memorial tribute for Walter will be held at the Santa Monica Museum of Art on May 3rd.

–Robt. Williams

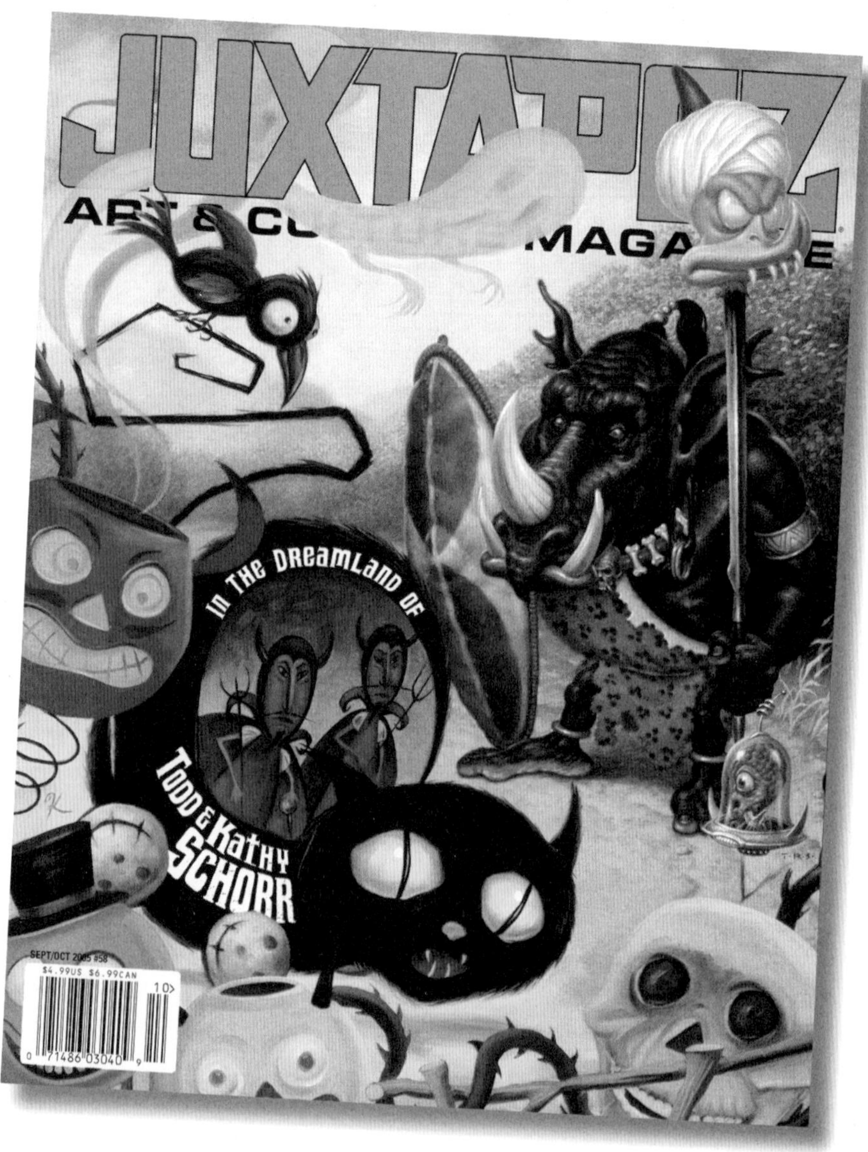

Cover art: Todd and Kathy Schorr *Autumn Sojourn*

Sept/Oct 2005 #58

Everything You Presume Is Wrong

WHEN I WAS TEN YEARS OLD, an older young man who was a grocery store bag boy told my mother and me a rather curious anecdote while bagging our groceries. He said, "You know, if you throw a live snake into a fire, its legs will pop out." I went another five years with this little misnomer stowed in my gullible head before I came to realize that this was nonsense. Nonetheless, it was a fantastic concept: a tortured serpent which all of a sudden sprouts limbs in the agony of its death throes.

Fifty years later I look back on that urban myth and appreciate it as sheer artistic license.

Long ago, I acquired a remarkable early-20th-century German print of the Swiss national hero, William Tell. This beautiful, large lithograph depicted William Tell shooting the apple off the head of his young son to appease the wishes of his Austrian oppressors. I had always understood Tell's importance to the nationalistic history of Switzerland. It was only in the last year that it has come to light that William Tell never existed. His legend was appropriated from an older tale with origins going back to a Norse saga from Scandinavia. The ignorance of the truth only adds to the story's lyricism.

Speaking of the flamboyant romance of Norse sagas, the Viking image also has its problems. We've always had a colorful vision of barbaric Vikings, with round shields and broadswords in hand, wearing horned helmets, plundering and hacking their way down the coast of Europe and ultimately the Mediterranean. This mental picture has been portrayed time and again, for almost a hundred years, in history books and adventure movies. But there seems to be one discrepancy; no contemporary or archaeological records have ever revealed evidence of the Vikings wearing horned helmets. There was one archaeological excavation (years ago) that produced a helmet belonging to a Norse warlord which was decorated with some kind of bulbous protrusions resembling milk bottles sticking up off the sides–but not horns. With the exception of Celtic design work on their shields, there is very little way of distinguishing Vikings from Byzantine or other late Iron Age soldiers.

"Art" has alone brought us this vision of these horn-headed devils. Not only are these false impressions important, they are the visual syntax with which we can identify "Vikings."

When I was the art director for Roth Studios, one of the top-selling T-shirt designs was a cartoon image of a knight in armor, holding a lance with a banner that read: "DO UNTO OTHERS AND THEN SPLIT." The shirt design was a favorite and sold in the thousands. The next logical step in the design was to make an improved version, depicting a new knight image, this time in accurate period-perfect Renaissance armor which stressed the manliness of the figure. This shirt was produced, and the sales proved it to be a flop. The earlier crude design was put back on the market, and, to our surprise, the sales once again climbed. What was the charm of the original retarded design? It shows how people think in symbols. This was very disappointing to me. I came to see successful art as the consequence of popularism–stupid sells.

My answer to this, and the only way I can gain emotional solace, is to take this lack of accuracy (and the lack of right and wrong) into the psychological and physical realm of poetic anarchy. An elephant isn't really an elephant just because it has big ears, tusks, and a trunk. It's an elephant because millions of people have agreed the word "elephant" doesn't mean giraffe. The space, mass, and volume which that pachyderm takes up is the "elephant." The negative vacuum left by the absence of the animal is the "not elephant."

Only to me, does the "not elephant" exist exactly in the same way the "not Viking helmet" exists, the "not William Tell" exists and the "not leg producing snake in the fire" exists?

–Robt. Williams

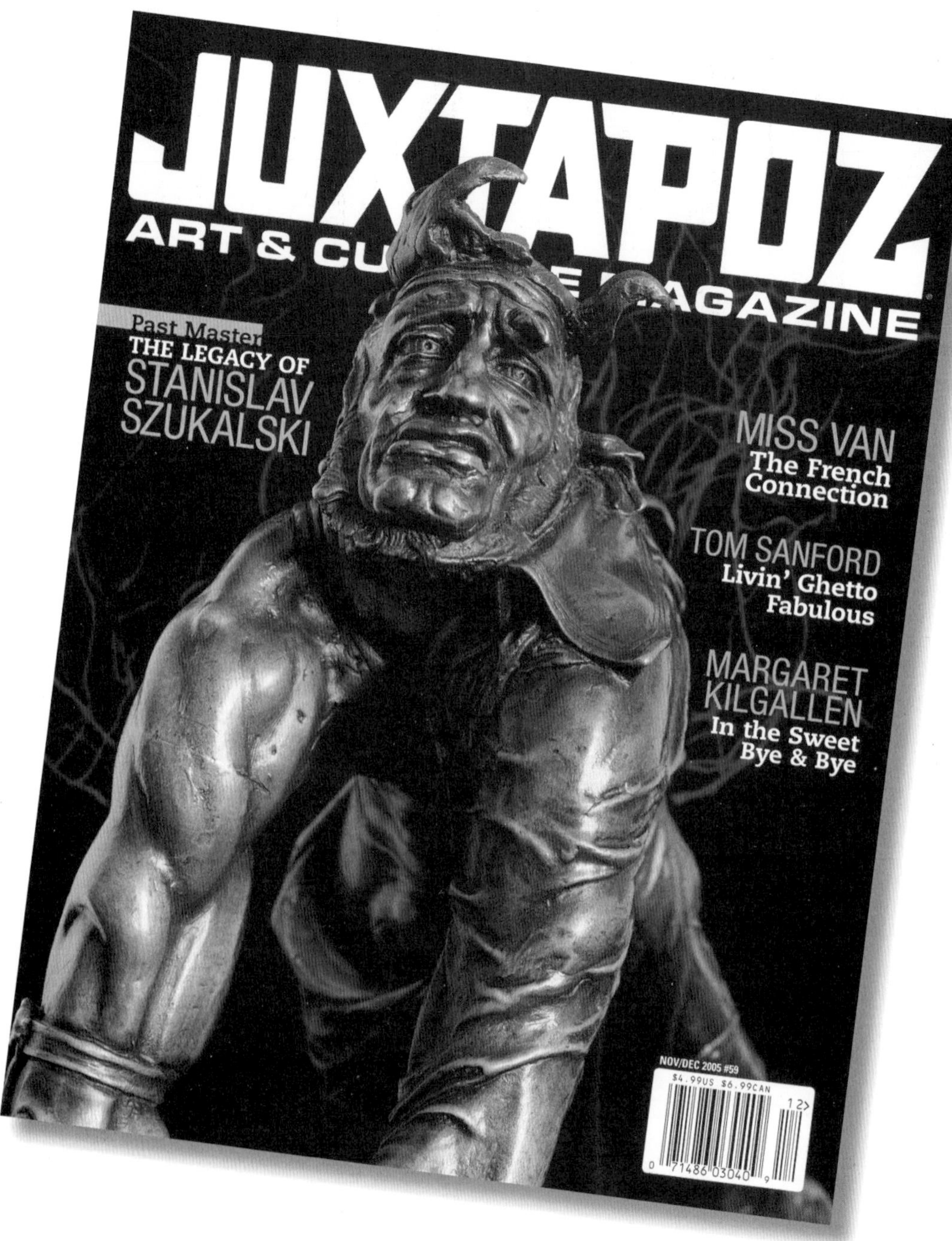

Cover art: Stanislav Szukalski *bronze*

The Ghost Of Aquarius

YEARS AGO, I had the opportunity to meet Chet Helms. I knew him as the coordinator of The Family Dog, which was the '60s San Francisco rock 'n' roll concert organization that put on rock shows and psychedelic light performances. I knew Chet only through my connections with the psychedelic poster artists Mouse, Kelley, Moscoso, and Rick Griffin.

By the late 1960s, I was an underground cartoonist and had little association with the concert promoters. But like the poster artists, I did run in the same underground art circles in San Francisco, and I did bump into Chet Helms often. He followed my work and always had kind words for me. When I found out he had just passed away, it caused me to reflect on our status those many years ago.

Chet was a hippie, but something of a businessman. I say hippie, but that was at the time, as it is now, a goofy term. Granted, Chet Helms seemed to be the prototypical flower child, but I don't know what his response to that would be–I just didn't know him that well. A lot of the older "hippies" were, in reality, coffee-house holdovers and throwbacks from the 1950s drug culture who basked in their bohemian "beatnikism." This flower child "hippie" appellation was actually a much publicized antiwar affectation which stereotyped an entire generation.

However, many of the later, younger adherents to "love and peace" revelled in the joy of thinking of themselves as "hippies." So I guess everybody who detested the government war policies and needed a haircut is now forever pigeonholed in that social classification. Believe me, back in the '60s, my long-haired friends and I were not hippies–we were unrepentant recalcitrants (born haters of authority).

The music scene during the mid-1960s was the driving force that propelled the youth movement that changed this country, which in turn extricated us from the Vietnam War. And Chet Helms, like his concert promoter rival, Bill Graham, was right at the forefront. Maybe I'm making too much of a hubbub over a bunch of old hippies. Maybe us old fools should just squat in the dirt, fiddle with our love beads, and quietly thump our bongos until our last moments slip away and free us to join Chet Helms in that big Woodstock in the sky. What's your sign, Chet?

–Robt. Williams

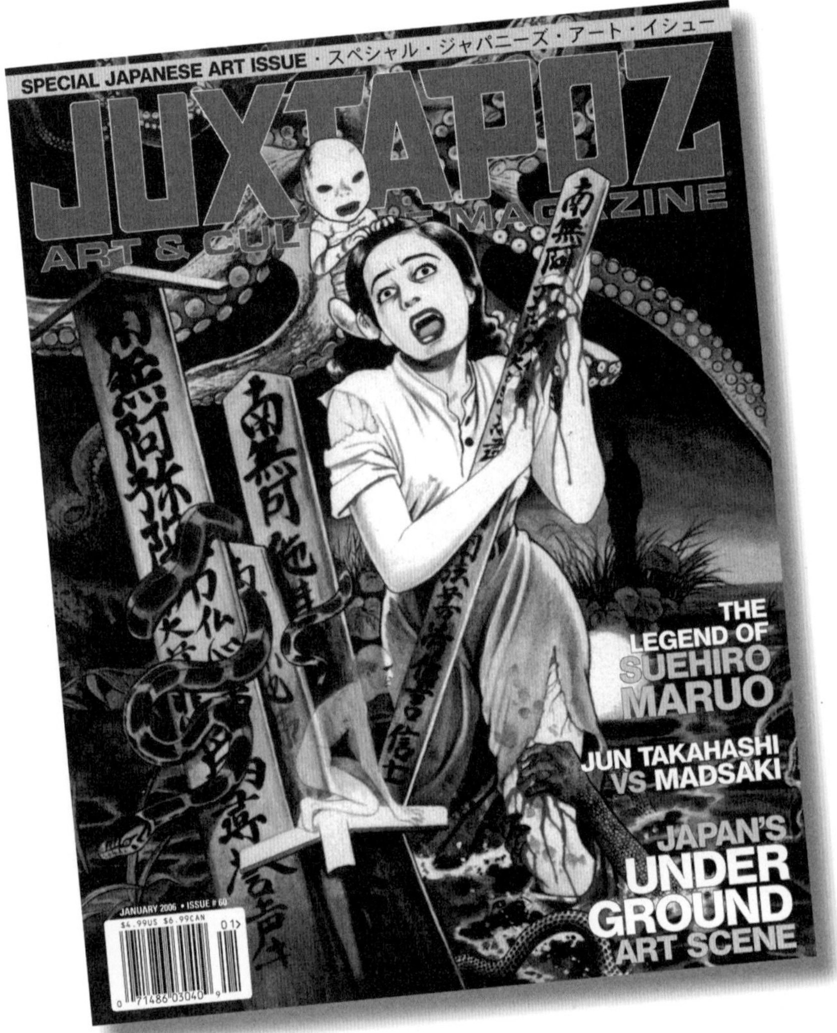

Cover art: Suehiro Maruo *Ero Guro*

Japanese Alternative Art ***A Gift From The Land Of The Rising Sun***

IN THIS SPECIAL *JUXTAPOZ* TRIBUTE to Japanese art, it would be easy to regress into the colorful history of Nipponese art evolution, to spirit back two millennia to the early Jomon culture, or study the works of Japan's indigenous faith, Shinto, and its sculptural shrines. Even to seek the cradle of Japan's early heritage in Kyoto and Nara, or further search out the vigorous and tumultuous art origins of the shoguns stemming from the influence of Zen Buddhism. It is apparent that all of these elements are still thriving today in the voice of Japanese expression.

But *Juxtapoz* doesn't celebrate the historical past of the upper academic and transcendental high ground of any art society. We pride ourselves on a presentation to the public based on art that emphasizes vitality, capability, and especially imagination. And young Japanese artists have always tended to meet these criteria.

Japan, often referred to as the England of the Pacific, has always understood the quick-changing tempo of a modern world, and has with humility and perseverance actively played a leading part in the arts.

As an example: the Japanese world of animation (once considered a silly form of cartooning) has now infiltrated and dominated entertainment and international art to the degree that saucer-eyed cartoon children with minuscule bodies are as ubiquitous as Barbie dolls.

Aggressive young Japanese artists now fill every echelon of alternative art, be it graffiti, rock poster art, comix, hot rod pinstriping, outlaw motorcycle styling, science fiction design, movie special effects, or even street-level pornography.

And, since I just mentioned pornography, let me express my appreciation to a culture that can freely live with normal bodily functions. Japan has never been under the yoke of guilt-ridden Puritanism, so its social values differ to some degree.

In my opinion, one of the premier artists in Japan is Hajime Sorayama. He is one of the boldest and most technically proficient artists of our time. But unfortunately, his spectacular pinup work is too erotically overwhelming for the American art market, and his name only finds recognition in more arcane circles. This is a burden Japanese artists will face if they pursue an American art following. We, as a country, revel in our inhibited provinciality.

Upon my visit to Japan, I found it to be a wonderful country, a little crowded for me, but having a real lust for the anticipated future, which I found exciting. I hope this feeling of manifest destiny and excitement will translate over to you in these pages of *Juxtapoz* magazine. Our energetic editor, Jamie O'Shea, has certainly given it his best, especially considering that beginning with this issue, *Juxtapoz* steps into 2006 as a monthly publication.

–Robt. Williams

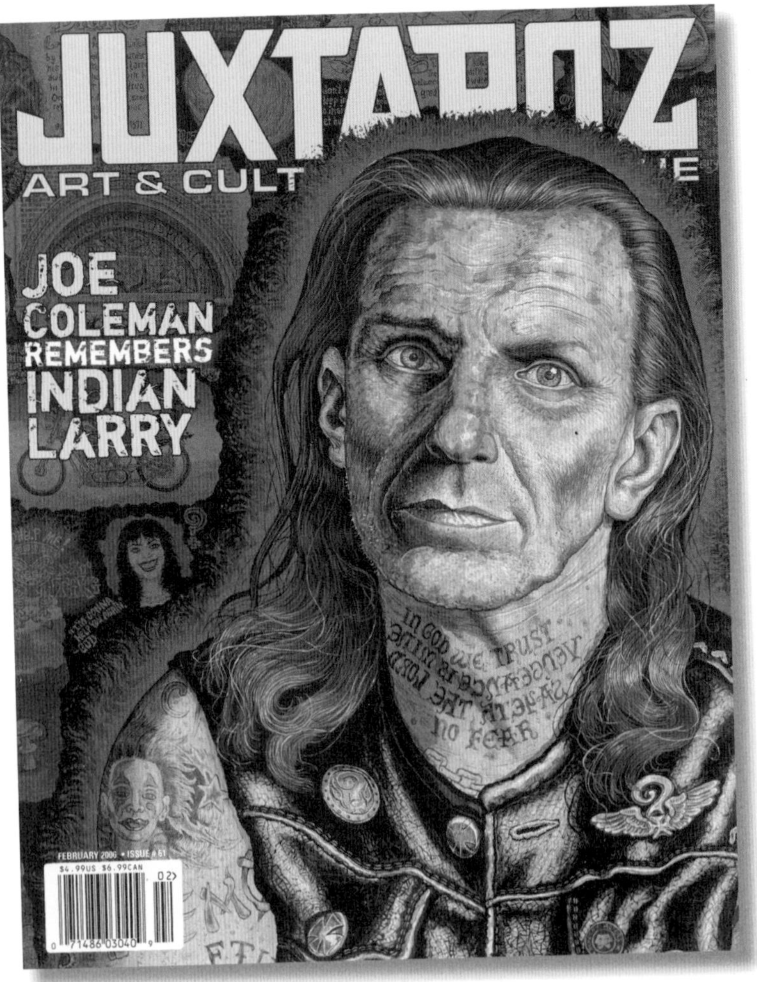

Cover art: Joe Coleman *Indian Larry*

Volume Thirteen Number Two February 2006 #61

Supra-Orbital Torus Art

A MONTH OR SO AGO, in *LA Weekly*, LA's largest liberal giveaway newspaper, there was a fine set of articles on the emerging specialty art dealing with progressive realism and, in particular, "Lowbrow Art." It seems that two *LA Weekly* writers, Holly Myers and Doug Harvey, have to some extent broken ranks with the usual editorial art program and come to the defense of the outlaw arts.

But one issue that appears to be a bone of contention with practitioners of this sub-bona fide art is the name "Lowbrow Art." And I for one certainly share this resentment.

About every three or four years I feel compelled to explain my position to the readers of *Juxtapoz* regarding this name, so let me again take this opportunity to shed some more light on this Lowbrow stigma.

During the mid-1960s in the United States, there were basically two quasi-surreal-fantasy painters who dared to confront the sterile, non-objective abstract art world presiding over culture at that time. In New York, that banner was carried by the very talented painter Mati Klarwein. And in Los Angeles, the battle standard was held aloft by (with all humble respect) myself. After a few years, Mati Klarwein caved in to the modernist pressures of the New York art scene and went into self-imposed exile on the island of Majorca. That left my insignificant artistic self to carry the torch for cartoon-tainted abstract surrealism.

At the time, I was still doing *Zap Comix* strips with Gilbert Shelton, the creator of *The Furry Freak Bros.* He also partially owned an underground publishing company called Rip-Off Press. In 1979 Gilbert offered to do an art book of all my paintings. No other publishing company anywhere would dare to undertake such an unorthodox project. It was decided at that time, since no authorized art institutions would recognize this form of art, to call my book *The Lowbrow Art of Robt. Williams.*

There was never any intention to make the title of my book the name of a fledgling art movement but, over time, that seems to be what has transpired. The original connotation was to suggest that this self-deprecating name would, over a matter of time, rise from the lowest cultural phylum of art to ironically (and much to the consternation of the art world) climb to the top–but this wasn't a serious conjecture.

The term "Lowbrow" was always unsettling to me because it made light of how seriously I took my art.

Curiously enough, a decade later a major art show was mounted and took New York by storm, and its name, *High-Lo*, implied Highbrow-Lowbrow. It did include a couple of underground cartoonists, but it was by and large a showcase for the usual conceptualists, pop artists, etc.

Since then the title "Lowbrow Art" has not met with much favor among alternative artists and the galleries who've indulged them.

In the 1990s, Greg Escalante dubbed the movement "Newbrow Art," but that hasn't met with much success. Recently, if I'm not mistaken, the New York art writer Carlo McCormick adopted the term "No-brow Art," but the jury is still out on that one too. The articles in the November 3, 2005 *LA Weekly* that I previously mentioned attempted to encapsulate these artists in a realm of art called "Uni-brow Art."

It just seems to me that any way you phrase it, the verbal description of the bone process above the eyeballs of humans, hominids, and apes (called supra-orbital torus) is just not appropriate for an art movement as vital and energetic as the work we see today. Since the advent of *Juxtapoz* magazine, virtually thousands of young artists have sprung up to involve themselves in this progressive form of imagist art.

Unfortunately, I am blamed for the name "Lowbrow" as if I've been responsible for trying to shove this title down artists' throats. In the late 1990s I heard grumbling from young painters remarking that "Robert Williams doesn't speak for me." Gee, I can certainly empathize with that. I, of course, wouldn't want anybody to presume to speak for me either. But on the other hand, if any of these young artists run afoul of the law, or government censorship, or malicious art critics, I would be disposed to come to their aid through the auspices of *Juxtapoz* magazine.

My suggestion for young artists who want to band together would be this: get your artist friends together and come up with your own classification before writers and art critics do. Your whole group might forever be labeled with a shitty name like "The Garbage Pail Kids School" or "The Etch-A-Sketch Generation," and believe me, these names stick.

Please take notice that as part of this issue, we've featured the fine painting Joe Coleman did as a tribute to Indian Larry.

–Robt. Williams

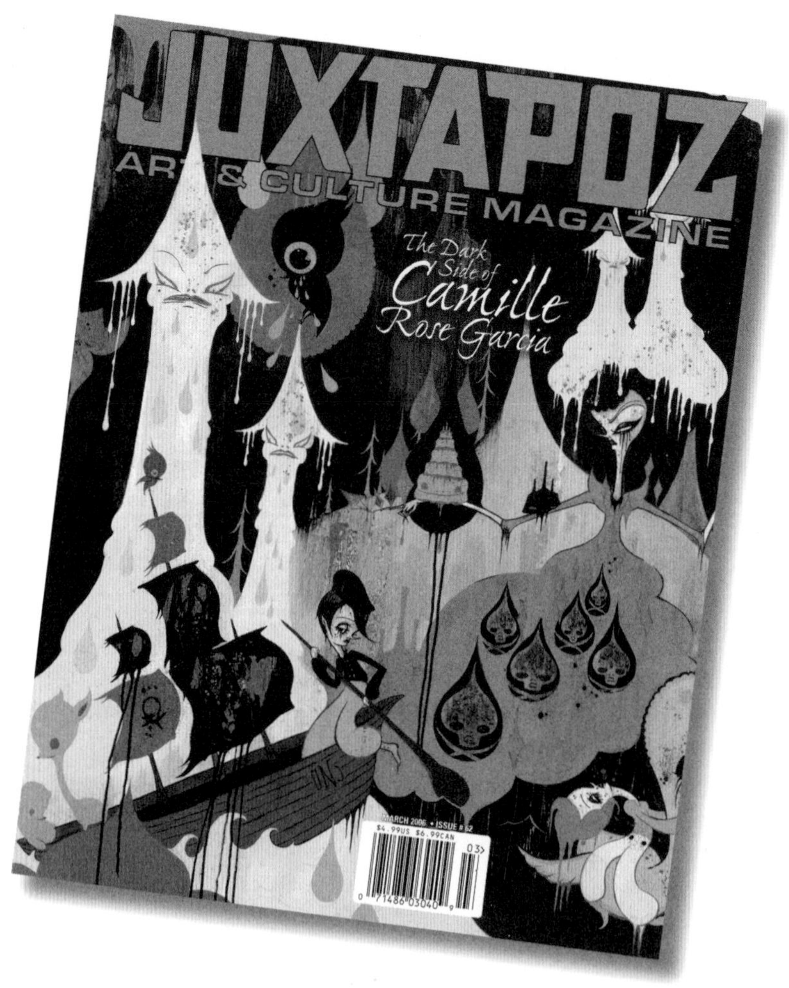

Cover art: Camille Rose Garcia (detail) *Orphaned Nihilist Escape Ship*

Volume Thirteen Number Three March 2006 #62

Bitch Slappin' Beelzebub

LAST YEAR A YOUNG MAN, while visiting a small town in New Mexico, was detained by the local police for exhibiting a windshield sticker portraying erotic interactions between two female devils. In my mind this form of censorship was an inevitability, and for *Juxtapoz* magazine it was just grist for our mill.

This was one of Coop's stickers, and for the last 15 years he has popularly emblematized the image of the Devil–especially she-devils. It seems that finally social indignation has caught up with him. This particular sticker depicts a kneeling, red female form submissively engaging in fellatio with another standing she-demon who has, in substitution of a penis, placed the tip of her tail near the recipient's mouth. Now, keep in mind, although both figures are nude and nipples are exposed, pornography has not been defined here. There is no physical penetration, nor is there any suggestion of bodily fluids or wastes.

For Coop, this accused misdemeanor was a validation of his artistic audacity. For the cop, it was his golden moment to show others that decency can be upheld beyond written law.

Thirty years ago, I too painted naked female devils pursuing the laxities of damnation. Like Coop, I created these imps to entertain a certain fringe audience and, maybe beyond Coop's following, a more specialized group. I knew that devil imagery was touchy to some, but I never guessed how touchy! To begin with, I'd roughly estimate that 60 percent of the US population believes in the Devil. The concept of Satan is a part of the enormous Judeo-Christian religion, which means that for the majority of people you come across on the street, Mephistopheles is a manifest reality.

What can also be signified is that if you, as an artist, show an inordinate amount of interest in devil, demons, etc, then you enter the realm of satanic worship or devil cults. Now, of course, the Devil represents the symbolic embodiment of all evil–the fallen angel. So if you tarry with notions of the Devil, you have inadvertently endorsed the validity and authenticity of the Old and New Testaments. And that implies you are only one repenting confession away from being a saved soul.

However, in the sup-positional sphere of art, the Devil is not rationally tangible. He graphically exists in the abstract. Like images of the Devil, Mickey Mouse has the same pictorial validity as the face of George Washington on a dollar bill. But, of course, not in the minds of those who impose emotional significance on these images. When a person is exposed to long-term amounts of pornography, they become marginally indifferent. Yet the large segment of the general public tends to emotionally unravel when confronted with the spectacle of open human sexuality.

When I paint portrayals of women in the nude, I fully realize whose provincial ethics I am violating. I ask myself: Are there carnal elements in this work that will drive moralists to take legal action against me? What about political correctness? To some of my liberal sisters (the feminists), any depiction of a posed female is exploitation. To my cretin constituency, lurid elements are addressed: are breasts sizably ample, and do I exhibit enough buttock and genitallic visuals? These would be the same questions for painting devil girls.

Everything mentioned up to this point has been a commentary on a ubiquitous characterization that most people can bring to mind. Now I'd like to take this she-devil subject further. We can abstractly alter the woman-devil concept to the degree that the average person loses sight of what an evil persona really is.

Just for artistic supposition, let's bring to mind a lovable cartoon character, a childish demon who can best be described as a cute little Kewpie Doll devil-waif. Let's say that she's about four years old, complete with darlin' little horns, abnormally big, brown eyes, and a perky little tail. Maybe give her a quirky little devilish smile with the sweetest dimples. Now let's stretch the point a bit. Say maybe, despite her gregarious personality, you do notice the poor little thing is an invalid with a crutch. And, oh yeah, one of those sweet, big, brown eyes has sadly been put out.

And now, remove the friendly aspect of her nature as being a cartoon. She is now represented in full realism, disfigured eye socket, crooked stance, and all. In fact, on closer inspection, her disposition isn't all that good either. Being a denizen of hell has probably subjected her to unmentionably physical abuse. Now she's no longer such a precious lil' mischief-maker.

And I guess since I've just fabricated this bitchy little pediatric slut, I'm tainted with the same antisocial position–in the opinion of some of our readers. Well, what if I reveal that this twisted little urchin is really an angel deceiver in disguise, secretly in the service of heaven? And this dangerous ploy is to save the souls of the entire population of hell.

Much like any good citizen, I hate crime, injustice, deceit, and greed. But, abstractly speaking (and I speak for myself, not *Juxtapoz*), the idea of spending the rest of eternity sitting on a cloud in an oppressive environment where I have to watch my language, not have unclean thoughts, and never see another naked woman is not my definition of heaven. I'll throw in with Lucifer's daughters.

–Robt. Williams

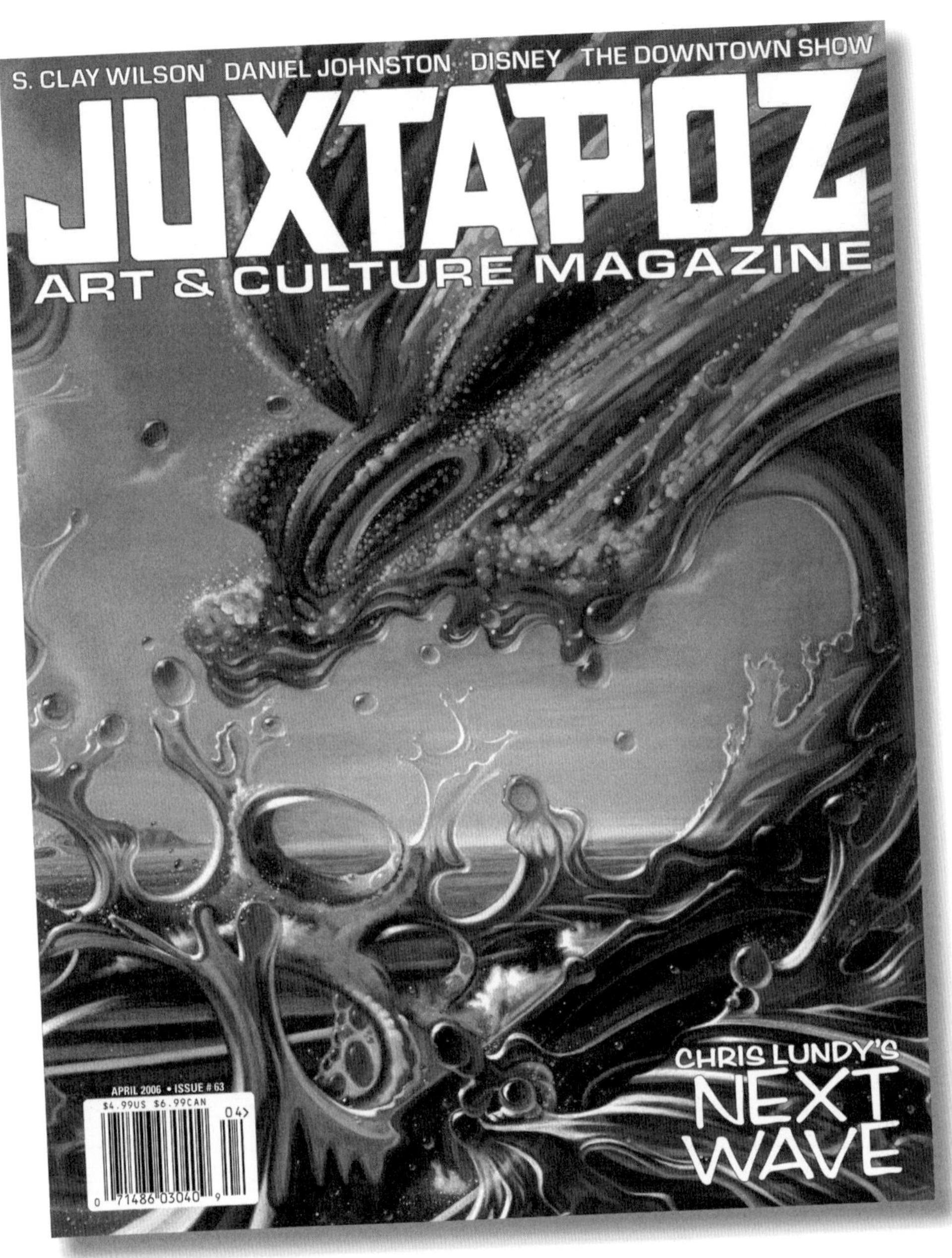

Cover art: Chris Lundy (detail) *Mama's Mad*

Point Of Interest

JUXTAPOZ MAGAZINE IS AN ever-changing journal that acts as a barometer for the trends and innovations which keep us on the cutting edge of emerging art. But, in the rush and excitement for Juxt-zeitgeist, subtle changes sometimes go unnoticed. In the February issue, we casually mentioned the exhibition *Masters of American Comics* in a cursory, but proper, two-page article. I thought the write-up was very well done, but also a bit inconclusive since *Juxtapoz* magazine at one time credited its origins to cartoon imagery.

To put these observations in focus, let me point out that since the advent of *Juxtapoz*, and the changing influence *Juxtapoz* has had on the graphic arts in the last 12 years, representational art has now become almost acceptable (I said almost).

To summarily get my point across, let me explain that 20 years ago, a comic book show with original comic book (and comic strip) art being exhibited in a major museum was out of the question–much less in two accredited museums at the same time. Now only is this show a blockbuster, but the layman art cognoscenti that haunt these venues take this cartoon material in their stride, as if comics have always been high culture.

The cartoon show presented by the Hammer Museum and MOCA in Los Angeles is absolutely magnificent. I can only congratulate the functionaries at these two museums for a commendable job on a presentation that was long overdue. The Hammer Museum took on the responsibility of showcasing the older, classic daily comic strips, and MOCA, downtown, presented works of the more progressive artists of our time.

There was the unusual squabbling about who was worthy of being included in the MOCA show. Many cartoonists were neglected, and there were accusations that Art Spiegelman surreptitiously stacked the deck, but if that's the case, more power to him. A number of people asked me why I was omitted, but I think my inclusion would have been inappropriate, since I had been long ago dis-ensconced from the outlaw comic fraternity.

Years ago, if a museum curator would have attempted to mount a show based on comic book originals, they would have had to tie the cartoon format to some relevance with pop art in order to pacify the controlling contingency of minimalists, conceptualists, and other modernist hard-liners. Times have changed.

This show remained in Los Angeles through March 12. Then it moved to Milwaukee Art Museum and is on exhibit from April 27 to August 20, 2006. Next it travels on to the Jewish Museum and the Newark Museum, September 15, 2006, to January 7, 2007.

As I mentioned before, I highly recommend this show. It contains works by some of our finest American draftsmen and storytellers, from not only the last hundred years but also current cartoonists that have formed our modern culture. This level of quality and imagination has long been overlooked by the formal art world.

–Robt. Williams

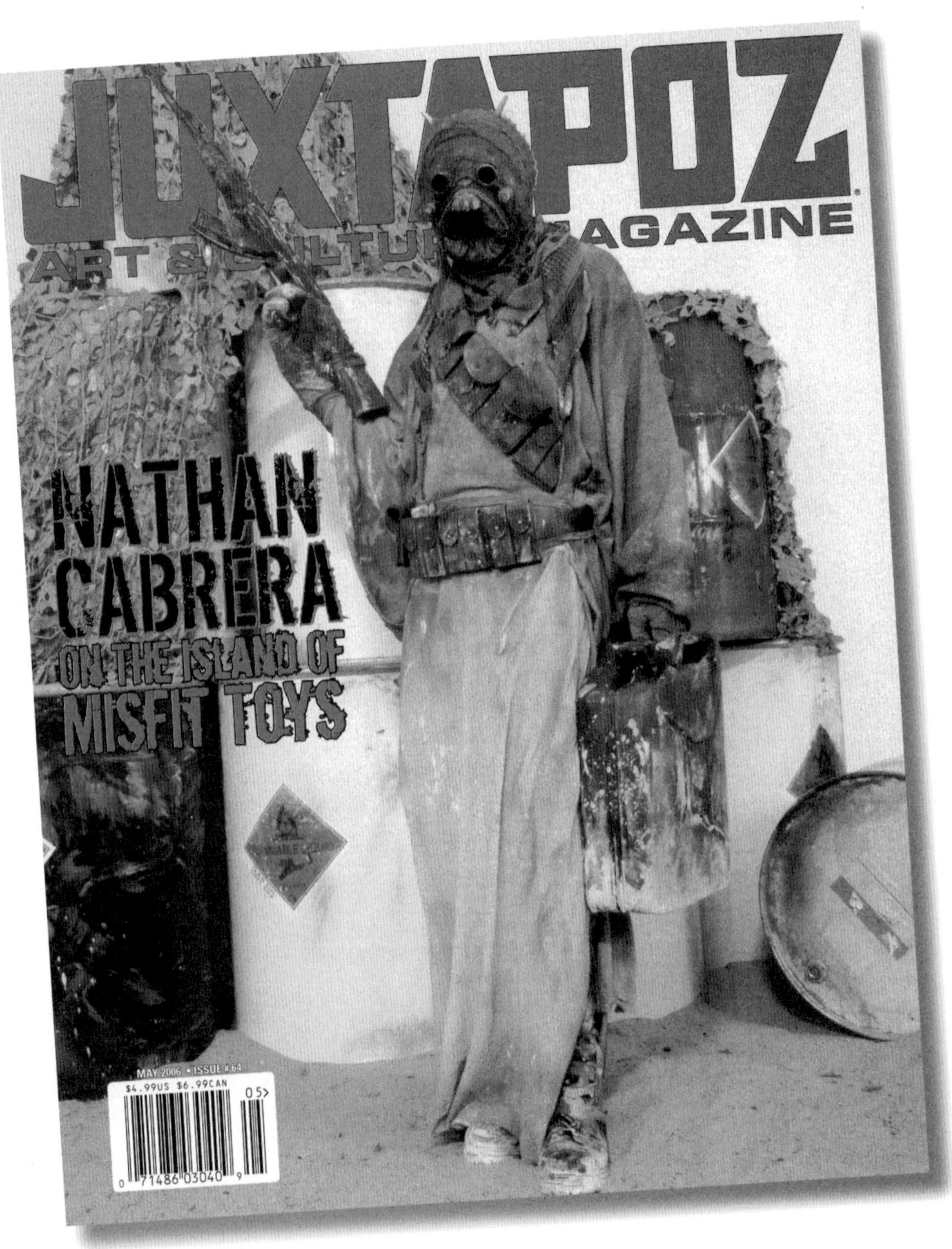

Cover art: Nathan Cabrera *Mixed Media Sculpture*

The Novelty Of Being Artistically Competent

YEARS AGO, WHILE IN ROME, I had the privilege to visit the Sistine Chapel. I was astonished at the sight of Michelangelo's remarkable frescoes that festooned this chapel's ceilings. Believe me being an artist myself I was immensely humbled. But one thing played on my mind: despite what I have been told over the years, it's hard to believe this highly acclaimed artist hand-painted the whole ceiling singlehandedly. That to me is like saying Teddy Roosevelt dug the Panama Canal himself.

Laying a fresco requires applying a preliminary coat of fresh wet plaster to the walls so the paint will absorb. I'm sure hired understudies must have performed many menial functions for him. And I doubt that the enormous expanse of painted surface was undertaken by him alone. However, I am confident the actual drawing transferred from the sketches, and the basic outline, was totally his hand application. Nonetheless, this is the way I would have carried out such a task.

I would have closely supervised the development of the forms and then personally made the corrections, to bring the figures into compliance with my initial ideals of the finished work. I certainly wouldn't have faulted Michelangelo for using subordinates to create this unbelievable work.

In my mind, any artist who attempts to undertake a piece of artwork which far exceeds the energy factor of one man is certainly justified in commissioning hired help. However, over time this entrepreneurial philosophy has gone a little apeshit. Don't misunderstand me, great ideas sometimes require the assistance of many talented people working together toward a common achievement–art is no exception.

The notion that art done by a single artist with their own hands seems to have fallen out of fashion with postmodernist art since the 1970s. Of the two great art giants of the 20th century (Picasso and Warhol)l it was Andy Warhol who taught us that art can really be greatly rewarding without the artist ever laying a hand on it. This concept was the cornerstone of conceptualism, and the premier ethic of the art world today.

Curiously enough, during the last decade, entire industries have sprung up that cater to "hands off" artists who can't be troubled with doing their own work. In fact it has become fashionable to avoid it. To take this notion even one abstract step further, some artists in the recent past have enlisted "idea men" to ease the cerebral burden. The most astonishing aspect about this delegationist form of art is the astronomical success some top artists are now experiencing.

Even though a few well-known art luminaries have suggested that skill and craftsmanship should be reserved for those marginal artists who compete for blue ribbons at state fairs, I personally take no offense. To me, art is an open and entirely free playing field. But I guess my remarks sound to some like the jealous ranting of a neglected artist who can't fend for himself in the common marketplace.

In the future, I can envision artists languidly laying on recliners, sipping cocktails, and whispering their flights of fancy to computer programmers who, in turn, enlist industrial robots to bring their every expressive notion to life. I'd like to join them.

But among the circle of artists I function with, there is one big difference. That discrepancy is the inborn, innate compulsion to personally do the work. A desire with a drive almost as compelling as sex, like a soul-cleansing catharsis to bring birth to expression, with not only two hands, but most important, a brain.

Juxtapoz magazine understands that art doesn't require a design staff and an obedient workforce to deserve a rightful place within galleries and museums. Artist prowess, competence, and virtuosity are more than a masturbatory sleight of hand.

–Robt. Williams

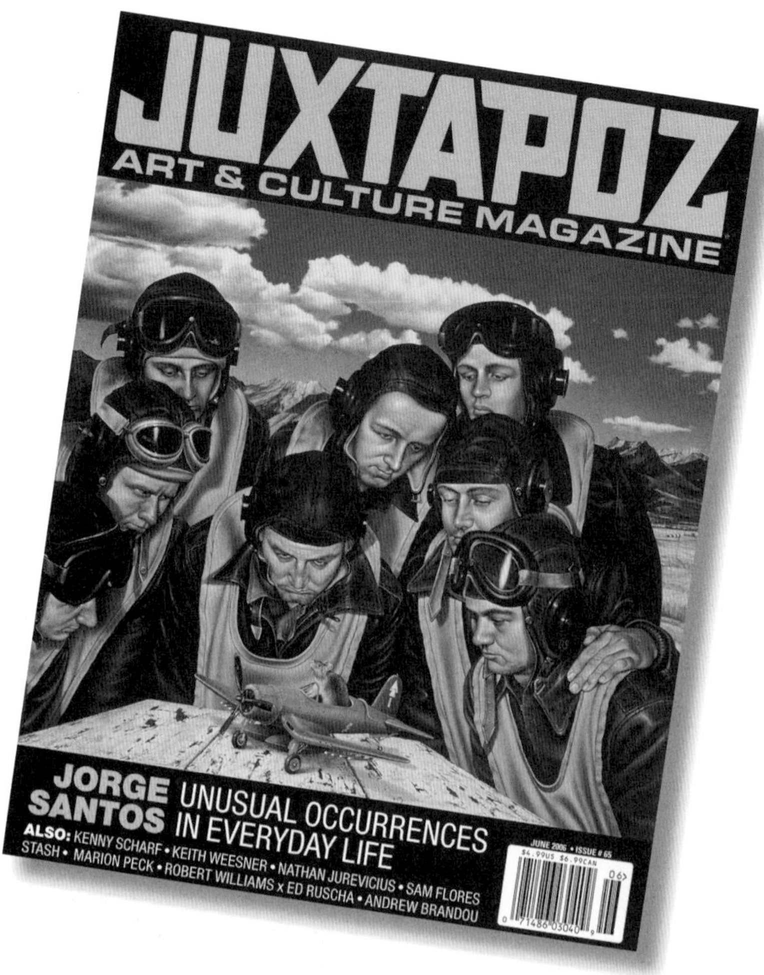

Cover art: Jorge Santos *Pet Project*

Volume Thirteen Number Six June 2006

The Art That Dare Not Define Itself

OVER A LONG PERIOD of time my wife, Suzanne, and myself have amassed quite a substantial collection of old and odd art publications. To look through a hundred and fifty years of art books and journals really puts young artists in an interesting perspective.

The oldest book in the collection is a dusty old tome titled *The Philosophy of Painting* from England in 1849. It is obvious that this book was intended for a very small, select group of cultural elites, and the artists of the time that pandered to them. The writing style is curious, in that it presumes it's the only world authority–sort of a pedantic baby talk. Only a tiny group of initiates would have had access to this book. This was during a time when many young artists were breaking away from classical and court painting to revel in the freedom of art bohemianism–something this English book would not dare acknowledge.

The next book of interest is a big, thick copy of *The Magazine of Art* (London, Paris, and Melbourne, 1892). This book bathes itself in the stoic boredom of the Victorian art academies of the late 19th century but does observe the pre-Raphaelite movement of the time. However, it completely disregards the birth of modern art, ignoring impressionism and expressionism. This constipated elitism lasted well into the 1920s. The First World War marked the beginning of the end for these exclusive, erudite power brokers.

The next interesting periodicals are those of the German expressionists that started to pop up around the First World War. By the 1920s the old Victorian art world was but a cold turd. Soon the Dadaists and surrealists had their periodicals, and modern art (now over 50 years old) was recognizable to the general public–I said "recognizable," not appreciated. World War II changed that. After 1945, the old European art scene was in a state of cultural apoplexy, and New York was the new art capital of the world.

But unfortunately, after another 50 years, the modern art power brokers took on the same characteristics of the old Victorian academies. For the last 25 years, America's top three art magazines, *ARTnews*, *Art in America*, and *Artforum*, have reflected this same absolutism.

Only two periodicals have stood alone, *Coagula* and *Juxtapoz*. *Coagula* is a gutsy little rag that stands right up to the art world and, in many respects, tries to cut the balls off their art champions. In the war on art, *Coagula* takes no prisoners.

Juxtapoz, on the other hand, though equally irrespective of the academic authorities, sees the ponderous art giant as a misinformed parent that won't let its child get a Mohawk haircut. Resistance to the art institutions only makes them more significant. The artists that find comfort in *Juxtapoz* magazine, for the most part, function without art subsidies and museum support, and remain free. Quite a phenomenon when you consider *Juxtapoz'* readership is nearly 80,000.

Nonetheless, things are changing. The other art magazines won't point this out, but take a copy of *ARTnews* today and compare it to *ARTnews* from 10 years ago. Representational art has slowly been replacing minimal and conceptual art. Things have been changing for *Juxtapoz* too. In the late 1990s, with the passing of underground influences, it transformed into an alternative art magazine with an emphasis on uncategorized art. Now, with such an enormous popularity base, it has become more egalitarian. It seems that young artists are creating an art idiom that brings them to success and financial reward by reaching the largest audience in the quickest possible time. The Internet has a lot to do with this. If this popularism, or mob art, does indeed replace postmodernism as the top art form, some intriguing residual slag is sure to be an interesting by-product.

Not every artist caught up in this popularist rush to fame will be an astute businessman and ambitious self-promoter. With a mad dash to swamp a new art movement, I'm sure there is going to be a small number of aberrant misfits with remarkable talent that are total failures at mercenary art exploitation. *Juxtapoz* magazine will be there to catch this failed group of prodigies who didn't make the cut.

–Robt. Williams

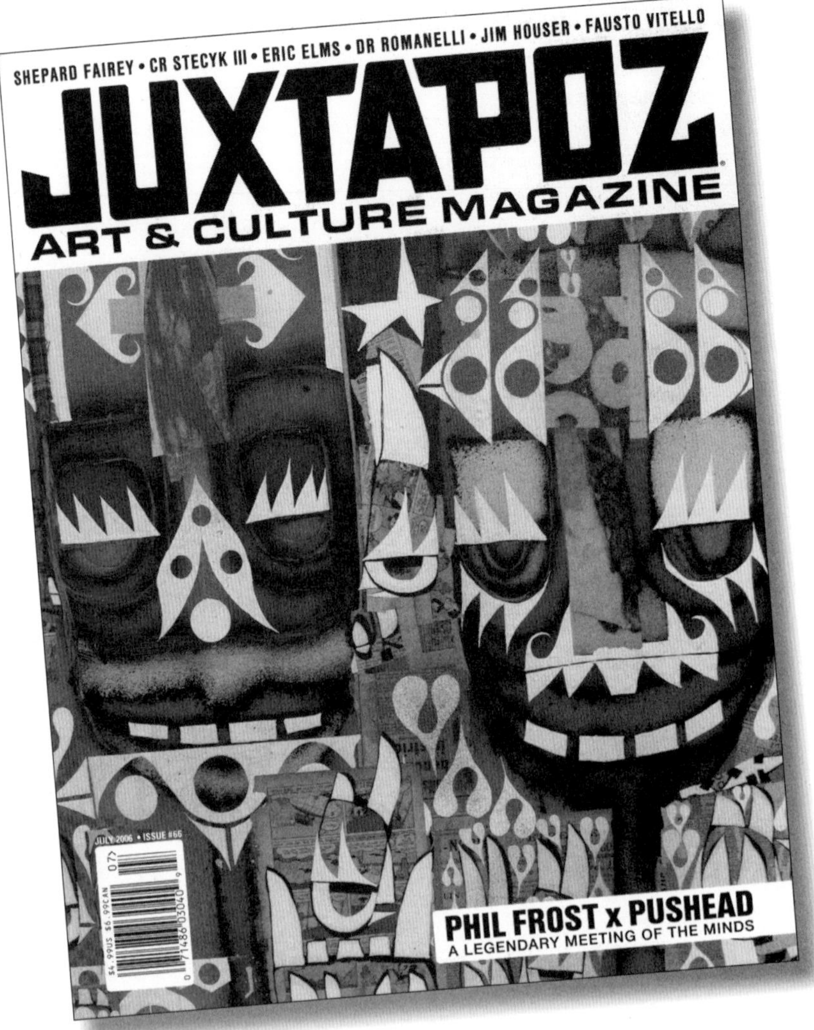

Cover art: Phil Frost *Untitled*

Volume Thirteen Number Seven July 2006 #66

In Memoriam Fausto Vitello
August 7, 1946 - April 22, 2006

THE GREAT 17TH CENTURY FRENCH writer and moralist François de la Rochefoucauld once wrote, "It is imperative to do unwitnessed what we should be capable of doing before the world." This highfalutin quotation, by a guy with a name no one can pronounce, would have fit Fausto perfectly. I say this in the past tense because we at *Juxtapoz* have lost our leader and executive director, Fausto Vitello.

This remarkable man died of a heart attack on Saturday, April 22nd. Fausto lived de La Rochefoucauld's maxim: No double dealing–don't do anything in clandestine circumstances you wouldn't do before us all.

Fausto burned more energy in his short 59 years than most of us would use up in a couple of lifetimes. He was the proverbial achiever, and he was an immigrant. His family was originally from Sicily but made their home in Buenos Aires, Argentina, where Fausto was born. He came to the States as a boy and was raised in the Haight-Ashbury district of San Francisco.

He built his empire on the skateboard culture of the 1970s and was instrumental in promoting the urban street use of skateboards when skate parks fell out of favor. Besides manufacturing skateboard trucks and hardware he, with his colleagues, created *Thrasher* magazine. Many have already written of Fausto's successes, achievements, and turbulent exploits in the skateboard world, but it should be mentioned that this is where he came to know and understand marketing among rebellious American youth. It was in this milieu of bad-boy street sports that Fausto learned to mix business with down-to-earth youth communications. To put it simply, Fausto had an innate sense of which way the cultural winds were blowing. He understood change because he was part of that change–he was an active member in what was happening, here and abroad.

After dealings with Fausto's High Speed Productions and *Thrasher* magazine during the late 1980s, I met Fausto Vitello with the help of Greg Escalante. This was in 1992, at my art show in New York City. I found him to be friendly, intelligent, humble, and unassuming. I had no idea how powerful and influential he was. A couple of years later, when we formed *Juxtapoz* magazine, the full scope of this man's command of business and organizational skills became apparent.

Fausto belonged to a new group of young entrepreneurs who started to appear on the California scene during the late '60s and '70s. These youthful business magnates sprung up primarily around beach towns, infiltrating surf culture, magazine publishing, and sportswear companies. Probably a better name for this group would be "cultural purveyors." This small, elite bunch was the caliber of wild, feral businessmen that Fausto fit in with. Barons without neckties.

Fausto Vitello had no pretensions, but his demeanor, his body language, his voice, and his piercing eyes were clues to alert one that this gentleman was not the person to force an issue with–and indeed this was the case. Fausto ran a democratic ship, but when decisions had to be made and his cohorts were indecisive and vacillating, his commanding personality always took charge, and, I might add, with the judiciousness of King Solomon.

Juxtapoz magazine was a whole new animal to him. With an art magazine, he had to change his way of thinking. It wasn't like the skate magazines that could enjoy an innumerable audience of young boys waiting to be rallied. *Juxtapoz* was a foray into unexplored territory. But both worlds had one thing in common, a characteristic Fausto was familiar with. Both were socially irreverent by nature.

As time went by, Fausto came to realize that an outlaw art magazine has virtually no limits. He must have loved it, because he had to put up with all its anguish and growing pains. On occasion Fausto and I had our differences, but we both understood *Juxtapoz'* significance with respect to young artists and its growing audience.

Fausto was a businessman first, but he was also a wonderful family man and a generous humanitarian. He understood the responsibility he had with young people. He had an active son (who was already involved in the business) and an attractive daughter, so consequently he could observe the vicissitudes and problems of young adults.

His business affairs will, I am certain, pass easily over into the competent hands of his wife, Gwynn, and longtime trusted *aide-de-camp* and publishing director, Ed Riggins.

Again, I speak for all of us at *Juxtapoz,* Fausto was our leader, our boss, our inspiration, and our friend. I am confident that all his endeavors will smoothly continue to succeed in his absence by the sheer force of the momentum he left with us.

Adios, Fausto.

–Robt. Williams

"BUT IS IT ART?!?"

Janet told Carl she wasn't going to stay one more day in the house with that ugly elephant statue on the mantel. Janet says when her friend Ruth comes over she always makes a snide remark about it, and you know Ruth teaches art at Beaverton High School. Carl was left with three ways to consider this. First: Is this sculpture really art? Second: Is it good enough art that it would supersede Ruth's taste parameters. Or third: Is the presence of the pachyderm bronze worth domestic friction and a possible separation with Janet.

This frivolous anecdote is actually a condensed embodiment of taste and academic sophistication that we have come to use as a justification for our own opinionated convictions. Personally I would put my money on Ruth and the entire "Ruthian Hypothesis." In other words, taste as a directive is all important, and the only idiom to exceed this would be the opinion having the most dominant ramifications.

Excuse me if I digress for a moment on Carl's behalf. The word "art" as a cultural aspiration actually only goes back as far as the late 1600s. Prior to that handcrafted objects were only valued with regard to their own individual aesthetic need required.

Ruth, with her experienced academic intuition has come to depend on the word art. However, now in the twenty-first century, both Ruth and Janet would hopefully come to understand that with the dadaization of art everything is eligible to be art, and Ruth's selective choices of what should be art is her conceptual expression.

Maybe Carl should explain this to Janet.

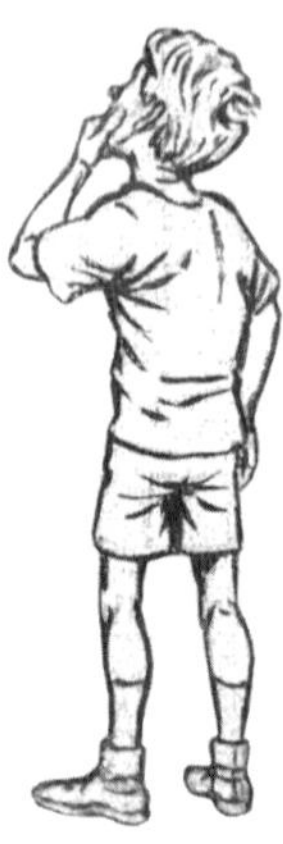

"IS EVIL REALLY ALL THAT BAD?"

I have always been surprized how many people react to the image of the Devil. I forget sometimes that most pious souls look upon fallen angels as evil incarnate. Followers of the scriptures see within Satan a malignantly wicked exemplification of mortal pain and the denial of entry into salvation. I must stress that this is a real, almost tangible fear for some who are confronted with the pictorial presence of Lucifer.

As an artist, I find the character and persona of Satan entertaining as well as an exercise in graphically portraying a creature who is both a debaucher and a psychologically powerful idiot who thinks because he lacks empathy he won't be taken in by subterfuge himself.

I don't fear the Devil, I fear people who want to be his embodiment, or even worst individuals who want to destroy what they see as the Devil.

Hence this story: When I was a young man, seventeen or so, living in Albuquerque, New Mexico, I worked as a construction supply worker. One day, while at lunch I heard an interesting story. I was sitting with two old Mexican-American laborers and they were talking among themselves. This was in 1960 and they were discussing events that occurred in their past, around the First World War. One elderly fellow told the other that he remembered that a neighbor woman gave birth to a child and it was a Devil so they had to kill it.

I said, "What, say that again!" and the nice old man calmly repeated it. "Yes, the baby was born a Devil, so we had to kill it." Then I asked, "How did you know it was a Devil?" I couldn't get any more information so I let the matter pass. Needless to say, my mind was cross-threaded for the rest of the day. Apparently it was a common practice for these simple folks for euthanasia of deformed children at birth. As the Devil himself would say, "Shit happens."

I can understand ancient primitive Satan worshipers carrying on but modern Devil cults really stump me. Believe me, there are some sizable groups that categorize themselves as "followers of Satan! Here is my problem with that: for an individual to perceive the Devil as a sacred deity and believe the Devil has magical and eternal power as indicated in the scriptures, one would have to also fully believe in God as the original deity-you know, the guy that created the Devil in the first place. In other words, a Devil worshiper with this admission is already halfway back to redempton. And besides, you can't be a real Devil worshiper if you are an atheist. You can't worship the Easter Bunny and reject Easter.

And then there is the question of how naughty do you have to be to be truly evil? I am sure there are some full-fledged criminals who find solace in the Satanic secret rights business. In my field, I have met almost every facet of adventurer-despots.

As an artist I find the Devil one of the most interesting personalities in Judaeo-Christian legends. I think, as a young preschooler, Satan was the first character I rendered–maybe because he was bright red. As a comicbook artist I found female Devils a natural to draw. I also tried to establish more controversial figures that would stimulate the imagination with equal dash and personal style. My eventual solution was the rendition of a seventeenth century, partially nude female harlequin. A true sinister arch-fornicatress--the one person that not even the Devil could resist or subjugate. My one comfort in using the Devil's image was that he is the only minority you can flagrantly discredit without bringing harm to an existing group (well, except maybe the Devil worshipers).

Whoever it was, way back in our long distant ancient past who dreamed him up came up with a winner. There have been many Gods in memorium but this horned bastard has outlived them all.

I have rubbed elbows with a few real Satanic acolytes in my time but they seem to be regular guys in it for the possible sex or shenanigans. I couldn't imagine going to one of these sacred, secret cabalas dressed in a black cape like Bela Lugosi and trying to keep a straight face.

ART . . . THE TRADING CARDS OF THE GODS

The renown and greatly respected museum director and art arbiter, Paul Schimmel had been heard on a number of occasions to express his very definite opinion with this characteristic remark, "I always tell it like it is!" Paul is of course referring to what will work, what won't, who's gifted, who isn't, what will financially fly and what will bomb. He, as an art functionary, is listened to and justly respected regarding academic cardinal rules and accepted practices of today's blue chip art business and is probably a good authority.

Coldly stated, art that is monetarily successful is a business. Art that economically flounders is a hobby. Consequently, to be a success an artist has to run an organized business or be tied to a gallery big enough to help operate a large, fully staffed studio. Hopefully, a known gallery that is willing to take a sizable chance, but this would usually be available only to an already proven artist. Other than this, the artist is either an aspirant or a wishful hobbyist.

To argue in semantics, today successful artists, in most cases, are actually not true artists by the old definition. According to the Funk and Waganalls Dictionary there are three established categories of artistic creators. Number one: the artist, the primary creative brains and power behind art. This is the individual who gives the inspiration for the project. Number Two: the artificer, the person who puts the project into motion with instructions and commands. And lastly, number three: the artisan, the person who actually does the hands-on work at the direction of the artificer.

An historical figure like Michelangelo had many helpers and secondary artists. He was also artist, artificer and artisan rolled into one. But a strange thing happened during the twentieth century. The conceptual art and pop art movements demoted the true artist, and elevated the artificer to the rank of project commander. This, in some cases with the need for many more artisan helpers. The fact that the artist could now just point to an object and declare it "Art" put him in the place of the decision-making artificer. The primary creative spirit had been transferred over to the original factory designer who designed the object in the first place.

Oddly enough, big money has substantiated this situation with theoretic conceptual art and pop art–so why worry who the real artist is. This is a question for museums, art schools, galleries and auction houses to ponder.

Back to Paul Schimmel's objective statement "I always tell it like it is!" But what is "it"?!? Does the word "it" challenge the liberal subjective freedoms of art? Since Marcel Duchamp immortalized the New York plumber, Richard Mutt in 1917 by enshrining his porcelain urinal the whole art world slowly became totally "subjective." This should have stopped "tell it like it is." The forces that backed Mutt's urinal either softened or erased most of art's tangible rules. Richard Mutt was, in reality, the real artist. If not Mutt, then the power of the art dealers, auction houses and the world of high financiers are the true artists.

Unfortunately, money turns "subjective" art theory into "objective" art theory. Less than one percent of all artists make ninety-nine percent of the big money. The other romantic ninety-nine percent of the artists are living off the anticipated glory of their imagined posthumous rewards. Unfortunately, of all the wonderful words that are connected to the arts "equity" is not one of them.

It is presumed that soon art auction sales will surpass the billion dollar mark for one single piece of art. With the dismissal of intrinsic worth, the prices are now the abstract factor in art. I think that is Paul's "It."

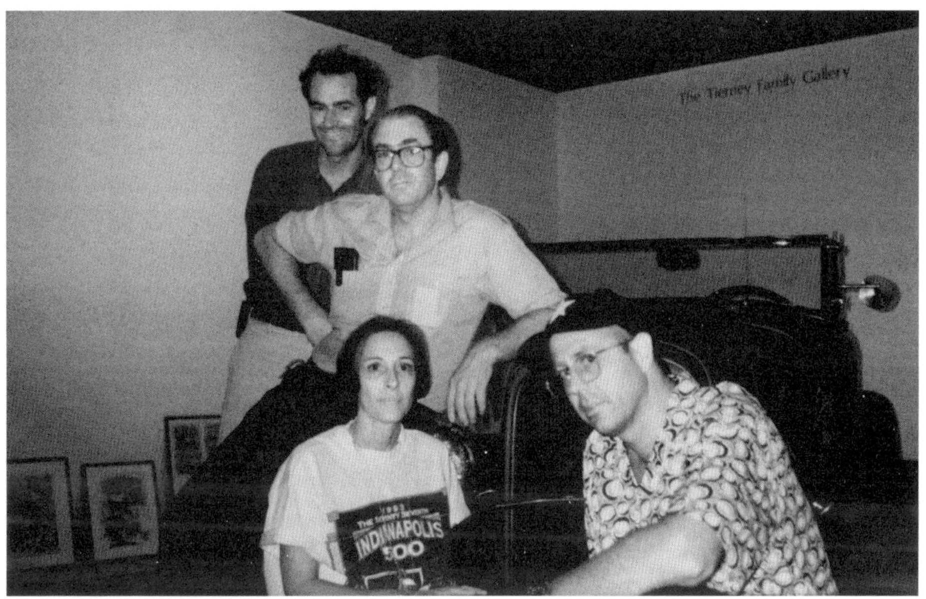

Greg Escalante behind Robert and Suzanne Williams with C.R. Stecyk.
Kustom Kulture Show, Laguna Art Museum Satellite Gallery in Costa Mesa, CA.
1993 (courtesy Williams collection)

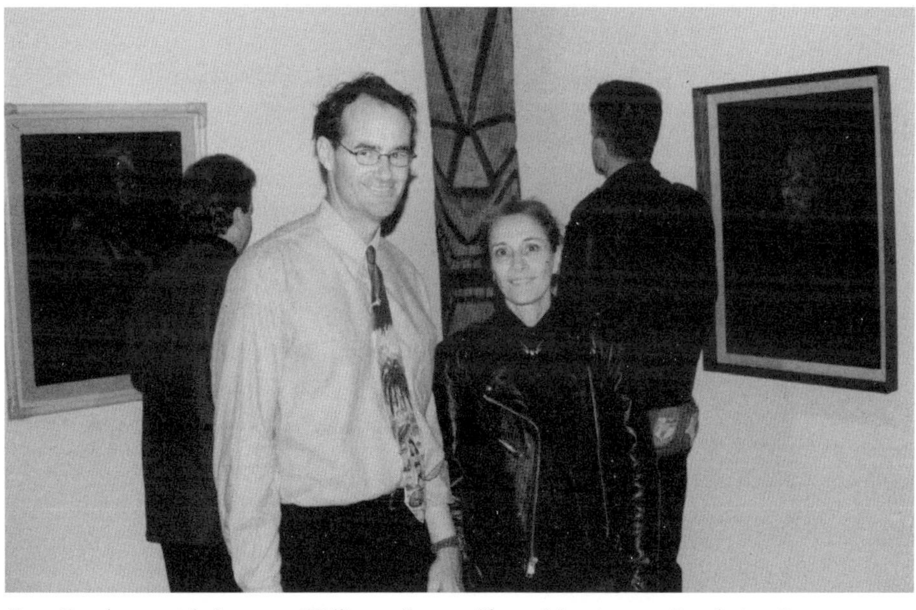

Greg Escalante with Suzanne Williams. Leetag Show, Huntington Beach Art Center.
1999 (courtesy Williams collection)

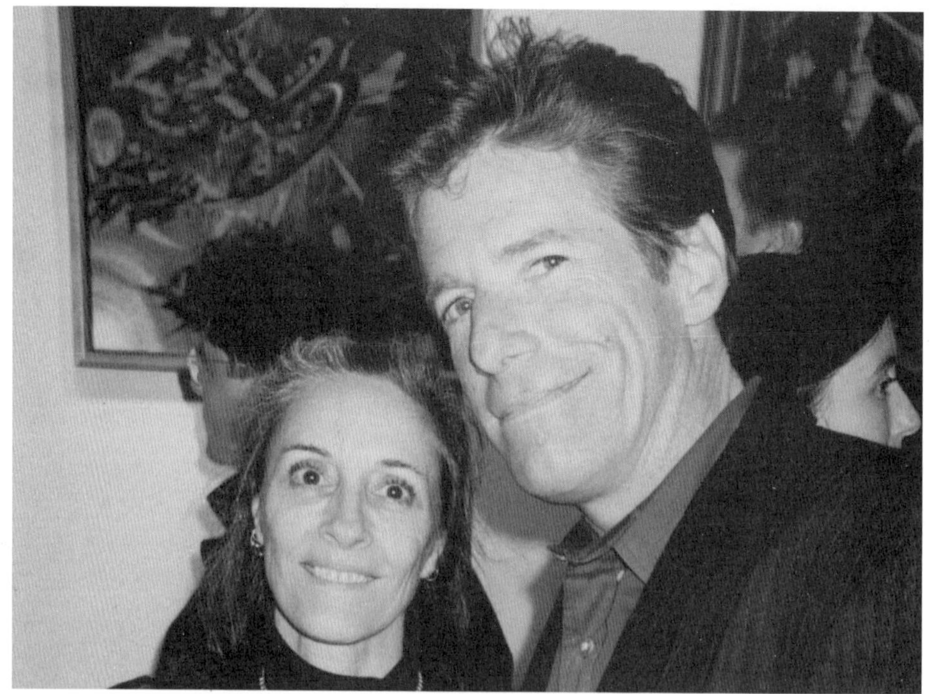

Suzanne Williams with Kevin Thatcher (first editor of *Juxtapoz*) at noted 111 Minna St. Gallery, San Francisco, CA. (photo Rebecca Wilson)

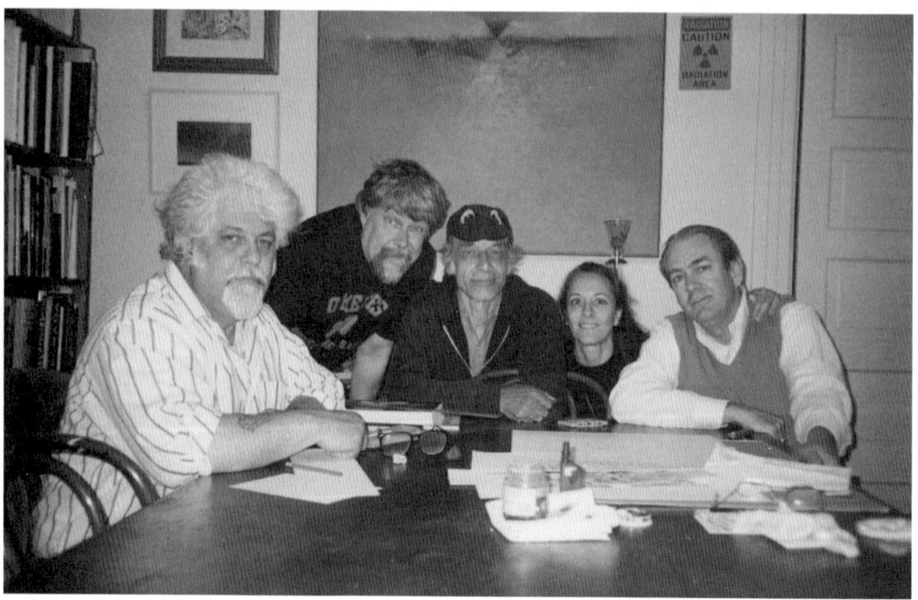

Zap Comix Jam.
from lt. to r.: Spain, S. Clay Wilson, Victor Moscoso, Suzanne Williams, Robert Williams.
1995 (courtesy S. Williams)

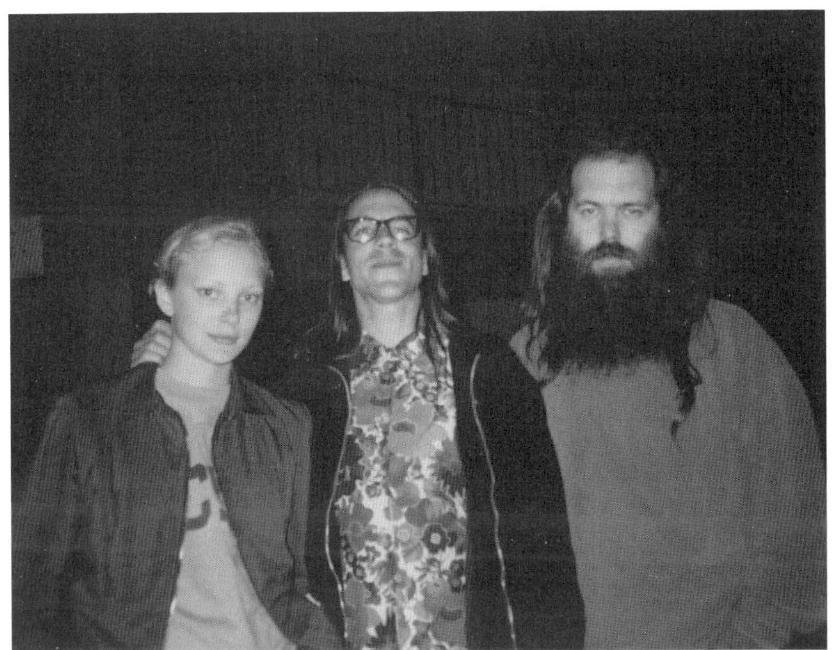

Guests of Robert's San Francisco Art Institute Show.
from lt. to rt.: Jamie, Red Hot Chili Pepper's Anthony Keidis and recording impresario Rick Rubin.

1995 (photo S. Williams)

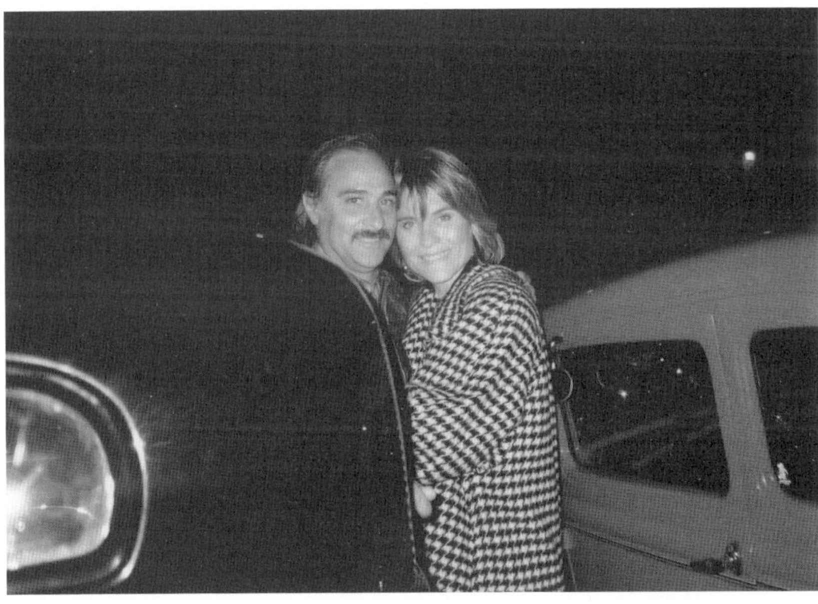

Photographed between two Hot Rod coupes, the late Fausto Vitello with his wife Gwynned. Fausto was publisher of *Juxtapoz* and *Thrasher* Magazines. After his passing Gwynned sucessfully filled the position.

1995 (photo S. Williams)

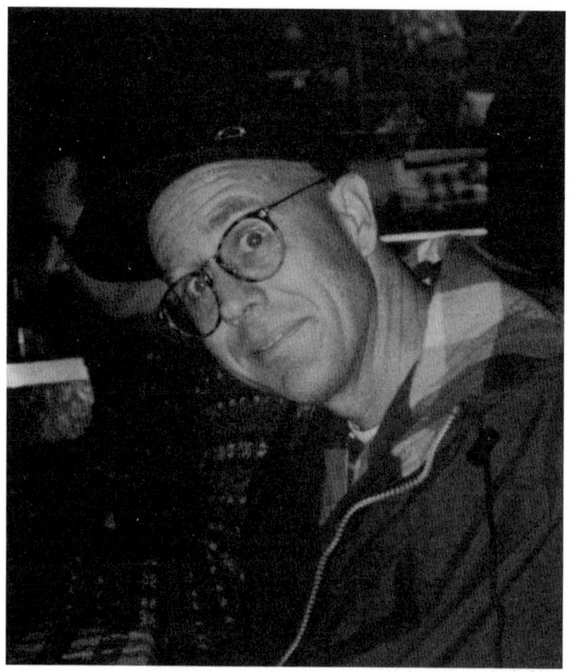

C.R. Stecyk at Williams' after party at Tommy's Joint.
San Francisco, CA.

1995 (photo S. Williams)

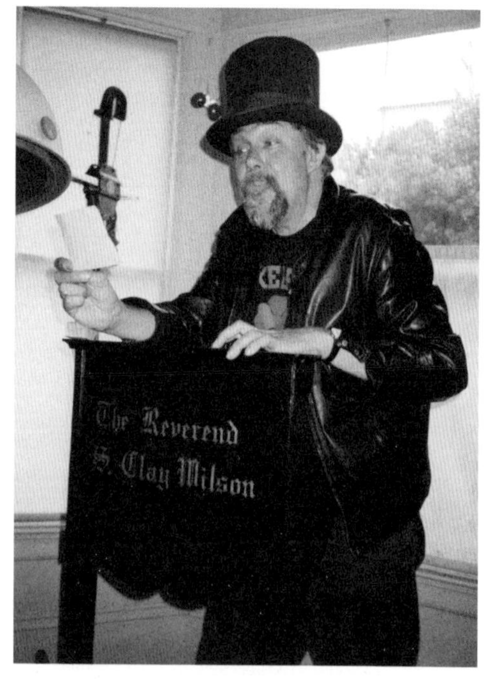

S. Clay Wilson in good form issuing a poignant statement during the Zap Comix Jam.

1995 (photo S. Williams)

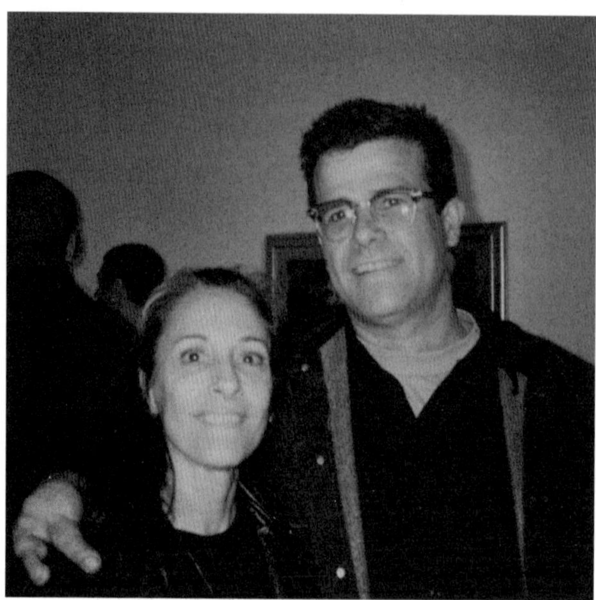

Suzanne Williams with Creative Monster Machine Wizard Mark Pauline (Survival Research Laboratories) at Robert's San Francisco Art Institute Show.

1995 (courtesy S. Williams)

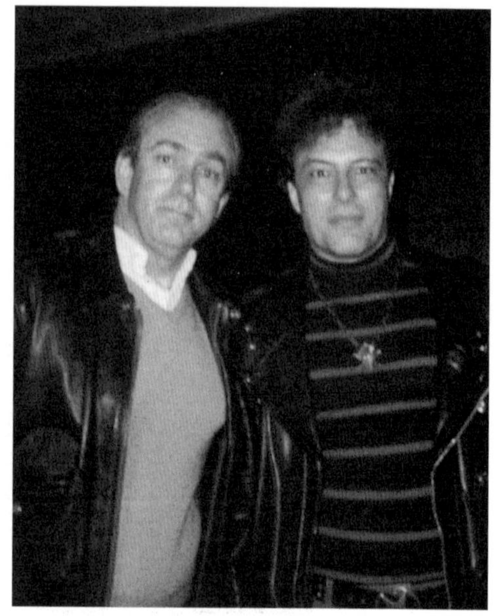

Robert Williams posed with punk legend Jello Biafra at Williams' San Francisco Art Institute Show opening.

1995 (photo S. Williams)

RUBBERNECK MANIFESTO

What is the worth of observation? Beyond the practical use of the eye for functioning successfully in everyday life, what are these values of simply seeing interesting things and enshrining them as art?

Nietzsche saw art as man's struggle against negative social forces by use of the imagination, which he considered a product of pure ego. Art for him was the highest form of clear lucid thought, a tool for the good. Schopenhauer envisioned art as a device of pleasure. Tolstoy viewed art as propaganda, and Oscar Wilde held to a doctrine of "art makes life," meaning art is sometimes more real then reality.

But there exists another facet and here is where I state my dictum: this is the act of simply being attracted to something visually; base curiosity! The purest form of art is to give way to simple visual interest. To look at what you find yourself driven to see. Higher notions of art tend to confine art with lofty moral restrictions. When art is passed off as a quasi-religion that can only be administered and interpreted by a special order of priestly elites, the system invariably stifles imagination–even when the art is as liberal as blobs, slashes, and spatters. Art that has to serve as the instrument of artistic revolution is limited by having to react to a greater force in a continual hope of some overthrow, hence becoming the tool of reaction. Even the great revolt is enslaving.

But when all predetermined prejudices are momentarily set aside and you are one of the many at the scene of the horrible accident, your libido will do the looking. Something dead in the street commands more measured units of visual investigation than one hundred Mona Lisas! It isn't what you like, it's what the fuck you want to see! Art is not the slave of decoration. Hail the voyeur, the only honest connoisseur!!

–Robt. Williams (1989)

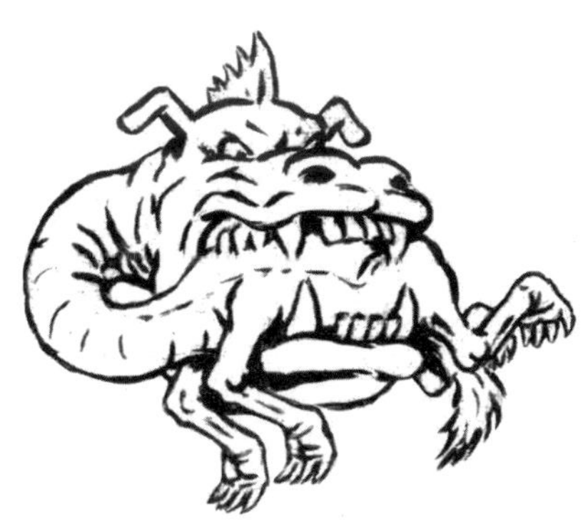

THE DICTUM MAGNUM MANIFESTUS
Humbly Phrased, The Great Pronouncement

Plain and simple, this following verbiage deals with the defense of art, its most expansive interpretations and the irrational.

First, it might be important to discuss just what is basic reality, its most serious application and the theory of no nonsense. Death and suffering are first and foremost measures of sober rationale. The leading tragedy for mankind is disease. Medical advancements have had a great effect on correcting man's many maladies but, still worldwide the premier remedies remain different forms of spiritual hope. Of course, this psychological treatment cannot be discredited, even though to some it falls into the category of mysticism. The next test of imposed reason is war. Mankind has come to appreciate war to such an extent that scholars have traditionally used it to mark the passing of history. Man, as a species, loves civil strife with opposing clans.

In the twentieth century alone, it is estimated that some 80 million people have died directly or indirectly due to war. I, myself think the estimate is a little high. I would roughly guess about 60 million but, still these are victims of serious rationale. The other big result of assumed straightforward objective no frills logic is politics. This is where facts and opinion run headlong into each other and create an incontinent train wreck. Political ethics are like a small child who goes crying to his father about his bicycle having been stolen only to find his father sitting on it. Governmental action is puerile theater intended to gloss over the fact that in the end only power will moderate.

One of the most famous proponents of cold rationale was the eighteenth century English cleric Thomas Malthus. He espoused the extreme philosophy that war, disease, famine, misery, suffering and death kept the world trim and healthy. Thus, this is the unspoken objective reality, or as the Devil so prosaically says, "My empathy for you is in my stool!"

There is another solution to find relief from these sullen laws of doom. The most elastic of all philsophy is already ours. It's the option to expand the pinhole of reason to an open gorge known as art. Unfortunately, the very word initiates thoughts of infantile pastimes and hobbies for shut-ins to a large portion of the general public. Even the higher echelons of the blue chip art establishment have limited public acceptance.

Influences of all the arts on our society has greatly fluctuated over time as the public has either adjusted to new nonessential trends or rejected them.

For example, it took people nearly fifty years to come to grips with modern art. Art today still hangs in limbo between a crackpot philosophy and a high society belief system. The real tipping point came at the beginning of the twentieth century with the birth of totally nonobjective painting and sculpture by artists such as: Wassily Kandinsky, Pablo Picasso, Piet Mondrian and Constantine Brancusi. With the advent of new achievements freeing art from being considered as decoration two other strong accomplishments followed.

Beginning with the horrors of the First World War the civil values of authority came into question. First through dada, an art movement against art and then Surrealism, an art trend that, borrowing from Dada pushed the idea that thought processes must proceed a search for beauty. From these two philosophical cultural steps conceptual art emerged in the late twentieth century. Modern art, especially abstract expressionism unfortunately had some negative tendencies. These drawbacks were the harsh suppression of realistic and narrative art as true fine art. This is a classic example of throwing the baby out with the bath water and then wondering where the water went.

Some may not understand or appreciate conceptual art. But with this questionable art movement there is no denying that art has finally been honored as philosophy. The problem with almost all modern art movements is they have tried to abolish the virtuosity of skill and craftsmanship under the guise that facile hand labor is for less mentally equipped menials. This begs the question, if a consummate violin virtuoso was required to wear boxing gloves while playing, would his performances be considered an encumbered masterpiece and no one would dare to mention that the piece was particularly hindered. If his musical audience is subjective they would require an encore but if the audience is objective everybody would have already left the room.

Struggling with consummate art critics and writers over the good or bad aspects of art is like fighting each other for aesthetic judgement of the preferred compositions of cloud formations. Now, with the exception of interior decorating, art is for all intent and purposes neutered. So how does my written directive pertain to art? Art has a much more powerful big cousin, far more poignant than a cultural or stylish pastime. It's the slick lubricant that all thought slides on–imagination. Far more aggressive than creativity, imagination is necessary for the advancement of thought. To create can be by accident but to imagine takes concerted effort.

Everybody is born with a fertile imagination but it seems to get stifled in childhood. Young children have rapacious imaginations but parents find it necessary to curb their flights of fancy before they become uncontrollable and cause harm to both the child and the family group. Conversely, the adults have no trouble in using fantasy as a control mechanism: The Sandman, Easter Bunny, Santa Claus and the old stand by, Satan–all scare phantoms. It is in some cases best that the wild notions of infants be regulated. It has been observed that criminal tendencies can be diverted through these counter measures. But then again, what is a real criminal tendency? Unfortunately, thieves and schemers have imagination too. That kind of acceptability of thought should be curtailed, however. The quicksand of jurisprudence is an undefinable stumbling block. Picasso was a thief, Van Gogh was a drunk and a whoremonger, and Salvador Dali was a flagrant print forger–all kings of imagination.

The issue that screams misuse of imagination is sex. This topic is far more sticky than it is with crime. Erotic thought bedevils everybody. It is said that consciously or unconsciously the average male mind has an erotic thought of some kind every fifteen minutes. Some people, maybe a large number of people can not deal openly with sex. Some feel that the reproductive functions are just too close to the elimination facet, and embarrassment is a good warning signal of lurid obsession. That's a shame because without a sex drive one would probably experience an ossified imagination. Progressive psychologists have long insinuated that sex drive is the premier driving force among vertebrates. This brings to mind the old maxim, life's primary responsibility is making more life. Granted not very poetic.

But, from that perspective it is not difficult to say that the concept of all beauty comes from the primeval appreciation of the female form. How this aesthetic philosophy prevails in the future, with new correct social values, remains to be seen. Of all the suppositions, the illusion of beauty is the most powerful distraction next to fear. And of course, beauty inevitably fits into the category of sex.

It should be made very clear that the thrust of this dialog is about the adulation and veneration of the human imagination, and a conviction that this area of thought has not been completely and thoroughly plumbed. The one villain that stands in the path of free inclusive thought is sophistication: "What will people think?" Imagination is "a gorilla in a birdcage," "a tornado in a thimble," "a drunk axe murderer in a mannequin factory," and a doorway to wherever anyone is capable of thinking.

Here is an example: You must know the distance between your bedroom and kitchen, say about forty feet. That forty feet is in your cerebral cortex, your brain. Okay, you know how to get to the grocery store and back home, it's about a quarter of a mile. That's in your head, and the information already belongs to you. Okay, from your home over to grandpa Bubba's house in Milwaukee, you understand that distance. Hopefully, you might have the esoteric knowledge that the moon is 238,000 miles away, which is the distance from your home. And, incidentally, it takes eight light-minutes for light coming from the sun some

93 million miles away to get to your front door. Okay, and you might have some science fiction knowledge and have heard that it is about four light-years to the nearest star system (Alpha Centauri).

I am sure you are aware that the stars around us are in a big wheel called a galaxy, and we live in a neighborhood of our galaxy called the arm of Orion. This location being two thirds of the way from the center of our galaxy (The Milky Way) is 100 light-years across. Now, continuing to develop a good idea of distances, the nearest big galaxy to us is Andromeda, some two million light-years away. Astronomers have discovered three trillion galaxies in the universe at its longest distance of roughly fourteen billion light-years away.

So, with this seemingly useless information in your head, your imagination will own that real estate just like your mind owns the familiarity of your trip from your bed to the refrigerator. What your mind has just tolerated was a crash course in comprehending remedial understanding of the universe. The human imagination is even bigger if you presume that before your mind stands a five dimensional forest, and the nature of this cerebral woodland is of your making. Yes, five dimensions: one is up and down, two is side to side, three is back and forth in depth, forth is representation of motion to indicate time passing and fifth is abstraction, the violation of physics.

You can envision a world of thick, challenging, impenetrable jungle, rich with illusive manifestations that require investigative thinking, or you can envision a modest shallow thicket that causes embarrassment for even allowing yourself to contemplate it. After all, why entertain one's self with preposterous ideas no one has thought up yet? Keep one adage in mind that all professional sex workers live by, "the best sex is between your ears." That ever expanding cerebral forest belongs to the quick-witted explorer who wades through the mental marsh to bring ideas back for others.

New ideas are multiple thoughts perversely shoved together in order to forge creativity. Five bad ideas stripped down make one brilliant original thought. Water alone does not make soup. The peer pressure and restrictive mores we face today will be reevaluated tomorrow. Among your friends, who would have ever thought that your idea of a tattoo on the side of a goldfish would end up in the future as a mural of the last supper on the flank of Moby Dick.

–Robt. Williams (3/31/21)

Postscript

ROBERT WILLIAMS, REVOLUTIONARY REACTIONARY

Robert Williams is one of the greatest storytellers of our times. Most of his stories are fictional, but he tells them so convincingly that nobody will notice the difference. Let us begin with his paintings. Even though we may not think of them in these terms, each one of his canvases is a self-contained micro-narrative, usually culminating in some spectacular and highly embarrassing failure of some of the protagonists. Excess and *Schadenfreude* inevitably enter an explosive symbiosis. Williams' background in underground comics is today part of his legend as a painter, a circumstance which obscures the fact that comics, as a genre, are located half-way between drawings and literature. When one studies the evolution of Williams' writing, one immediately notices parallels with the development of the style and subjects of his canvases. If the famous declaration of the 1989 *Rubberneck Manifesto* that "something dead in the street commands more measured units of visual investigation than a hundred Mona Lisas" stands for the bold, attention-grabbing stunts in Williams' art and prose of the 1980s and 1990s, his recent retrospective assessment of his career, "My Misinterpretation of Fine Art," strikes us by its measured self-reflectivity about history's place in the artist's life and that of the artist's life in history. The great importance of the present collection of Robert Williams' writings resides in the circumstance that the idea of narrative is what links Robert William's art to his role as a writer, and vice versa. It is time that we discover and celebrate his literary contributions and pungent linguistic skills with the same degree of appreciation for his exceptionalism that we bring to bear to his place in the history of painting and sculpture.

Words routinely stand at the very beginning for pictorial ideas in Robert Williams' creative process. Not coincidentally, a central place of the artist's library-study room in his Chatsworth residence is reserved for a large lectern that holds a phenomenally bulky, old-fashioned dictionary. When conceptualizing new artworks – or even during casual conversations – the artist will consult this dictionary frequently to re-assure himself and any visitor present of the nuances of a word's meaning. Robert Williams' "literary career" has its roots not only in underground comics, but also in the idiosyncratic choices for the titles of his artworks. He is, of course, not the first painter who is also a gifted writer. In fact, the history of art begins with the biographies of famous artists and architects compiled during the late Renaissance by Giorgio Vasari, who was foremost a painter and who contributed major artworks to the Mannerist style. Williams furthermore shares with the famous Symbolist painter Gustave Moreau the habit of turning overboarding, descriptive titles conceived to explain densely painted iconographic content into a pathway to art writing.

Beginning in the 1980s, Williams introduced the convention of composing three different titles for his paintings: a "general title" by which the painting would be known, a longer "museum catalog title," and a more concise "colloquial title." It goes without saying that the reader's/viewer's interest is immediately drawn to the tension between the museum title and the catalog title, which can yield to a clash between, for instance, *Three Zen Bopsters [Who] Find Beet Culture in the Farmer's Almanac* and *The Generation Of Contemplation Put in Association With the Vegetable of the Same Name, Denotes a Remarkable Similarity Between the Philosophy Of Passive Inaction And Agrarian Horticultural Osmosis*. The astute reader will have noticed that the "museum catalog title," despite its erudite pretentiousness, often moonlights as a Dadaist exercise in automatic writing. When Last Gasp of San Francisco published in 2005 an exhibition catalog of Williams' work entitled *Through Prehensile Eyes*, the three-tier title system was enhanced by a fourth feature, a page-long, deadpan iconographic analysis of each work, interspersed with salacious anecdotes. Such wordsmithing complements the notion of Lowbrow art, with which Williams is associated, as Lowbrow deliberately plays up the contrast between the snobbism of cultural capital and a real or alleged colloquial lack of sophistication. It took somebody no less than a member of the venerable French Academy, Marc Fumaroli, to note how much low brow/Lowbrow is a uniquely American phenomenon, when he wrote in *Paris-New York, Travels in Art and Images:*

> I am compelled to speak American when speaking about the antithesis of *low brow – high brow*, which is impossible to translate into French or any other European language. [...] *High brow* gets dangerously close to *egg head*, an insult thrown at the pretentions of intellectual pedants who only swear by European models, while *low brow* designates the happy and modest pride of the native born who knows how to appreciate all sorts of crude products for what they are worth without turning up his nose like a little Europeanized milord would do. (Marc Fumaroli, *Paris-New York, Voyage dans les arts et les images*, 4th ed., Flammarion, 2011, pp. 309, 311)

Despite their Americanness, in terms of visual content, Williams' paintings and sculptures have their closest historical cousins in the genre scenes of seventeenth-century Flanders and the Netherlands. Lowbrow is the Pop term for lowlife scenes that genre elevated for the first time in history to the status of art. After the year 1600 or so, the walls of aristocratic art galleries began teeming with peasants, hoodlums, street people, and rat catchers by David Teniers the Younger, Rembrandt, Adriaen Brouwer, and others, who released onto their interiors or landscapes armies of figures drinking, smoking, pissing, beating each other, or engaging unashamedly in public sex acts. How can one not see in them the precedents of Williams' hippies, pole dancers, violent clowns, flea market sellers, victims of food poisoning, homages to still sewage, or even his lovingly rendered used chewing gum stuck under restaurant tables?

The tone for Robert Williams art writing career was set by the *Rubberneck Manifesto*, published in *Visual Addiction* as part of a series of monographs about recently created works which Last Gasp and, later, Fantagraphics began publishing by the late 1980s. Although it is an apology of the base instincts of voyeurism in the visual arts, the *Rubberneck Manifesto* was peppered with literary references ranging from Nietzsche, Schopenhauer, and Tolstoy, to Oscar Wilde. Perhaps because it presented itself in the guise of that ultimate portend of twentieth-century avant-garde writing, the manifesto, it earned Robert Williams subsequently a dishonorable mention in the November 1993 issue of *Artforum*.

The *Rubberneck Manifesto* was but a prelude to the bi-monthly editorials Williams wrote over roughly a decade, beginning in 1994, for *Juxtapoz* Magazine. Of course, a lot of his writing is autobiographical in the sense that it relates the visual information contained in artworks – both his and those of others – to anecdotes and lived experiences. But an even more important aspect of Williams art writing is concerned with his coming to grips with the history of modern and avant-garde art of twentieth-century art, as well as the social and aesthetic conventions that validate it. The critical re-valuation of these questions – and their inherent contradictions and misunderstandings – turned into an intellectual quest of central importance.

Robert Williams came into his own as an artist during the post-World War II years. It was bad timing.

> As a young man, I erroneously presumed that 'fine art,' like theater, motion pictures, music and literature would embrace adventure, sensuality, daring, and boldness, and celebrate the romantic stimulation that heralds the pathos of life. But I was wrong. (Robert Williams, "My Misinterpretation of Fine Art," in *The Father of Exponential Imagination*, Fantagraphics, 2020, p. xxxii)

Whereas Williams grew up with traditional notions of the nature of art grounded in the academic training system and in nineteenth-century ideas of culture and beauty, he found himself in an era when art schools discarded their collections of classical plaster casts used for drawing lessons, when academies were occupied by student protesters more intent on starting revolutions than creating artworks, and when art fairs, like that in Venice, were "reformed" to exclude traditional media, like painting and sculpture, because they were allegedly corrupted by the art market. Williams' own conspicuous skills as a draftsman and his fervent imagination did not earn him the expected kudos in California's art education system of the early 1960s; it did not even offer him an intellectual home of like-minded individuals that he had hoped to find; instead, his peers labeled him derogatively "the illustrator."

Many of Williams' *Juxtapoz* editorials and related writings are concerned with his coming to terms with the manifold deceptions, if not hypocrisy, of the art world, an inquiry which extends far beyond these early years and the subjectivity of his own art. Williams raises larger philosophical and historical discussion points, which led him to re-think the structural development of the history of art during the twentieth century. A significant portion of Williams' writing is a criticism of the avant-garde and its rhetoric observed from the rear mirror of our own age.

A pivotal figure is Marcel Duchamp and his *readymades*, which "freed" artists from the obligation of producing hand-crafted objects and paved the way for later twentieth-century conceptual art. No art historian has ever managed to summarize as succinctly the dilemmas of mid-twentieth-century modernism as Williams when he wrote that "where Abstract Expressionism made everybody an artist, Conceptualism made everything art" ("My Misinterpretation," p. xxxiii). Avant-garde art comes with its own ideological baggage, which includes such notions as truth, freedom, and honesty. Who would ever want to argue with anyone of these values? Moreover, the writings of Clement Greenberg and others, which were largely responsible for legitimizing the rhetoric of the avant-garde, came with a dichotomy that labeled academic art as reactionary and abstract or conceptual art as progressive. Reactionary is originally a political term. In the early nineteenth century, it referred to tendencies in France to make the French Revolution undone by the regime of the restored Bourbon monarchy, including an ill-fated attempt to restore a divine-right monarchy and a return to Catholicism as a state religion. As the idolization of progress accelerated during the twentieth century, defending apparent regress seemed ever more like a losing proposition.

As a postmodern artist and writer, Williams has repeatedly affirmed to be a defender of *all art* – what could be more Duchampian than that? – but he also wrote that "an appreciation for academic art and its legacy should be greatly valued" ("My Misinterpretation," p. xxxiv). Those familiar with Williams and his art know that he carefully cultivated over half a century the position as an outsider and a dissident of the mainstream art world. There once was a time when modern, abstract, and conceptual art was in the outsider position, but, during Williams' own lifetime, it became the default position to assume. It is still part of the dogma of museums and most art institutions to the present day, including even the art market, which is why lowbrow could assume the role of a minority voice.

Interestingly, Williams is not alone in debunking the modernist rhetoric of progress and regress in the fine arts. An increasing number of observers have come to share his views since the beginning of our own *fin-de-siecle*, and his cavalry surprisingly issues forth from some of the last strongholds of allegedly elite culture. Compare for instance the following passage from "My Misinterpretation of Fine Art," published in *The Father of Exponential Imagination*, with an excerpt of the writings by Marc Fumaroli:

> For the first time in art history, anyone could now wear the honored laurels "artist." This was a joyous time [the 1950s of Abstract Expressionism]! The trade-off: fine draftsmanship and craftsmanship became taboo. (Robert Williams, "My Misinterpretation of Fine Art," in

> *The Father of Exponential Imagination*, Fantagraphics, 2020, p. xxxiii)

> In the era liberated from all straitjackets, Art prospers like never before in the ruins of the ancient art that preceded it. The new creativity of image makers *(plasticiens)* and their dealers, replacing the ancient artist, former patrons and genuine collectors, found a natural leadership figure in Andy Warhol, like Michelangelo had been the leader of the Mannerists in Vasari's *Lives*. While Michelangelo selected as his motto *Ut pictura poesis*, Warhol multiplied – thanks to the magic wand of the contemporary – the *readymade* of Marcel Duchamp into so many three-dimensional masterworks, exhibited by galleries and museums in limited-edition series offered to consumption by an elite of billionaire collectors. (Marc Fumaroli, *Ut Pictura Poesis: What Language to Say the Arts?*, LSU Press, 2016, p. 12)

Fumaroli illustrates his observations with an anecdote from the aftermath of a lecture by Arthur Danto at the University of Chicago, during which the inventor of the "art world as an atmosphere of art theory" was taken to task and had to confess that "as a private person" (as opposed to his "public task as an authority in philosophy and as an expert in aesthetics"), he much preferred the eighteenth-century painter of still lifes and children at play, Jean-Baptiste-Siméon Chardin, over the conceptual, "cutting edge" art he promoted. Fumaroli sees the main enemies of art in its bureaucratization and institutionalization, on the one hand, and, on the other, in the publicity machine and the marketing "hype" surrounding especially contemporary art. Otherwise, however, the structure of his criticism follows remarkable similar lines of that of Williams.

Such voices are growing in number. In 2016, I had the privilege to be invited in Paris to a private audience with Pierre Rosenberg, the legendary, longtime director of the Louvre, who (in reference to my partiality to the fantastic realism of Claude Verlinde's art) told me: "You have reactionary taste." Friends familiar with the context later told me that his words fell in the highest category of praise to be possibly bestowed. In this spirit, I would like to pass on the badge of honor at this point: being reactionary never rocked so hard as in Robert Williams' art and writing!

Darius A. Spieth, Ph.D.
San Diego Alumni Association Chapter Alumni Professor of Art History
School of Art
Louisiana State University

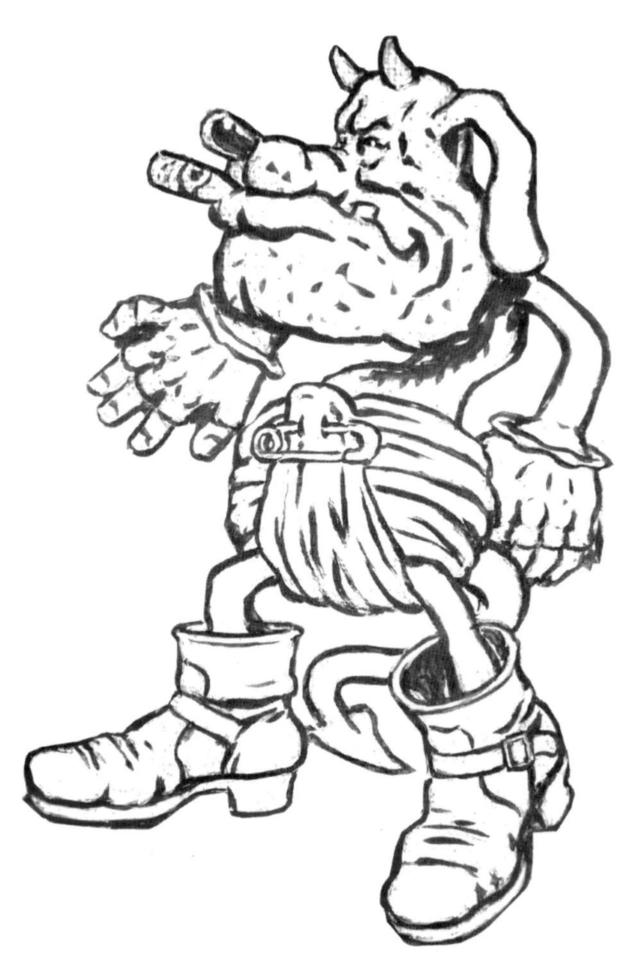

ACKNOWLEDGMENTS

This book was far more than one person's labor of love. It was the combined efforts of a group of dedicated and talented art enthusiasts. Fortunately, over the many years these fine people have understood the continued desire for an alternative to the inflexible and demanding creative environment fine art requires and a need for a voice that is more than a whisper in the wind.

First, it would only be fitting to honor our two late supporters, Fausto Vitello and Greg Escalante, along with Gwynned Vitello, Evan Pricco and the staff at Juxtapoz.

Special thanks to Colin Turner and the crew at Last Gasp Publishing, and to Richard Blue Trimarchi at Art Works Fine Arts in Los Angeles for photo lab work and layout.

Our sincere gratitude to so many spanning the years, of supporters, acolytes, benefactors and artists.

Thank you to my wife Suzanne Williams for the energy and wisdom that helped reinforce the alternative realm that this book documents.

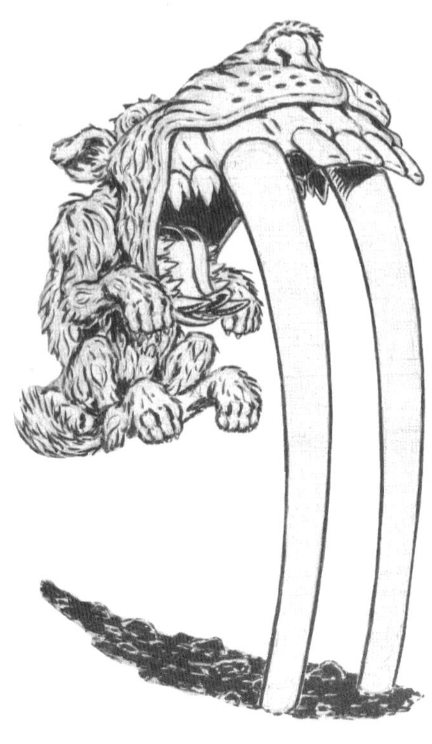

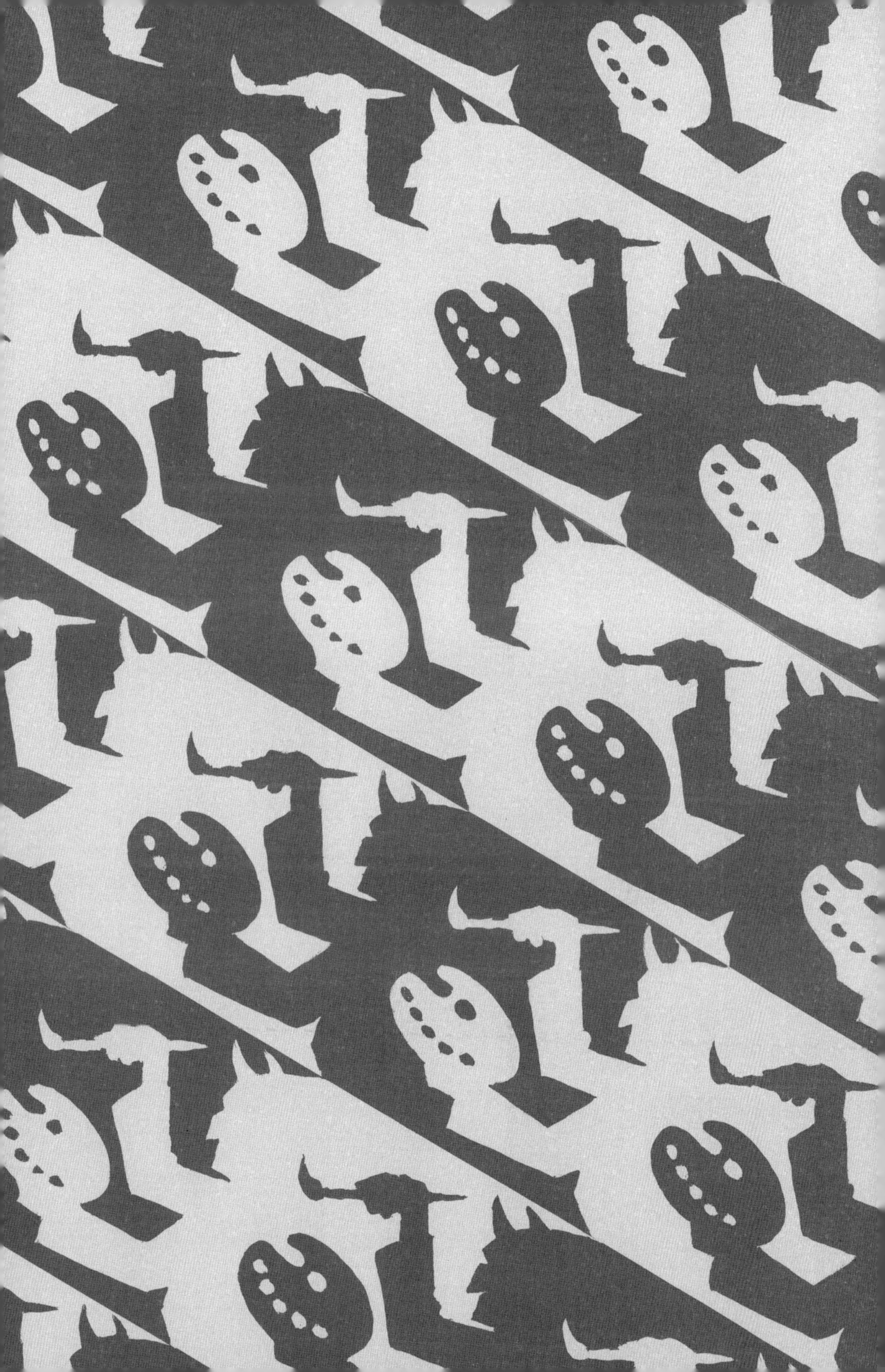

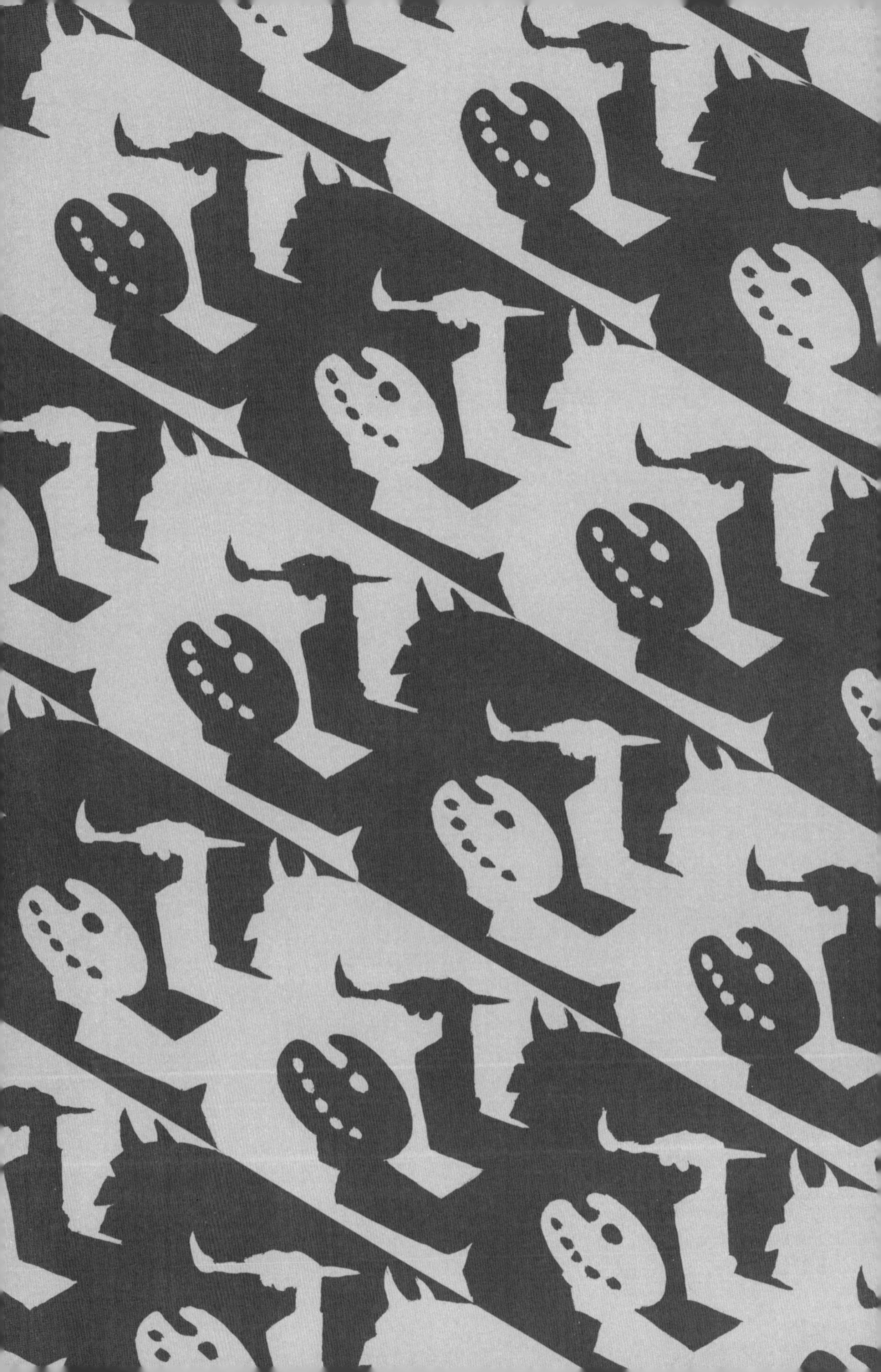